AF564487

TRADE IN SERVICES

A Case Study of India's Higher Education Sector

TRADE IN SERVICES

A Case Study of India's Higher Education Sector

BISWAJIT CHATTERJEE
Professor of Economics
Dean, Faculty of Arts
Jadavpur University, Kolkata

DEEP & DEEP PUBLICATIONS PVT. LTD.
F-159, Rajouri Garden, New Delhi - 110 027

TRADE IN SERVICES

A Case Study of India's Higher Education Sector

ISBN 978-81-8450-303-6

Printed in India at MAYUR ENTERPRISES
WZ Plot No. 3, Gujjar Market, Tihar Village, New Delhi - 110 018

Published by DEEP & DEEP PUBLICATIONS PVT. LTD.,
F-159, Rajouri Garden, New Delhi - 110 027 • Phone : 25435369, 25440916
E-mail : ddpubs@gmail.com • ddpbooks@yahoo.co.in
Showroom :
2/13, Ansari Road, Daryaganj, New Delhi - 110 002 • Telefax : 23245122

Contents

Preface

Following GATS Agreement, trade in educational services has become one of the important components of global trade in services. Considered as non-tradeables earlier, some of these services like education and training are now increasingly being traded globally, and this is one tangible effect of the globalisation process. India being one of the founder members of the WTO, is also an early signatory to the Articles of Agreement under the GATS, and after some years of grace period, has to open up its higher educational sector to the forces of international trade. What constitutes the direction of effects of globalisation of educational services in India is an important issue of policy research on international trade, and the present study is an attempt to undertake this research. This study was undertaken under the Global Trade Programme of Jadavpur University with the support of University with Potential for Excellence Scheme of UGC. Spread over six chapters, the present study discusses the theoretical literature on trade in services, the GATS provisions in the WTO and globalisation of service sector trade and their implications for less developed nations like India, and set out the rationale for the study of the effect of trade liberalisation on an hitherto non-traded sector, namely, education. It also analyses the possible effects of opening up of trade in educational services as per the GATS provisions on grounds of quality of education and costs of education, and outlines the policy implications. While I thank Jadavpur University and the UGC for the generous financial support to this study, different research assistants associated with the different phases of the study Mallika Roy, Dolly Naskar, Sangeeta Kundu and Nabaneeta Chatterjee, deserve special mentions for their sincere help and meticulous support towards the completion of the study. I also thank Professor Asok Nath Basu and Professor Shyamal Kanti Sanyal, former Vice-Chancellors, Jadavpur University, Professor Pradip Narayan Ghosh, and Professor Siddhartha Datta, present Vice-Chancellor and Pro-Vice-Chancellor respectively, of Jadavpur University for their continuous encouragement and support. Shri Rajat Bandyopadhyay, former Registrar, and Shri Gour Krishna Patnaik, Finance Officer of Jadavpur University, have always been supportive of my academic endeavours. Needless to say, the infrastructure supports of the Planning and Development Unit and of the Economics Department of Jadavpur University have helped me to complete the work. I record my sincere thanks to all of them.

It is important to recognize that an academic exercise on a theme like this is handicapped by the unavailability of the relevant data in right form. This may be due to the very recent and yet fluid nature of the Indian higher education market which is exposed to the process of globalisation. But as the art of empirical research in Economics lies in making the imperfect data talk, I have used indirect indicators to assess the impact of trade based on comparative costs and product quality on India's higher education system. The policy conclusions that emerge from my detailed work is that government's regulatory framework needs be designed appropriately and applied carefully to prevent the adverse impacts on the India's higher education sector in particular, and the economy in general. I sincerely hope that the product will be useful to serious researchers in economics and policy-makers.

Kolkata BISWAJIT CHATTERJEE

1

Introduction

International trade in services has been expanding in recent years and now constitutes an important component of global trade. The importance of the service sector in the growth process of nations has also been impressive in recent histories of development experience in the world, particularly in the developing nations. The most crucial aspect of this service sector trade in recent years has been trade in educational services. As a result of GATS agreement, this sector—which was traditionally been a part of non-traded sector of the economy are now being exposed to global competition through trade. The present book is an attempt to evaluate the impact of globalisation in the form of trade in educational services in the Indian economy.

The book is organized in the following manner. In chapter 1, we discuss the theoretical literature on trade in services, and set out the rationale for the study of the effect of trade liberalization on an hitherto non-traded sector, namely, education. Chapter 2 discusses the GATS provisions in the WTO and globalisation of service sector trade and their implications for less developed nations like India. Here we also discuss the different modes of supply of services trade across the nations and the implications thereof for the Trade in educational services. Chapter 3 provides an analytical assessment of the higher education sector in India—its profile and the constraints it faces. In Chapter 4, we present a profile of the costs of education in different countries and in India to judge the potentials for trade based on the principle of comparative advantage. In Chapter 5, we analyse the possible effects of opening up of trade in educational services as per the GATS provisions on grounds of quality of education and costs of education. The trends in recent years are depicted and their implications for the Indian higher educational sector are examined in details in this chapter. Chapter 6 summarises the conclusions of the study and the policy implications.

There is no denying the fact that the share of services sector in the GDP of nations has gone up in recent years. Recent years have also experienced phenomenal increase in the trade in services in different regions of the world and annual report of the WTO (2006) corroborates this a fact. According to the Annual Report of WTO, 2006, the world economy had expanded by 3.3 per cent in 2005, less rapidly than in 2004, but still slightly faster than the decade average. Economic growth remained strong in most regions although less buoyant than in the preceding year. In 2005, the value of world merchandise exports rose by 13 per cent, to US $ 10.1 trillion, and that of world commercial services exports by 11 per cent, to US $ 2.4 trillion. For both merchandise and commercial services, this represented a marked deceleration in growth if compared with the preceding year. Cross-border commercial services exports expanded for the third year in a row less rapidly than world merchandise exports. World economic output of goods and services is estimated to have expanded by 3.3 per cent and real merchandise exports rose by 6 per cent in 2005. However, at the more disaggregated level the actual outcome deviated from projections, but the impact of these deviations on output and trade tended to offset each other. Among the broad commercial services categories (transportation, travel and other commercial services), expansion rates have been similar, ranging from nearly 10 per cent for travel to 12 per cent for transportation services. Europe, the largest trader among the major geographic regions, recorded the lowest export and import growth for both merchandise and commercial services of all regions in 2005. Over the last five years, the growth of North America's merchandise and commercial services exports was about half the 10 per cent average annual growth observed globally. South and Central America and the Caribbean region not only recorded very high merchandise trade of nearly one-quarter in 2005, but also the strongest expansion in commercial services trade of all regions. Asia's commercial services exports and imports have been far more dynamic than world commercial services trade. China's and India's services trade expansion exceeded that of other Asian countries by a large margin, although incomplete information (China) and methodological changes in recording (India) exclude a precise year-to-year comparison at this moment. Asia's largest services importer, Japan, saw a near stagnation of its total.

This is a general trend across nations, but since many services were non-tradables in many developing countries with cheaper labour costs, they became attractive for trade/exports on grounds of comparative costs, when globalisation induced institutional changes in the form of WTO's articles of agreement on services permitted international trade in some of these services. Moreover, as the demand for services like education, health, etc. are numerically higher in populous developing nations, making them attractive destinations of suppliers of services, as well as of investments (financial capital) in these services. As a result, both from the supply and the demand sides, developing countries' participation in global trade in services like education, have been on the increase. This trend needs be explained, and more importantly the likely effects of globalisation-induced trade in services on the higher education sector in India needs to be analysed to derive policy options available to the country in the changed economic environment. The important analytical issue that merit discussion is how far the present higher education system in India is poised to face global competition, and with what likely effects. The importance of governmental regulation on the functioning of foreign educational institutions in our country, and the direction of movement of resources are important considerations in a study on trade and educational services in India. Accreditation of foreign educational institutions entering or operating in India to compete with domestic public/private sector units of higher education is an important task to be accomplished to safeguard quality of educational services. Perhaps the most important issue for consideration is whether the degrees offered by these foreign institutions for their Indian students are acceptable in their own country or not, as this would determine the employability of the candidates in the international labour market.

Cross-country differences in immigration laws are important deterrents to labour flows across the nations and liberalization of educational services as per the dictates of the GATS would be inimical to the interests of such nations which still wants to control international labour supply in their respective countries—the classic example is the USA, which has not virtually allowed any foreign academic institutions to open their branches in the country. This would warrant detailed rounds of negotiations at the level of the WTO. The issue of fair trade based on the principle of non-discrimination gets to the forefront as the advanced countries like the USA prefer to impose restriction on the exports from developing nations, and do not reform their own domestic regulations which are protective in nature and therefore are discriminatory to the interests of developing countries. For India in terms of quality and costs, exports of educational services overseas are comparatively advantageous in certain areas, and the major blockade in the export of such services are the rules and laws in advanced countries like the USA and the European Union. The inflow of foreign educational institutions or groups to provide educational services to the Indian residents, though on the rise in recent years, does not always provide viable alternative supply of general higher education to domestic consumers, many of whom are poverty-constrained to pay low for education of their child(ren). Education and training in emerging subjects like hotel or hospitality management, computer-aided digital library services, or even BBA or BCA types have been coming—but we do not find any attempt to establish education or training centers for Micro-biology or Bio-technology, Centres for Statistical or Economic Forecasting like the ISI or IIM type of high quality management education centers or for that matter another IIT type ventures to provide high quality rigorous education on technology by foreign service providers in the field of education in our country. Perhaps the investment and sunk costs are too high for these enterprises to venture into these high quality frontier areas of education in India. The threat of globalisation to our indigenous very high quality service providers in the field of higher education are therefore virtually non-existent, and these providers have strong comparative advantages for export of their products abroad, whose realization would, of course, depend on the regulatory framework in our education-importing nations. For example, although USA is a signatory to the GATS treaty, its federal and state laws do not permit opening up of educational institutions by foreign sources—government or private—within their geographical territories. As a result, although many of India's education providers have comparative advantage in export of educational services, the scope for such exports in the near future to countries like USA and European Union appears limited. The non-tariff barriers in countries like USA and European Union countries, and not quality and cost of education in India, which restricts export of high quality education to some such countries, but there are places where such exports could take place.

The other category of educational institutions, have large stock of physical infrastructure, but poor quality of human resources like teachers, so that quality of education that these institutions provide, remain low, and their costs are also not very high, giving them an iota of comparative advantage on cost terms only. They would be ideal recipients of foreign collaborators offering degrees on subjects like hospitality management, hotel management, and collaborative degree proposals or joint ventures in higher education may ensue in the process of globalisation. The bottom layer—both on cost grounds due to inefficiency and corruption, and quality being very poor—cannot survive international competition and even domestic private competition, and would gradually be wiped out. Such wiping out would have implications for employment contraction, but such contraction would be balanced by expansion in the new private/foreign institutions. The product of such educational enterprises needs to be accredited by the government, and it is matter of conjecture to know what status of these joint venture degrees have in the foreign countries wherefrom capital for joint venture had come. National policy on regulation of such foreign degree providers should be framed to tackle many of the problems that are involved in such pattern of higher education in our country in the years to come.

The plan of the report is as follows. *Chapter I* makes a critical review of theoretical issues in international trade in services. This is followed in *Chapter II* of the thrust of globalisation and GATS treaty in the context of trade in educational services. *Chapter III* provides an analytical review of higher education system in India and of cross-country evidences on educational exports and FDI flows. *Chapter IV* deals with costs of higher education in India and abroad to assess the cost advantages of different categories of higher education in India. *Chapter V* provides an analytical review of the policies on higher education that are likely to emerge in near future and the implications of globalisation of higher education in India are summarized briefly in *Chapter VI,* which concludes.

2

Trade in Services

2.1. INTRODUCTION

The service sector accounts for about 70% of the GNP of most developed countries and an even larger proportion of employment, yet its role in international trade (with some notable exceptions like transportation and shipping, finance, and insurance) had been rather low. This situation reflected the fact that most of the services, by nature, were inherently less tradable than goods because they could not be stored (except when they are embodied in goods as with films: diskettes, computer tapes, etc.) and, therefore, production and consumption had to occur simultaneously, if not at the same place. There were also the facts that, for a variety of reasons, services were subject to heavier domestic regulation than goods and only recently, there has been GATS agreement by the WTO which has made rules for international trade in services. Times are changing as advances in communications technology are breaking down many technical barriers to trade in services, and many countries are beginning to deregulate many of their service industries, and WTO's articles of agreement on services have made penetration of the forces of international trade into the arena of services.

In simple economic terms globalisation means free trade in goods and services and in the factors of production. Among the factors, only capital mobility is quite common, labour mobility is still restricted by different countries regulations for migration of labour. Financial capital is however, quite mobile across countries. The basic principle of goods trade is the principle of comparative advantage, based on relative costs of production of goods and services. Of course, quality differences are also important factor behind trade of goods and services, but it is difficult to get data on quality based trade.

Like Adam Smith's "Vent for Surplus", where international trade broadens the scope of home market, and taps hitherto untapped resources into productive use, thereby increasing productivity and growth, globalisation induced penetration of international trade transforms hitherto non-tradeable activities into tradeables and brings them to the forces of international competition based on the principle of comparative advantage. Certain service sectors which were non-traded final goods produced and consumed, now becomes important elements in a country's trade basket and the scope of world trade in services have seriously widened over the last decade. We therefore need to explain trade in services, and the different theoretical attempts in the literature to predict the pattern of trade in services under alternative market structures.

The conventional view about international trade in services is that it is feasible to trade in service factors, but not in service product, because services must be consumed where and when they are produced, but the factors specific to the provision of services can be employed in either one country or the other. International trade in services occurs when factors specific to the service sector and whose ownership resides in one country are allowed to co-operate with factors located in the other country to produce the service product there. The key point is that the provision of the service requires the joint input of the service factor of one country and the inter-sectorally mobile factor of the other country. The situation has changed considerably over the years, and hitherto non-tradeable service products are also brought into the ambits of service trade service. There is also the possibility of commercial presence of foreign factors of production in domestic production of services flow, may in the form of subsidiary to foreign institutions, or joint ventures between say a domestic university and its foreign counterparts.

2.2. DEVELOPMENT OF THE PRODUCER SERVICES SECTOR

The growth of modern industrial economies has been accompanied by dramatic growth in the services sector. The classical theory of stages of development suggests that, as industrialization takes place in an economy, the share of the 'primary' or agricultural sector, in total output and employment, gradually diminishes while that of the 'secondary' or manufacturing sector increases. This is followed by a gradual rise in the share of the services sector in national income as well as in employment, and a further contraction of the share of primary sector. The rise and decline in the shares of manufacturing and agricultural sectors, and residually in the services sector can in general be explained by the differences in the rate of growth of productivity in these sectors, the impact of the international division of labour as well as changes in their income elasticities of demand. Sir William Petty as early as in 1690 recognised the significance of comparative advantage in explaining, in this respect, the growth of the services sector activities like trade and commerce and shipping in Holland. Over a century later, certain writers of the so-called German Historical School, notably Fredrich List, formulated a stage-theory of development which in certain respects had anticipated the Fisher-Clark thesis. By the turn of the twentieth century, statistical studies began to show not only a relative decline in the share of agriculture and a relative rise in that of manufacturing, but also an increase in the share of some services both inside and outside the manufacturing sector. In 1933, Allan G.B. Fisher in a pioneering paper, for the first time, distinguished three broad sectors of 'primary', 'secondary', and 'tertiary' industries in the economy, and suggested that transition from the relative shares of each sector with economic development takes place in stages. Colin Clark's (1940) restatement of Fisher's hypothesis appears to suggest a rising share of services in income associated with economic growth. His observation was that the share of labour devoted to the production of services goes up with income. Clark emphasized the role of income levels, arguing that the reasons for the growth of the tertiary sector had to be sought on the demand side. Simon Kuznets's terminology, on the other hand, was 'neutral' in the sense that he described the sectors as agricultural, manufacturing, and service. The relative rise and decline of the shares of the manufacturing and agricultural sectors, as already noted, was basically attributed to the changes in comparative costs and income-elasticities of demand. The importance of the role of supply factors in bringing about these changes in relative income and employment shares was noted, among others by Hollis B. Chenery. Victor Fuchs's time-series study shows that the income-elasticity of demand for services in America is not significantly greater than unity, and the cross-section study of the shares of the three sectors in the national product and total labour force undertaken by Simon Kuznets indicates that the dispersion of the share of services between the advanced and the underdeveloped countries is less than those of the other sectors.

Thus there are two problems with regard to the development of the service sector : (i) whether the pattern of sectoral development of services is a significant function of changes in income per capita, and, if not, what other explanatory factors might be important, and (ii) analyse the factors that may explain the relatively smaller dispersion of shares of this service sector in the developed and underdeveloped countries. Like new products, new services have come into being during the process of economic development and as per capita income rose, the demand for many of these new services have shown to be income-elastic. The role of comparative advantage in expanding these new lines of services has been recorded through the colonial history of the nineteenth century, and as the WTO annual reports indicate, in the current century through the pattern of service trade among the developed countries in large numbers and among the developing worlds in a slowly growing patterns. The expansion in trade-induced services have been facilitated by the gradual replacement of old types of services which, by nature, were unmovable and strictly non-tradeables. As the less developed nations progress on their path of economic development with rise in real per capita income, even though with more iniquitous income distributions, the demand and supply of these new types of services have been growing and with that the overall shares of services in the national income and employment in these economies. Technological breakthrough, which constitutes the basis of comparative cost advantage seems to be a major factor in these expansion of the relative shares of the service sector in developed as well as developing world. M.A. Katouzian (1970) provides a historical account of the development of the service sector.

Summers (1985, p. 48 n) has argued that Clark's view was concerned with the share of employment devoted to production of services, and was not strictly that consumer services which were income inelastic. Because of the changing employment and price patterns observed by Clark and more recently by Kravis, Heston, and Summers (1982), an important issue in the theoretical literature on services has been to find the correlation between final-expenditure service prices and per-capita income levels. This includes work by Balassa (1964), Samuelson (1964), Bhagwati (1984a, 1985), Clague (1985) and Panagariya (1988). The emphasis of this literature has been on consumer rather than producer services, and on why the price of non-tradable final expenditure services varies systematically with per-capita income levels. While the share of services in final expenditures has been found to increases systematically with income levels, the most important changes observed in terms of employment have been for producer or intermediate services. For the US, the employment data for the US for select years from 1929 through 1985 indicate that the producer services sector, which accounted for 6% of US employment in 1949, accounted for 14.8% of employment by 1985, and the employment share of consumer services, in contrast, fell from 10.77% in 1929 to 4.24% in 1985.

Bhagwati (1984b) has suggested that producer services appear to be a growing sector in part because firms are externalizing service activities once performed inside the firm. While the "splintering" away of activities once performed inside manufacturing firms may explain part of the shifting pattern of employment in producer services, it does not fully explain the rise of the producer services sector. In fact, producer services also represent an increasingly important share of the remaining activities that are still performed within manufacturing firms. Greenfield has suggested that the importance of services in production is related to the emphasis placed in modern economies on specialization in production. He observed that, with economic development, there are important qualitative changes in the input mix of the labour force in expanding firms-increased output at the firm level requires the creation of additional departments within the firm and the increased specialization of personnel and equipment. The changing input mix of the labour force is an important qualitative change associated with economic development

2.3. TRADE IN SERVICES—ANALYTICAL ISSUES

Since the decade of 1980s, there has been growing interests among economists in service sector development in general, and international trade in services in particular. There are a number of reasons for this changed perceptions. Firstly, in most countries, the service sector has been growing at a fast rate, as reflected in the growing share of this sector in the gross value-added or national income of these economies. In countries experiencing structural unemployment, the empirical importance of services, however measured, is reinforced by the importance of actual and potential employment in services. The second reason is the range of new possibilities for the development of services generated by technological changes in the service sector, the scale of which changes may amount to a services revolution like the industrial revolution of the 19th century. Thirdly, perhaps the most immediate reason, is the GATS treaty in the WTO, which has focused on liberalization of international trade in services

Traditionally, service sector activities were not traded internationally, because such trade was technically impossible and/or prohibited by domestic regulations. As a result, price and output in markets for services were characterized by the equality of domestic demand and supply. These products were treated as non-tradeable because of impediments to trade such as high transportation costs, tariffs and quotas. In addition, certain physical characteristics of goods and services also render them non-tradable. Bhagwati (1985) and Sampson and Snape (1985) had distinguished between various groups of transactions according to the physical proximity of the suppliers and the receivers of services:

- Transactions, which can be executed at arms length, i.e. suppliers and receivers of services can be geographically separated. An individual living in New York can obtain an insurance policy from Lloyd's of London without having to be in London or without the insurance company being present in New York.
- Transactions, which require the receiver to move, at least temporarily, to the country where a particular service is provided. International tourism is a case in point.
- Transactions, which require the receiver to move, at least temporarily, to the country where a particular service is provided. Development of a coalmine in Brazil requires a foreign constructor to be on the site.
- Transactions occurring in a third country where neither the supplier nor the receiver resides. An American bank established in London can take financial operations for, say, an Australian customer.

The above classification is important because it shows that many so-called trade transactions actually involve no trade but international movements of factors of production. Only the first category of service transactions is comparable with trade in goods. The obstacles to the exchange of services between countries, thus consist not only of trade measures but also of limits to the foreign investments, rights of establishment, visa requirements and so on. It is quite clear that complete liberalisation of the international exchange of services would also, or even primarily, involve removal of obstacles to factor movements. Bhagwati (1984) argued that technological progress allowed more and more services to be traded, just like good, by relaxing the requirement of physical proximity. Advances in telecommunications and information sectors rendered many banking and insurance services tradable at long distances. But in other sectors, the natural barriers still continue to limit direct trade in services for a long time to come.

In the 1980s, a set of papers, e.g. Djajic and Kierzkowski (1986), Burgess (1990) and Melvin (1989) using a variety of models, had interpreted trade in services as trade in service factors—these factors combine with local specific factors produce a non-tradable service product. This interpretation follows the tradition of Hall (1977) who had characterized services as involving the simultaneous location of consumption and production, thereby ruling out the idea of a tradable service product. Deardorf (1985), on the other hand, looks separately at services as both final products and intermediate inputs. Melvin (1987) has noted that there exists a range of services which permit a separation of the location of production and consumption in space as well as in time, so that service trade may take place either at the factor or at the product level. Such service products include certain management consulting and accounting services, engineering services, legal services, data processing and telecommunications services, and financial and insurance services. When there are more than one option for international trade (i) there can be either trade in the *service factor,* where it can combine with local specific factor to produce a non-traded service product, or (ii) there can be trade in service product itself, involving no further production in the foreign country. For a country wishing to liberalise its service sector, the choice before the government is between facilitating trade in factor services by allowing foreign companies right to establish in the home country and seeking reciprocal agreements for its own companies, and the facilitation of trade in service products, which the government can do by negotiating right to do business for companies. GATT negotiations on service trade had primarily focused on product trade rather than on factor trade.

There have been some notable exceptions to the general neglect of services by trade theorists. Bhagwati (1984), for instance, provided an explanation for the well-established fact that the relative price of services is higher in the developed countries than in developing countries. The basic argument is that factor endowments differ substantially between countries and hence the factor-price equalization theorem does not hold.

If service industries employ labour intensively, production costs should be higher in the countries well endowed in capital. Hindley and Smith (1984) have argued that the theory of comparative advantage is equally applicable to goods and services. The fact that services differ from goods does not imply a need to construct new theoretical models. Indeed some researchers used the standard Heckscher-Ohlin model to provide an explanation for the existing trade patterns in services. In particular, Sapir and Lutz (1981) attempted to explain net service trade flows in freight, insurance and passenger services of developed and developing countries by using variables related to the factor endowments. Their results, however, suggest that the Heckscher-Ohlin model has only limited explanatory power to explain the actual pattern of service trade.

Will trade liberalization in the service sector necessarily improve national welfare? This is tricky question, and there are positions that can arise following trade liberalization in service sector products or service sector inputs, which involve costs which may outweigh the benefits. David F. Burgess (1995) argues that if one abstracts from the possibility of gains from eliminating imperfectly competitive markets and exploiting scale economies in the service sector, and if one recognizes that for a variety of reasons countries have chosen to impose distortive taxes on factor income, then trade liberalization in services could produce a real income loss. Since international flows of goods specific and service-specific factors may be either complements or substitutes, trade liberalization in service by a small country may involve either a hidden benefit or a hidden cost when foreign-owned goods-specific factors are subject to tax depending upon whether trade in the service factor is complementary or substitutable with trade in other factors already subject to tax. If an influx of the service-specific factor from abroad causes the economy to demand more of the goods-specific factor, trade liberalization in services will involve a hidden benefit; but if an influx of the service-specific factor causes the demand for the goods-specific factor to decrease there is a hidden cost. Whether the two factor flows are substitutes or complements depends upon details of the technology and preferences that cannot be determined *a priori* and can only be resolved empirically. If the distortions contribute to the incentive for trade in services then allowing such trade will be harmful, but if the distortions weaken the incentive for trade in services then allowing such trade will be beneficial. So, while there is a presumption that trade in services will be beneficial for a small country simply because of the principle that freer trade is better than restricted trade, one must be wary when there are distortions in the economy that cannot be removed. If these distortions strengthen the incentive for trade liberalization in the service sector then it will not be wise policy to pursue such liberalization.

The fact that these diverse outcomes depend upon empirical knowledge about elasticities of substitution in production and consumption, relative factor intensities, and expenditure shares makes the issue of whether there are overall benefits or costs from trade liberalization in services a contentious one. The results of the paper can be related to the literature on exogenous *versus* endogenous capital movements under protection as discussed in Brecher and Diaz (1977), Jones (1984) and Neary and Ruane (1988), among others. According to that literature, an exogenous influx of capital under protection may be beneficial or harmful, but if the influx is an endogenous response to protection it will necessarily be harmful. Burgess (1995) shows that trade liberalization in services at either level will lower the price of the service product and the return to the service factor in the home country. If it has a technological comparative advantage in services, liberalizing trade at the factor level will reduce the price of the service product by more than liberalizing trade at the product level, thereby offering greater potential for welfare gain. However, the influx of service factors from abroad could draw labour from the goods sector and reduce employment opportunities for goods-specific factors whereas the influx of service products from abroad will shift labour into the goods sector and increase employment opportunities for goods-specific factors. The increased demand for goods-specific factors that occurs when service sector trade is liberalized at the product level is a hidden benefit associated with this option when there is a divergence between the private and social costs of goods-specific factors, and it may suffice to reverse the ranking of the two options for liberalizing service sector trade in certain cases.

Findlay and Kierzkowski (1983) have developed a Heckscher-Ohlin type model to investigate the formation of human capital through educational services. The two goods in their model, viz. industrial good and the educational services are produced with the help of neoclassical production function, each using two factors of production, skilled and unskilled labourers, but no use of physical capital. They demonstrate that, *ceteris paribus*, a country with a larger stock of educational capital or a lower discount rate will end up having more skilled labour. Consequently, when trade in goods is allowed this country will specialize in exporting the skill-intensive commodity X and importing Y. The relative factor endowment has been endogenised in this model along the Heckscher-Ohlin mechanism. Trade in educational services in such a framework will generate skill differentials between sectors and affect product quality through changes in the composition of output. Liberalisation of trade in educational services would have to involve eliminating restrictions on international movement of the educational capital, K, or the international movement of students. Whether such a liberalisation would be welfare increasing or not depends on the degree of unequal distribution of the world stock of K. Free movement of capital (K) would increase world welfare by improving the allocation of resources.

Melvin (1989) has developed a neo-Heckscher–Ohlin model of international trade where one good and the services of capital are tradeable commodities. All the standard assumptions of Heckscher-Ohlin model of international trade including endowment differences between nations are made. The combination of goods and factor trade in different scenarios in his model produces the following interesting results : (a) If the tradeable commodity uses the mobile factor service intensively, then efficient world output is possible; however, the country well endowed with capital will import the capital-intensive good, even though the relative commodity price of this good was lower in autarky; (b) When the tradeable commodity uses immobile factor intensively, free trade of commodities for factor services will *always* result in efficient world output regardless of the initial endowment of factors; (c) If the imported commodity uses the immobile factor intensively, then in a service trade model, tariffs will produce the usual commodity price effects, whereas if the imported commodity uses mobile factor intensively, then a tariff will reduce the relative price of imports. Thus, when capital is the mobile factor, no matter which good is imported, a tariff will raise the relative price of labour-intensive good; (d) With internationally mobile capital services and with commodity service trade, a tariff on either commodity will increase the real and relative return to labour, and more generally, any tariff will increase the return to the immobile factor; (e) When factor services are imported, a tariff takes the form of a tax on repatriated service income—thus countries that are large service importers may resort to differential tax taxes on foreign sources of income if they become involved in tariff wars with service-exporting countries; (f) With trade in factor services and both commodities, there is an indeterminacy in trade patterns, and as a consequence, traditional commercial policy interventions like tariffs or quota restrictions will reduce trade in the commodities on which they are imposed, but need not produce welfare reductions for either of the two economies. Thus, the removal of tariffs or trade liberalisation policy need not result in the welfare improvements even though commodity trade may well increase. In this scenario, since service trade and commodity trade are substitutes, trade policy liberalization may result in small welfare changes, they may produce significantly different trade flows and trade patterns. The above analysis hinges on the fulfilment of strict sufficient conditions for the validity of factor price equalization, and in the real-world such conditions hardly exist. Therefore, analytical results apart, the policy conclusions of this general equilibrium model must be read with caution, and need not be really suitable for applications. This is important in the context of liberalization of tariff regimes, which in the presence of service trade combined with commodity flows under the observed situation may yield results which are not deducible from this cogent model of James Melvin.

James R. Markusen (1989) has developed a model of trade in which trade occurs in differentiated or specialized intermediate products produced with increasing return—increasing returns characterize both capital-intensive intermediate manufactures and knowledge-intensive producer services. Many of these inputs are differentiated and complementary to domestic inputs. These inputs are produced with increasing returns and so differentiation is limited by the extent of the market, and increases with international trade in specialized inputs or services. Permitting trade only in final goods is an imperfect and inferior substitute for permitting trade in specialized services in two well-defined senses. (a) Free trade in inputs/services is Pareto-superior to autarky while free trade in goods only may not be. (b) Free trade in inputs/services is superior to free trade in goods from the point of view of the world as a whole, although not necessarily the point of view of each individual country. These results have special relevance to current discussions about the liberalization of trade in services. Because of the need to move people and/or establish a foreign presence, trade in producer services tends to fall under restrictions imposed by immigration and foreign investment laws. In most countries, these laws tend to be significantly more restrictive than barriers to trade in goods. Combining this generalization with the welfare results of the previous section suggests the possibility of significant gains from liberalized trade in producer services.

It is generally recognized that the services sector represents an important and growing aspect of employment in industrial economies. Until recently, however, formal analyses of the services sector have tended to emphasize final expenditure services, even though the most dramatic growth in this sector has not been in consumer services, but rather in producer or intermediate services. Joseph F. Francois (1990) explores the relationship of producer services to market expansion and integration and the division of labour, highlighting the role of services as a complement rather than a substitute to the manufacturing process. He has analyzed the implications of the relationship between intermediate services, scale, and specialization, with explicit role for producer services in the linkage, coordination and control of specialized, interdependent operations, through both internal market expansion and changes in the extent of the market due to increased opportunities for trade. His analysis follows the important theoretical literature of Grubel and Walker (1988), Jones and

Kierzkowski (1988), Markusen (1989) and Rivera-Batiz and Rivera-Batiz (1988), and Greenfield (1966), where the important function of the service sector in coordinating and linking together specialized operations in production process in an open economy is not analysed, but rather concentrated on trade in specialized or differentiated intermediate services. Francois's model shows that trade liberalization in services sector, accompanied by an increase in the scale of individual firms and a rising employment share for services, results in the realization of returns due to specialization. The cost and availability of producer services may be a limit to the realization of increasing returns due to specialization. The disintegration of production into specialized intermediate stages depends on both scale and on the supply of producer services. This suggests that an expanding producer service sector is an important aspect of growth. Access to producer services through multinationals or through direct trade may help developing countries to take part in this process of specialization. Traded services may facilitate both increased specialization within borders and participation in a process of international specialization in various stages of production, playing a critical role in the realization of "international returns to scale".

In a paper in *The Canadian Journal of Economics* (Feb., 1990), Joseph F. Francois further shows that liberalizing trade in services, while yielding efficiency gains associated with comparative advantage, may yield additional gains for both importing and exporting countries because of an increased division of labour. He develops a one-sector, two-country, differentiated product model characterized by Chamberlinian monopolistic competition to demonstrate that the cost of producer services is an important determinant of the degree of specialization in production and that restrictions on trade in services limit the realization of the increasing returns from enhanced specialization. Liberalization of trade in services will have effects similar to those of growth, which lead to changes in the production techniques selected by firms in the service-importing and exporting countries. In fact, the gains associated with comparative advantage are augmented by the returns associated with a greater division of labour. However, a redistribution of the increased income that results from trade may be necessary to assure that both skilled and unskilled labour gain from such liberalization. With the introduction of additional sectors to the model, such liberalization would still be desirable from a world point of view, though additional transfers may be necessary to ensure that both service-importing and exporting countries share these welfare gains. The opportunity to trade for management, information processing, engineering, and a myriad of related intermediate services undoubtedly affects the choice of production methods and the organization of production. Liberalization of trade in producer services affects the extent to which specialization is applied to the production process and the realization of returns associated with such specialization. These returns are in addition to the standard comparative advantage-based arguments for liberalizing trade in services..

The growing importance of services or in domestic economies and international trade is due largely to an increase in the production of producer services, that is private services satisfying business of intermediate demand. Firms increasingly delegate costly, knowledge-intensive intermediate-stage processing activities in their production processes to specialized outside producers in order to gain cost advantages. They tend to exploit more fully the scale economies that are often associated with the provision of knowledge-intensive producer services. Countries generally differ in the extent to which producers in final goods sectors have the opportunity to gain cost advantages by using knowledge-intensive producer services. But services markets are among the most regulated markets of an economy, and the extent of a coherently and efficiently operating market for producer services depends crucially upon how stringent the regulatory barriers are. Such regulations are often found in less developed countries. To investigate the structural difference of the producer services sectors on trade patterns and welfare, C. van Marrewij, J. Stibora and A. Vaal (Economica, Nov., 1996) have developed a general equilibrium model in which two countries, Home and Foreign, are similar in all respects, except that in Home there is an efficiently operating market for knowledge-intensive producer services. Both countries produce two goods, manufactures and food, and, whereas Home manufacturers can establish efficiency gains by delegating specific tasks to outside services producers, Foreign initially lacks such a possibility and generally faces a comparative disadvantage in the manufactured good. Opening up to trade in goods is not necessarily beneficial to both countries : whereas the Foreign always gains, Home may lose if the extent of the market for services is not large enough. Opening up to trade in goods and services reverses this result. In this case, it is Home that always gains, whereas Foreign needs a sufficiently large number of imported services in order to gain. The results of trade in goods and FDI in services—services are often non-tradables—are truly mixed, and depend on the exact mode by which FDI takes place—both countries may lose or gain. They distinguish between three ways of modeling FDI : free transfer of technology scenario, the subsidiary scenario and the labour movement scenario. In the first scenario it is the technology of services provision that is transferred from Home to Foreign—in return for the profits made in the Foreign services sector—so that in the trade equilibrium Foreign becomes a replica of Home-in-autarky. Consequently, welfare in Home remains the same *vis-a-vis* autarky, and Foreign country gains only if the extent of its services market is large enough. In the second scenario, the transfer of technology takes place in the form of Home's services firms establishing subsidiaries in Foreign. It then follows that the welfare effects for each country are the same as if services are tradable, so that setting up subsidiaries for services abroad is a perfect substitute for trade. Home thus always gains, while Foreign gains only if the extent of the market for services is large enough. The distribution of the welfare gains changes dramatically if we consider the third scenario, in which it is assumed that the know-how required for the production of services is embodied in its fixed-cost component. In that case, either country may win or lose from trade—the country that in equilibrium exports the manufacturing good that gains from free trade. However, whereas this is a sufficient condition for Home to gain, in Foreign this is true only if the export of manufactures is accompanied by a large enough services market.

The policy implications of their analysis are as follows: First, the welfare effects of free trade in services qualitatively depend upon the nature of the services involved, and countries will differ in their preferences regarding the liberalization of each specific services category, irrespective of whether or not they have a services sector. Consequently, in order to achieve success, any negotiating procedure to liberalize trade in services must acknowledge the fact that different types of services require different types of treatment. Second, within the group of non-tradable services, the accrual of welfare effects depends on the particular mode of services. As such, trade negotiations between a country with a producer services sector and a country that lacks such a sector can be expected to take a long time. Moreover, once such an agreement is reached, if it involves permanent cross-border labour movements, it is conceivable that countries will subsequently engage in a distortive game of favouring their own manufacturing sector, as it is this sector that is instrumental in order to seize the welfare gains of trade liberalization.

Jones and Ruane (1990) have focused on the options for trade in services from an initial state where all types of service products and factors are sheltered from global markets. Assuming that all production, including services, makes use of a factor used only in that process as well as local input, labour, available to all sectors. While labour, which is sectorally mobile, is trapped by national borders, every specific factor in non-service activities is assumed to be internationally mobile. Assuming free trade and perfect competition in all markets for a price-taking small open economy, with difference in technological knowledge (with comparative technological advantage in favour of the home country) and factor endowments between nations, they have arrived at the following results :

(a) When factor endowment differences outweigh the differences in technological knowledge at home and abroad, (i) trade in service factor moves output of local service sector in a direction opposite to that taken when trade at the product level is opened up instead; and (ii) of the two alternative trading options, the one corresponding to expansion of the service sector yields greater gains, given the initial assumption of home country having comparative technological advantage.

This involves overshooting of the gap between the autarky and world prices of the service product, when the country has super-abundance of the service factor in its endowment bundle, or between the autarky and world prices of the service factor, when the service factor is scarce at the local level.

(b) Opening up trade in either service product or factor, in the competitive framework, shall improve unambiguously national welfare, independent of the country's relative factor endowments, and whether or not it has a technological comparative advantage in service sector or not. The extent of welfare gain shall, however, depend on which trading option—product or factor trade—is chosen, if technologies differ between nations. However, following one of the trade options may widen the divergence between home and foreign prices in the local market. Therefore, for a government, wishing to choose between trade options, comparisons of domestic and world prices for the service product and factor in autarky may not be sufficient to indicate the preferred pattern of trade, one need to look at technological comparative advantage or disadvantages in services of that nation.

(c) As the service sector is gradually liberalized to free international trade, when technological knowledge differs across nations, relative factor endowments do not influence trading patterns—technological superiority in services would under complete free trade lead to complete specialization in the production of services, whereas technological inferiority in services will lead to complete specialization in manufacturing, thus reflecting a Ricardian pattern of international specialization.

(d) While following the either option for opening up of trade in services results in welfare gains, the rewards are asymmetrically distributed across factors, and the magnitude of difference in relative rewards depends on the trade option chosen. The option which generates larger welfare gains also involves greater disparity in changes in relative factor rewards. Thus, depending on

> their distributional objectives, government may face an equity-efficiency trade-off in its choice of the trade option. In the extreme endowments case, the option involving greater welfare gains involves overshooting of the factor rewards of either the service factor or of labour and the non-service factors, compared with final completely free-trade equilibrium

Thus services can be incorporated into the traditional trade framework by articulation of the Heckscher-Ohlin model. But this requires some care in specifying the nature of a particular service and of demand and supply conditions. There are cases of services trade as middle products, and the scope for scale economies and imperfect competition in input and output markets. Furthermore, given the nature of some services transactions, the standard trade model has to be combined with the theory of foreign investment, with regard to such services as banking and insurance, international transactions coupled with investment by foreign companies and multinationals assume importance, and risk and uncertainty associated with such investment are to be incorporated in the formal dynamic analysis of trade in such services, and the result of deregulation and consequent liberalization of such services. Quite clearly, however, risk would have to be introduced into the analysis.

2.4. PRODUCT QUALITY AND TRADE

International trade in goods are guided by quality factors also, and recent researches in trade theory have tried to identify factors that affect international transactions in goods which are differentiated by quality. The factors include technology, demand elasticities—price as well as income—in home and foreign countries, skills of the domestic workers and the distribution of income and wage inequality that it generates. Liberalisation of trade would tend to drive away dirty bundles or poor quality goods from the consumption set of the domestic residents provided their real income increases as a result of the regime shift in policy. Comparative advantage in terms of cost differences apart, comparative quality differences constitute the rational basis of trade in commodities, and similar logic applies to trade in services, where quality differences are reflected in the efficiency of factors engaged in services production in different locations or countries, and influence international transactions in such services.

Exports of dirty goods by developing countries, and export of poor quality unskilled labour-intensive products by East European countries in the 1990s have been the basis of concern regarding the link between product quality and international trade. Murphy and Shleifer (1997) have argued that high income countries both produce and demand high quality goods, whereas low income countries both produce and demand low quality goods. This is primarily due to endowment asymmetry between these set of countries with respect to stock of human capital or skilled manpower which provide each with comparative advantage with regard to production of good and bad quality products respectively, but demand preference for quality products, which is reflected in willingness to pay, which is a function of the level of incomes of these countries, may neutralize such supply side advantages such that in equilibrium no trade may take place between countries. More specifically, countries rich in human capital produce high quality products, but also demand high quality goods because human capital has made them wealthier. On the other hand, countries poor in human capital produce low quality goods aplenty with their low skills, and also prefer lower quality goods than rich countries because their willingness and ability to pay for better quality is low. Therefore, countries rich in human capital typically have comparative disadvantage at lower quality goods relative to high quality goods, and therefore cannot profitably export them to poor countries. Because countries tend to be good at producing goods similar to the ones they prefer to consume, countries with very different stocks of human capital may not trade amongst themselves in equilibrium—only countries with similar human capital endowment would tend to trade more with each other—a pattern predicted by Linder's hypothesis, which is extended by Markusen (1986), with regard to capital intensity of products, rather than product quality. The empirical evidence from survey of individual plants on Linder's hypothesis gives mixed result. With imperfect substitutability between product quality and quantity, Murphy and Shleifer have shown that, unlike in the standard Ricardian or Heckscher-Ohlin set-up, tastes and endowments are correlated in the sense that countries with low (high) endowments of human capital prefer to consume fairly low (high) quality goods, in which they themselves have comparative advantage in production, and hence might not trade with countries which are very different from themselves. Imperfect substitutability between quality and quantity generates consumer's preference in each country for a particular type of quantity/quality combination, and generates results which would not be obtained in the standard hedonic pricing model of Lancaster (1966). Very similar countries have a low volume of trade with each other because they make similar goods, and very different countries have a low volume of trade because they demand very different goods. The volume of trade is the largest for some intermediate difference in human capital endowments between the two countries. When extended to multi-country framework there shall be chains of trade—an intermediate country exports moderate quality goods and imports X, but then turns around and imports high quality goods from a rich country and exports X to that country. Thus, each country, when it trades, imports quality goods from its best available trading partners, meaning the ones whose most efficient quality is closest to the country's ideal quantity demanded, but gains from trade with the closest country might be lower than gains from trade with a country that is further away.

Acharyya and Jones (2001) have developed a dynamic general equilibrium model for a small open economy to explain the two-way causality between income distribution and export quality. Their result is quite revealing : *A country with relatively smaller endowment of capital or more unskilled labourer typifying a less developed labour surplus economy, will have a higher return on capital relative to unskilled wage and shall produce low quality variety of exports compared to other advanced nations endowed larger stock of physical capital.* Their model also echoes the results of Fulvey and Kierzkowski (1987) whereby a country endowed with superior technology will in general export better quality variety. Trade policies by affecting income distribution at home may affect the quality of exports, and since the export sector competes with rest of the economy for scarce capital, quality variations also affect domestic income distribution. The result would be invariant to the liberalization of tariff rates for imported intermediate inputs used intensively in the non-traded service sector-tariff rate liberalization would promote expansion of this non-traded service sector, which would affect domestic income distribution by tilting the return on capital relative to unskilled wage. Imposition of minimum quality standards would also expand the labour-intensive non-traded service sector and raise return on capital and reduce unskilled wage rate. Such minimum quality restrictions introduce distortions in the system, leading to loss of real income and hence lower demand for both non-traded services as well as traditional exports. The implication of this general equilibrium analysis for trade in services is that quality differentiated services also affect domestic income distribution and hence domestic demand for both tradeables and non-tradeables, and affect the rewards of different factors differently. But quality differences also segment the market for services, and the marginal willingness to pay for services also varies as the levels of income of domestic and foreign buyers are affected by liberalization of trade regimes. The opening up of trade in services where the services provided by developing countries are quality-differentiated, forces the following outcome in a otherwise competitive free trading distortion free regime :

(a) Low quality domestic services, though have comparative cost advantages, may not be demanded by developed countries' consumers with higher levels of income—these low quality low priced services cater to huge domestic demand at low willingness and ability to pay by majority of domestic consumers of services like education, health services, etc.
(b) The competition from high quality service providers from abroad would tend to eliminate the existing low quality service providers who have been surviving due to protection of home markets by the government's hitherto pursued protectionist policies favouring indigenous enterprises; but these imports would constitute the consumption basket of the upper income ladder in the income distribution. It is possible that

providers of lower quality indigenous services, because of shrinkage of their home market, would face exit threat, and this would further degrade the quality of these services for the poorer consumers—the complementarity between domestic demand and technological capability thus affects the pattern of specialization and trade in developing countries.

(c) The high quality service providers at home, who have attained the technological or otherwise capabilities comparable to the world level providers will continue to survive and even grow with abilities to export their services to foreign markets where consumers preferring high quality services are able and willing to pay better prices for quality products, would be guided by comparative costs of these services exported from a developing country and produced in their home country. How the export revenue from such services are distributed among the consumers would determine the net effects of liberalization of trade in such services on national welfare.

According to Acharyya (2005), the marginal willingness to pay and the cost of quality are the two basic forces underlying the choice of product quality. The demand side determinants include tastes and incomes and technological asymmetry across firms constitutes the supply side explanation, and market concentration rather than competition raises product quality through its favourable influence on average industry quality. Given the heterogeneity of tastes and income levels by the consumers, market would offer both high and low quality products, and when different types of quality of services goods coexist, the effect of liberal trade policy would be to accentuate the market segmentation.

In case of domestic monopoly of the supply of services, the high-type consumers will be offered the same high quality of the services, whereas the low-type consumers will get lower quality of product variety. Thus, there will be quality distortions at the lower end of the market and incentive on the part of domestic monopolist to degrade the quality of services offered to low-end consumers increases as the size of the relatively affluent and high type consumers increases, and this would also be reflected in the differential prices for different quality of services in the economy. When both the preference and cost structure is linear, the monopolist would offer a pooling menu with the topmost quality to both types of consumers. This result is independent of the number of types of consumers or whether they are distributed discretely or continuously over the types. However, when costs involve positive spillover effects so that production of high quality variety lowers the costs of lower quality variety of products, the higher category of consumers may be offered a lower quality product than are offered to lower spectrum of consumers at the socially optimum equilibrium. Thus quality distortions may occur for both category of consumers, with the higher type consumers getting still better quality of product or services, whereas for the low category of consumers, the quality is definitely degraded.

The above analysis presumes the existence of consumers with differential tastes but with identical income levels, but they are not constrained by the paucity of purchasing power. Thus all of these higher type consumers can afford to pay for even the highest quality of products, even if such a high price charge for such products take away all of their consumer surplus. In the presence of such binding purchasing power constraint faced by the consumers, even if the marginal willingness to pay does not vary with the income levels and all consumers have identical tastes and hence identical marginal willingness to pay, there is a possibility of quality discrimination and differentiation at equilibrium and when international trade opens up and the domestic monopolist is in a position to cover a sizeable part of global market, the product or service quality will be differentiated for all types of consumers. When there exists technological asymmetry between producers/suppliers from developed and developing countries, the range of qualities produced at home would become a lower subset of the qualities of the range of services produced by technologically advanced developed countries. Such a technological backwardness in developing countries is mainly due to low level of R & D expenditure or investment in products or services and inflow of foreign suppliers to the domestic market in a liberalized set-up does not necessarily ensure the bridging of this technological gap, and therefore, does ensure reduction in costs or improvements in product quality in developing countries. High protective wall in the form of prohibitive tariff may be the reason for low incentive to domestic supplier to innovate or incur R & D expenditure for improving product quality, and maintain monopoly in low quality products or services in the protected domestic market, but when entry of foreign suppliers are permitted into the domestic market, they come with superior or low-cost technology and uses cheaper domestic resources like land or credit to expand production of higher quality products/services, and domestic suppliers, instead of benefiting from knowledge spillovers, would be constrained to operate on low quality products for consumers of lower income strata. Given the disparity in income distribution in developing countries, and the possibility of purchasing power constraint among a large number of consumers, there is a likelihood of prevalence of low quality products or services in such countries as compared to range of high quality products/services available in developed countries in the world.

A further problem of poor product/service quality in developing economies arises in the presence of asymmetric information whereby the producers face moral hazard and adverse selection. Absence of perfect warranty system, high cost of maintaining reputation through high quality and the informational externality prohibit the suppliers in developing countries to overcome these problems. In developing countries most of the markets are characterized by the presence of numerous small producers without any sunk cost and free and easy entry and exit. There is no incentive for the incumbent supplier to build reputation, and the potential entrants, being transient in nature, do not care in building reputation and supply quality products. Because of inherent informational externality, efforts to enhance individual quality enhances average industry quality and, making social marginal benefit exceeding the private marginal benefit. Thus quality offered by an individual producer falls short of socially optimum levels. Whereas the contestable markets diminish the incentives for maintaining good reputation to overcome the moral hazard problem for the producers, poor perceptions regarding average industry quality generates lower willingness to pay for goods and services produced in developing countries. The problem can be explained in case of educational services provided by many private enterprises in a country like India, where there is also a public sector. Because of informational asymmetry and externality, these producers could not or do not care for quality upgradation of education, as result of which we have bad or ill-reputed institutions providing educational services, which are far below the international standards, and therefore faces the danger of being wiped out in the face of competition from international institutions/service providers on quality grounds. There is also the problem of technological gap in capability, and given the uncertainty in the market for education services, and quality differentiation at different income levels there is no incentive for them to innovate or improve quality, and there exists plenty of domestic demand for inferior quality of educational services compared to international standards.

3

Globalisation, GATS and Trade in Educational Services

3.1. GLOBALISATION

The conclusion of Uruguay Round of negotiations under the GATT led to the formation of World Trade Organisation in 1994 to facilitate multilateralism in global trade and investment flows as integration in the world economy took place in a significant manner through expansion of trade and financial flows during the decades of 1980s and 1990s. Globalisation in its present form has opened up new challenges for trade, investment flows and financial movements across the different regions of the world, and a world body assigned with the task of providing the regulatory framework necessary for the free trade in goods, services and financial flows across the nations and to set-up the rules and norms for opening up multilateral transactions in these areas of goods and services across the globe. Trade in services has been included as one of the major aspects of the agreement of the formation of WTO and in this chapter we shall review critically the role of GATS treaty in facilitating global trade in services in general and trade in educational services in particular.

The meaning of the term globalisation appears differently to different persons depending on the perceptions and perspectives. In economic terms, globalisation means a process of transition to free trade in goods, services and factors of production across the globe. Ideally, on a theoretical plane, explanations of the effects of the operation under such a globalised and liberalized trade regime can be made in terms of general equilibrium models of international trade, but the actual world operation of trade regimes in different countries are far from the ideal world, and therefore the effects of liberalization of such a varied and differentiated trade regimes in the world economy are likely to be inherently complex, diverse and difficult to predict. There are therefore many advantages as well as disadvantages of trade liberalization induced participation in the globalisation process. One of the most important aspects of such trade liberalization has been to transform the hitherto non-tradeables into tradeables. This may be due to changes in the technological capabilities, and changes in the rules and institutional reforms that follow expansion of foreign trade in many countries. Such a change has very important implications for the domestic economy's resource allocation, efficiency, growth and welfare, both in the short and the long-run. The implication of the expansion of the domains of international trade on domestic economy has been varied across different countries and regions, and therefore we see that the benefits of globalisation has been rather mixed. In the words of Joseph Stiglitz (2002) : "Globalization itself is neither good nor bad. It has the *power* to do enormous goods, and for the countries of East Asia, who have embraced globalisation *under their own terms*, at their *own pace*, there has been an enormous benefit, in spite of the setback of the 1997 crisis. But in much of the world it has not brought comparable benefits. For many, it seems closer to an unmitigated disaster." And he continued to add, "Today, with the continuing decline in transportation and communication costs, and the reduction of man-made barriers to the flow of goods, services, and capital, we have a process of 'globalization' analogous to the earlier processes in which national economies were formed during the nineteenth century.

Unfortunately, we have no world government, to oversee the globalization process in a fashion comparable to the way national governments guided the nationalization process. Instead, we have a system that might be called *global governance* without global government, one in which few institutions and few players dominate the scene, but in which many of those affected by their decisions are left almost voiceless." There is no denying the fact that benefits of globalisation are asymmetrically distributed among the participants in the liberalization process, and this has caused anxiety and tensions regarding the effects of globalisation in many countries, including the less developed ones.

There can be benefits from liberalization of trade in services, accompanied by the reform of complementary policies, both to sectoral and economy-wide improvements in performance. Among the sectoral effects, the removal of barriers to trade in services in a particular sector can lead to lower prices, improved quality, and greater variety of services. As in the case of trade in goods, restriction on trade in services reduce welfare because they create a wedge between domestic and foreign prices, that lead to a consumers' loss which is greater than the increase in producer surplus and government revenue. Several empirical studies support this contention. Since many services are inputs into production, the inefficient supply of such services acts as a tax on production and prevents the realization of significant gains in productivity. As countries reduce tariffs and other barriers to trade in goods, effective rates of protection for manufacturing industries may become negative if they continue to be confronted with input prices that are higher than they would be if services markets were competitive. Furthermore, trade liberalization is likely to provide access to a wider variety of services whose production is subject to economies of the scale. There can also be an indirect benefit to consumers because a wider variety of more specialized producer services, such as telecommunications and finance, can lower the costs of both goods and services production (Ethier, 1982; Copeland, 2001). In such circumstances, smaller markets can have a strong interest in liberalizing trade in producer services, since this can offset some of the incentives that firms have to locate in larger markets. (Markusen, 1989).

The economy-wide effect of liberalization of trade in services varies from country to country, ranging from under 1 percent to over 50 percent of GDP, depending on the initial levels of protection and the assumed reduction in barriers. In simulations of global service-trade liberalization, developed countries are found to have more gains in absolute terms—which is not surprising, given the relative size of their economics—but developing countries also see significant increases in their GDP. One econometric model has predicted gains of between 1.6 percent of GDP (for India) to 4.2 percent of GDP (for Thailand) if tariff-equivalents of protection were cut by one-third in all countries (Chadha *et. al.*, 2003). The gains from liberalizing services may be substantially greater than those from liberalizing trade in goods, because current levels of protection are higher and because liberalization would also create spur. For instance, one model has found that the welfare gains from a 50 percent cut in service-sector trade liberalization would be five times larger than the gains from non-service sector trade liberalization (Robinson *et. al.*, 1999). These results are particularly striking because they are derived from models that do not fully allow for the temporary movement of individual service suppliers, which is potentially a major source of gain. Temporary movements of workers offers arguably the neatest solution to the dilemma of how international migration is best managed, enabling the realization of gains from trade while averting social and political costs in host countries and brain drain from poor countries. Recent research finds that if OECD countries were to allow temporary access to foreign service providers equal to just 3 percent of their labour force, the global gains would be over $ 150 billion more than the gains from the complete liberalization of all trade in goods (Walmsley and Winters, 2005). Both developed and developing countries would share in these gains, and they would be largest if both high-skilled mobility and low-skilled mobility were permitted.

There is a relatively strong econometric evidence for the financial sector and less strong but nevertheless statistically significant for the telecommunication sector, that openness in services does influence long run growth performances. After controlling for other determinants of growth, countries that have fully liberalized the financial service sector grew, on average, about 1.0 percentage point faster than other countries. An even greater impetus on growth was found to come from fully liberalizing both the telecommunication and financial service sectors. Estimates suggest that countries which fully liberalized both the sectors grew, on average, about 1.5 percentage points faster than other countries. Furthermore, barriers to entry in a number of service sectors, ranging from telecommunications to professional services, are maintained not only against foreign suppliers but also against new domestic suppliers. Full liberalization can, therefore, lead to enhanced competition from both domestic and foreign suppliers. Greater foreign factor participation and an increased competition together imply a larger scale of activity, and hence greater scope for generating the special growth enhancing effects. Even without scale effects, if greater technology transfer accompanies service liberalization—either embodied in FDI or disembodied—the growth effect will be stronger. Of course, the success of liberalization of trade in services would require adoption of complementary domestic economic policies to prevent and preempt the adverse consequences of foreign competition leading to monopoly and extinction of domestic services.

Opening up essential services to foreign or domestic competition could have an adverse effect on the poor which is often cited as a reason for the persistence of public monopolies. However, a more efficient solution is to have regulations with a social purpose. If a country is a relatively inefficient producer of a service, liberalization and the resultant foreign competition are likely to lead to a decline in domestic prices and improvement in quality. But the twist is that in many cases in developing countries, the prices pre-liberalization are not determined by the market, but are often set administratively and kept artificially low for certain categories of end-users and/or types of services products. Such a structure of prices is often sustained through cross-subsidization within public monopolies or through Government financial support. And liberalization often threatens these arrangements—elimination of restrictions on entry may actually lead to an end to cross-subsidization because it becomes no longer possible for firms to make extra-normal profits in certain market segments, and new entrants may focus on the most profitable market segments (cream-skimming), such as urban areas, where network costs are lower and incomes higher. And privatization could mean the end of government support. The result is that even though the sector becomes more efficient and average prices decline, the prices for certain end-users may actually increase and/or availability decline. The evidence on relationship between competitive market structures and wider access to services is mixed. In some cases, a positive relationship has been observed in services like basic telecommunications, especially in countries where initial conditions are feeble, as exemplified by a low tele-density or service rationing (long waiting lists for obtaining connections). However, there is also evidence that financial services liberalization in some countries has had an adverse effect on access to credit for rural areas and the poor. There is thus a need to create mechanisms to ensure that the poor have adequate access to services in liberalized markets.

Economic globalization had led to huge expansion of international trade. The expansion since 1945 had been phenomenal, despite ups and down periodically and slowdown in the world economy after the oil price shock and the consequent downturn that affected world trade. The adoption of protectionist tariff policies by many developing countries to promote domestic industrialization, and use of non-tariff barriers by many developed nations despite proclaiming principles of free multilateral trade with the purpose of domestic stabilization did affect the growth of world trade during 1970s and 1980s. The scenario began to change in the 1990s when breakdown of the socialist regimes in Eastern Europe and free flows of goods and services to the transition economies, and gradual dismantling of tariff and non-tariff barriers by both developing and developed countries have helped the expansion of world trade significantly. In 1997 the value of global trade has reached US $5.47 trillion and non-government services of developed economies was found to be is US $ 12 trillion, i.e., over 60% of GDP of industrialized countries and 50% of developing countries. The situation had progressed further in the new millennium, but in recent years there had been some slowdown in the world economy which affected trade performances. According to the Annual Report of WTO, 2006, the world economy had expanded by 3.3 per cent in 2005, less rapidly than in 2004, but still slightly faster than the decade average. Economic growth remained strong in most regions although less buoyant than in the preceding year. In 2005, the value of world merchandise exports rose by 13 per cent, to US $ 10.1 trillion, and that of world commercial services exports by 11 per cent to US $ 2.4 trillion. For both merchandise and commercial services, this represented a marked deceleration in growth when compared with the preceding year. Cross-border commercial services exports expanded for the third year in a row less rapidly than world merchandise exports. World economic output of goods and services is estimated to have expanded by 3.3 per cent and real merchandise exports rose by 6 per cent in 2005 (Table 3.1). The year-to-year deceleration of global economic output and trade was rather close to the predictions made in early 2005. However, at the more disaggregated level the actual outcome deviated from projections, but the impact of these deviations on output and trade tended to offset each other. The negative impact of higher than predicted oil prices on global output and trade in 2005 was partly offset by more resilience than expected to the oil price hikes, illustrated, for example, by the stronger than projected economic activity in Japan.

TABLE 3.1

World Trade and Output Development, 2002-05
(At Constant Prices, Annual Percentage Change)

	2002	*2003*	*2004*	*2005*
Merchandise Exports	3.5	5.0	9.5	6.0
Merchandise Production	0.8	3.5	4.0	—
GDP at Market Exchange rates	1.7	2.6	4.0	3.1
GDP at Constant PPP	3.0	4.0	5.1	4.3

Source : WTO; IMF, World Economic Outlook.

Expansion of trade and investment flows across the globe has important consequences, some of which are unintended. The acceleration of growth profiles, accentuation of income and wealth inequality between nations and across groups within many developing countries, the trade-off between equity and efficiency, and the diversification in production in many countries are result of globalisation in the sense of freer mobility of goods between countries. But one novel consequence of this process of specialization has been to draw some of the non-traded sectors into the ambit of tradeables, and trade in services is a case in point. Services are not only final consumption goods, most of them have the feature of producers' goods as well. Therefore, trade in services as a consequence of globalisation-induced expansion of trade affects national welfare, the order and extent of effect depending upon the returns to scale that technology reflect and the market structure in which production and exchange takes place. But the world is not of free trade, there are distortions and conflicts that needed monitoring and control at the world level, and sometimes this task of coordinating trade policies of different countries, which aimed at national interests only, becomes crucially important, yet difficult. Distortions in the domestic economies some inherently structural and some policy-induced hamper maximization of social welfare at the national level and lead to non-tariff barriers to prevent entry of cheaper and cost-effective products in the respective domains of national interests. For about past 50 years, the task of monitoring and regulating international trade was done by permanent negotiating forum. GATT (General Agreement on Tariff and Trade), which acted as a permanent forum for negotiations and execution of international agreements relating to trade, investment and financial flows across nations. In 1995 GATT was replaced by an international organization consisting of 134 members, called the World Trade Organisation (WTO) which is responsible for the implementation of agreement during the Uruguay Round of GATT negotiations. While the functioning of GATT was confined to only trade in commodities, the WTO agreement includes investments, services and copyrights. WTO now plays a central role in governing international trade in the world and the different articles of agreement of the WTO provides regulatory framework for international trade and development of trade policies. The agreement establishing the WTO had *three* major objectives : (a) Promoting trade liberalization; (b) Progressively increasing this liberalization through negotiation; and (c) Establishing mechanism for settlement of dispute.

The history of evolution of the multilateral trading system since the Second World War has been replete with ironies. Firstly, growth and liberalization of the international trading system has been the most important success during the post-war period, even though the participating nations could not produce a charter for an international trade organization that was acceptable to key governments like the USA. Secondly, the remarkable success of multilateral tariff negotiations under the aegis of the GATT has made the world truly interdependent at a phenomenal rate, and there was increasing concern about a "level playing field" for all competitors. Although the ramifications of increased interdependence gave rise to great gloominess over the success of the Uruguay round of negotiations, yet the outcome was an overwhelming success, which included not only a framework of agreement on services trade, agreements on intellectual property rights and trade-related investment measures, a timetable for phasing out all quantitative restrictions on trade, first steps to bring agriculture under multilateral purview, but also the establishment of the WTO, completing the triads with IMF and World Bank, as was designed under the Washington Consensus. The role of USA shifted from being a protector of its domestic inefficient industries in the form of numerous tariff and non-tariff barriers to a player in fiercer global competitor in world trade, facilitating thereby transition to a world body to coordinate and regulate international trade in goods and services in the world and lay down the rules governing such trade and trade negotiations in case of disputes between countries, and or violation of these principles.

3.2. SERVICES AND DEVELOPMENT

The traditional role of services is related to the provision of physical infrastructure such as health, housing, water and sanitation and education, as well as the availability of financial services (which is an integral part of national development strategies). Policies with respect to these sectors are in general influenced by consideration of national security, attainment of particular strategic objective, infrastructure for economic activities and consumer protection, social dimension and universal provision are also important. The national governments play a major role in service sector and regulate it. The need to reconcile this complex objective with economic efficiency and international competitiveness raises a dilemma for developing countries, wherein the service sector is characterized by both highly regulated and open sector, presence of a number of small and medium sized enterprise and also include transnational corporations. Inefficiencies in the provision of service sector outputs by the monopoly suppliers in the government sector have put pressures on private firms to improve management and operational efficiency for ensuring quality, reasonable price and adapting it to advance technology, so as to afford international competitiveness of their products. The need for new regulatory framework by the government was also evident to cope with the new dynamism in the activities of the service sector, where not only domestic private enterprises but also enterprises with foreign ownership have entered as big players in many countries of the world. The image of service as non-productive sector has been replaced by a more dynamic role of service brought about by communication technology and efficient producer services.

The developed countries contribute 2/3 of their GDP and developing contributes to over 40% of their GDP to service sector activities. New information technologies have increased scope of trade in many "knowledge-intensive" services. The establishment of international networks has led to substantial economies of scale and scope, greater value-added is created, and limitations are eliminated. But, trade statistics and service transaction do not reflect this. Services are fastest growing component of trade growing component of trade and FDI accounting 20% of world trade and 3/5 of FDI flow (mainly among developed countries). Service share in foreign trade is smaller than production and employment. Since 1990's share of commercial service on BOP remain unchanged. But in 1998 world trade in commercial services has increased to US $ 1.3 trillion. The share of top ten exporters of commercial services is over 65% of total trade. Computer and information services, royalties and license fee, construction services constitute over 90% of exports in financial services. In most developing countries, services do not make a positive contribution to the external sector, except where there are benefits from an active international movement of person. Some developing countries, with vigorous growth in export of manufactures, also exhibited their strength in trade in service, in 1999, for example, some developing countries in North America and Asia have their comparative advantage in labour-intensive services from trade in accounting, legal, health and advertising services. International service trade by developing countries also reflects internal weakness of trade in goods and services. Advances in telecommunication and information technology have created new opportunity for developing countries to find niches for themselves in both developed and developing economies. There are nice opportunities for expansion of trade in six sector (professional and business service, health, tourism, construction, audio visual and transport) in which developing countries have potential comparative advantage through movement of natural person. India received US $ 76 billion in 1996, which was three times as high as net direct investment inflow in 1996. Many service markets are dominated by relatively few large firms from developed countries. So, developing countries' service providers, who are small and medium size enterprises, face competition from large service multinationals with massive financial strength with access to the latest technology worldwide network and a sophisticate information technology infrastructure. This high degree of concentration is often a consequence of the enormous volume of capital and the complex network of interdependent organization needed to maintain technological advantage to exploit several products simultaneously and maintain economic of scale. UNCTAD's studies on air transport, construction, health and tourism highlighted the possible anti-competitive impact of these new business techniques. A number of key competition issues are also raised by the manner in which distribution channel and information network for several service are structured. Due to increasing globalization it become difficult for service firm to succeed without entering into some form of strategic alliance. And a strategic alliance may develop into *de facto* industry standard-setters or price-setters. Given the critical role of service (as intermediate processes in the production of goods, contribution to value-added, FDI) specific policy initiatives are required to improve the efficiency and competitively of service sector. Policies, which are preconditions for benefiting from liberalization of trade in services relate to capacity building in human resources and technology, upgrading of telecommunication infrastructure, incentives and financing for service firms to increase their competitiveness, and pro-competitive economic policies, including progressive external market opening and encouraging FDI flows, improving access to market information and presence in major market, institutional reforms providing for independent regulatory supervision, establishing service industry association to put their members in touch with potential partners in target market and to voice the need of service industry, and so on.

Adoption of national export strategy is important for country's economic development. Developing countries would need to strengthen their efforts to expand trade and investment opportunities and co-operate at the regional and inter-regional levels to diversify markets and to take advantage of global trading opportunities. In particular, developing countries need to devise measures so as to develop specific sector/sub-sector/activity which would strengthen the sector itself through introduction of competition, efficiency and transfer of technology, strengthen other goods and service sectors, including expansion of export of goods and services, infrastructure building, and attracting of FDI flows through opening of commercial presence with appropriate limitations and performance requirement could contribute to domestic capacity-building.

Negotiations on service under GATS involve a stake for developing countries as much as developed countries. Reforms in domestic policies by developing countries are as important as reforms in external policies and developing countries need carefully to consider the costs and benefits of policy reform and further market opening. Benefits of liberalization in terms of access to lower cost imports, reduction of price-cost margins by limiting the power of suppliers to restricting output to raise price, increasing competition, efficiency gains, dynamic innovation gains through knowledge spillover and transfer of technology and potential trade opportunities should be balanced against the cost liberalization in terms of structural adjustment and impact on BOP. While liberalization may lead to loss of business by nascent service suppliers which may result in loss of future growth opportunities in the sector where there is scope for rapid learning and productivity improvement opportunities. Employment loss particularly amongst lower skilled and social loss in terms of access to key services could also result from liberalization. The opening up of the service sector, and policy reforms to encourage growth in these activities, may be coupled with transfer of technology and foreign direct investment to promote expansion in employment opportunities and unleash a process of high growth trajectory in the service sector leading to expansion of income and purchasing power in the poor developing countries and thereby reduce the incidence of poverty.

3.3. WTO AND GATS

After the Uruguay round of negotiations, GATT, which began in 1947, was replaced by the formation of WTO in 1995 through the Marakaash Agreement with the objective of broadening the scope for trade liberalization across the globe and gradual dismantling of non-tariff barriers imposed by many countries over the years. WTO proposes to broaden the scope of international trade by including in its ambit international trade in services which were hitherto considered as non-tradables. This was done by WTO through the General Agreement in Trade in Services (GATS). The major aims of GATS treaty has been (a) to expand free trade in services; (b) to open up markets for services; and (c) to facilitate economic growth of nations through trade. In the field of higher education, the aim has been to remove restrictions to market access and barriers to competition in higher education.

Under GATS, while extending trade in services, including education and health services, the member-nations are bound by two guiding principles. First, is to disallow bestowing 'most-favoured-nation status', the degree to which a WTO member opens a sector of its service market to any country must be the same for all member-countries. The second is 'principle of national treatment', this requires all members to treat service providers, whether domestic or foreign, in the same way by the member Governments. However, the degree to which individual members commit to open their markets to foreign health services providers is quite flexible. However, GATS commitments do not explain whether they represent liberalization from previous policies, thus, does not capture how trade policies have changed over time and also do not consider the range of DR that often has a strong effect on services' trade. To address the latter problem of DR, the World Bank is developing a database on measures affecting trade in services. This would allow researchers 'to address a range of questions about services trade policy, including identification of barriers to trade; how such barriers differ across services sectors and across countries; and the implications of liberalizing trade in services for overall economic performance'.

GATS commits WTO members to successive rounds of negotiations "with a view to achieving a progressively higher level of liberalization" in their service sectors. To achieve this, WTO members make liberalization requests of other member-countries in secret, bilateral meetings in Geneva so as to open up to competition those sectors, which are of most interest to their own service providers. Although developing countries officially have the right to choose whether to commit a sector to GATS, in practice they come under intense pressure in these negotiations to meet the demands of more powerful WTO members—pressure which the smaller and poorer countries are often powerless to resist. In this way, GATS is primarily a mechanism for the service corporations of developed countries to expand their reach into new markets around the world. This is widely acknowledged by official negotiators: the European Commission has confirmed that GATS is "first and foremost an instrument for the benefit of business, and not only for business in general, but for individual service companies wishing to export services or to invest and operate abroad."

GATS defines the scope of the agreement as follows:

> "Services" includes any service in any sector except services supplied in the exercise of governmental authority. However, the article further clarifies that "a service supplied in the exercise of governmental authority," means any service that is supplied neither on a commercial basis nor in competition with one or more service suppliers, e.g.: social security schemes other than public such as health and education provided at non-market condition. In most countries health services are also provided by the private sector and even the government sector charges for certain services. Annex on Air Transport Services are also exempted from coverage measures affecting air traffic rights and services directly related to the exercise of such right.

Under GATS, supply can take four modes: *one,* Cross Border Supply, where the service is provided remotely from one country to another (e.g., international telephone calls, Internet services, telemedicine); *two,* Consumption Abroad, where individuals use a service in another country (e.g. tourists traveling abroad, patients taking advantage of health care in foreign countries); *three,* Commercial Presence, where a foreign company sets up a subsidiary or branch within another country in order to deliver the service locally (e.g. banks, private health clinics); *four,* Presence of Natural Persons: where individuals travel to another country to supply a service there on a temporary basis (e.g. software programmers, nurses, doctors). Although it is generally agreed that international trade is possible only through the physical presence of both the producer and the consumer, in many instances in order to be commercially meaningful, trade commitments must extend to cross-border movement of consumer, establishment of commercial presence within market or temporary movement of service provides himself. GATS acknowledges the right of the member-country to regulate supply of services in pursuit of their own policy objectives and does not seek to influence them. The GATS agreement establishes rules to ensure that service regulation are administered in a reasonable, objective and impartial manner, and do not constitute unnecessary barriers to trade.

The GATS obligations are grouped into two categories : General obligations, which apply directly and automatically to all members and service sector; and Specific obligations which are laid down in individual country schedule whose scope may vary widely between members. Two guiding principles are market access and national treatment.

(a) Under General Obligations

The MFN Treatment was to extend immediately and unconditionally—"treatment no less favourable than that accorded to like services and service suppliers of any other country". This provision therefore prohibits preferential arrangement or of reciprocity provisions which confine access benefits to trading partners granting similar treatments. All exemptions are subject to review and not to last longer than 10 years. GATS allow members to enter into mutually recognize regulatory standards, economic integration certificates and the like if certain conditions are met. The clause of transparency requires all GATS members *inter alia* to publish all measures of general application and establish national enquiry mandated to respond to other member's information requests. It also requires all members to establish administrative review appeals procedures and disciplines on the operation of monopolies and exclusive suppliers.

(b) Under Specific Commitments

Market Access is a negotiated commitment, subject various types of limitation such as—limitation imposed on number of service supplier, service operation, and employees in the sector, value of transaction, legal form of service supplier or participation of foreign capital. Under the clause on National Treatment, concerned Member does not operate discriminatory service, or service suppliers, and the key requirement has been not to modify in law or in fact the condition of competition in favour of Member's own service industry. Extension of national treatment clause in particular sector is subject to certain conditions and qualifications. While the members are free to tailor the sector coverage and substantive content of such commitments as they see fit, commitment on national treatment provides for actions to be taken to coordinate with overall objective and constraint on national policy, and in selective individual sectors. Existence of specific commitment trigger further obligations, *inter alia,* notification of new measures that have a significant impact on trade, avoidance of restriction on international payment and transfer. And each WTO Member is required to have schedule of specific commitment on the service on which member-country guarantee market access and national treatment, and any limitations that may be attached and also for additional commitments undertakes with respect to 4 modes of supply. Such schedules would consist of both Horizontal and Sectoral sections. The horizontal schedules apply across all sectors which are subsequently listed in the schedules, and limitation mentioned here often refers to a particular mode of supply (e.g., commercial presence and natural person), while the sectoral schedules apply only to the particular service. There are specific exemptions in the GATS to cater for important national policy interests: GATS permit its members in specific circumstances to introduce or maintain measures in contravention of their obligation under the Agreement. Measures such as: (i) Protect public morals or maintain public order; (ii) Protect human, animal or plant life or health; and (iii) Secure compliance with laws or regulations not in consistent with the agreement including among other measures necessary to prevent deceptive or fraudulent practices. The Annex on financial services permits members to take measures for prudential reasons, including for the protection of investors depositors, policy holders or persons to whom a fiduciary duty is owned by a financial services supplier, or to ensure that in the event of serious BOP difficulties, members are allowed temporarily restrict trade, on a non-discriminatory basis, despite the existence of specific commitments.

All the 144 signatories of the GATS treaty have agreed to abide by general GATS obligations of MFN, transparency, adjudication of dispute, impartial enforcement of measures affecting trade in services. They also make specific commitments to reduce tariff and other impediments to trade in services. These national commitments also serve as basis for negotiation between members of GATS. One may distinguish between two levels of commitment: General obligation (e.g.: most favoured nation and transparency, etc.), of which MFN implies equal treatment to all; and Specific commitments, i.e., member-country's commitments to market access and national treatment for specific sector (such as education) and each government identifies these in schedule of specific commitments. It may be noted that "National Treatment" implies treatment of GATS partners in the same way a nation's own citizens are treated, whereas "Market Access" implies market commitment in a specific service sector, with respect to number of service supplier, value of transaction, total number of service operations, total number of people employed, participation of foreign capital, etc. But members are free to tailor sector commitment as they wish, as long as limits are stated of outset. Each member may make additional commitment also.

Part III of the GATS refers to "Specific Commitments", which comprise the provisions governing the scheduling of commitments (Articles XVI to XVIII), is the centerpiece of the Agreement. All the access and country specific trade obligations under the GATS are specified in and assumed under these three articles. Nevertheless, their full implications can only be properly understood in the context of a broader framework of disciplines that are laid down in Part II. These disciplines essentially fall in two groups. First, there are those that must be respected by all members in all sectors covered by the GATS, regardless of existence of specific commitments ("unconditional obligations"), and secondly, there are disciplines ("conditional obligations") whose scope is confined to those sectors and modes for which a Member has undertaken specific commitments. Both these sets apply as they are, and cannot be modified by way of scheduling limitations.

Unconditional Obligation

The unconditional obligations contained in Part II can be grouped into three broad categories.

Accordingly, all members are required in all sectors under the Agreement :

- Not to discriminate between other WTO members (—most favoured nation (MFN) treatment pursuant to Article II and related disciplines (e.g. Article VIII: 1));
- To ensure transparency in the use of measures (—publication and information equirements, including establishment of enquiry points, under Articles III: 1 and 4); and
- To comply with some additional duties, mostly procedural in nature, *vis-a-vis* other members and their suppliers (—access to domestic judicial mechanisms (Article VI: 2); consultation requirements concerning restrictive business particles (Article IX) and trade distorting subsidies (Article XV:2)).

Given the relatively modest levels of many access commitments, it is fair to say that the most immediately palpable result of the Uruguay round, concluded in 1993, was the entry into force of the MFN requirement. In pursuant to Article II of the GATS, all members regardless of economic weight, political affiliation, levels of liberalization, etc. are automatically entitled to anti-trade benefits, whether or not covered by specific commitments, that a member extends in areas falling under the GATS. All foreign services and service suppliers must be treated on a par. As in the case of merchandise trade, the MFN requirement is a powerful instrument in particular from the perspective of small countries that do not have the economic leverage and administrative resources to negotiate effectively with large trading partners. If there is a continued disadvantage of small members, it is not rooted in discriminatory treatment, but unequal agenda-setting power. A Sub-Saharan country will certainly find it far more difficult to make itself heard and articulate its trade interests than a large developed country. Nevertheless, the GATS helps to contain such imbalances insofar as it provides a forum for information exchange, cooperation and coalition building among all members, large and small, that does not otherwise exist. Even for such core obligations as MFN treatment, the GATS offers more scope for accommodating country—and sector specific peculiarities than is the case with the GATT. This was necessary for mainly two reasons. First, the Agreement's broad policy coverage, including investment-related issues under mode 3, extends its reach into areas with a long tradition of bilateral accords. These had certainly not been drafted in view of an MFN obligation that might be contained in a future multilateral agreement, and it could take years for them to be adjusted. Second, sector-specific reciprocity concepts are particularly widespread in services trade. Since reciprocity alludes to notions of fairness and burden sharing, governments have found it easier to overcome domestic resistance to foreign competition if access remained confined to countries that offer comparable conditions. Reciprocity considerations are particularly widespread in professional services and transport. There was thus little alternative for the drafters of the GATS but to include provisions, in Article II:2, that allow for the grandfathering of existing MFN-inconsistent measures. The Annex on Article II Exemptions should not exceed a period of 10 years in principle and be subject to review, the first to take place five years after the WTO's entry into force (i.e. in 2000), and be negotiated in any subsequent trade round. About two-thirds of WTO members considered it necessary to attach a list of MFN exemptions to their services schedules in order to obtain legal cover. In total, more than 470 MFN inconsistent measures have been listed. The relevant lists are in standard format, indicating the sector concerned, the relevant measure and its inconsistency with the MFN obligation, affected countries, intended duration, and the underlying policy needs. In over 90 per cent of all cases, the exemptions are intended to apply for an indefinite or otherwise non-specified period.

The possibility of listing MFN exemptions still exists for new WTO members at the time of accession, but not for current members. The only option for them to obtain cover for additional measures would be a waiver under Article IX:3 of the WTO Agreement. However, no such waivers have been sought to date for MFN inconsistent measures. There are additional GATS rules that allow for departures from MFN treatment in specified circumstances, which may have been inspired by precursors in the GATT and certain multilateral trade agreements for goods. Relevant provisions allow members to facilitate exchanges of locally produced and consumed services in frontier zones (Article II:3); to conclude economic integration agreements (Article V) and labour market integration agreements (Article Vbis); and to recognize educational degrees, licenses, certificates, etc. from particular countries (Article VIII). Unlike the ten-year time frame for MFN exemptions, softened by the insertion of "should" and "in principle", application of the latter provisions is not subject to any time limits. However, there are other constraints to prevent abuse. Article II:3, by its very nature, is strictly limited in its geographic application; Article V requires an economic integration agreement, *inter alia,* to have "substantial sectoral coverage" and provide for the elimination of "substantially all discrimination" between participants in the relevant sectors; while recognition agreements under Article VII must be open in principle for third countries to join. Unlike Article II:3, whose application is virtually impossible to monitor, Articles V, Vb and VII contain notification requirements. However, doubts have been expressed by some WTO members as to whether these are always properly complied with. In addition, the general exceptions contained in Article XIV, already referred to before, allow members to disregard the MFN obligation, if necessary, for the attainment of the specified policy objectives, including protection of life and health.

Conditional Obligations

The conditional obligations of GATS apply additionally to sectors and modes for which bindings are being assumed, basically to protect the commercial value of what has been inscribed in schedules and prevents commitments from being gradually undermined, intentionally or otherwise, by ongoing policy changes. The GATS does not entail any disciplines or constraints on domestic regulations on a government's ability to pursue the regulatory objectives that it deems appropriate. The Preamble explicitly recognizes the right of members to regulate and introduce new regulations on the supply of services in order to meet national policy objectives. These basic principles have since been reiterated, *inter alia,* in the Ministerial Declarations in Doha (2001) and Hong Kong (2005). The intention has been to avoid unnecessary trade restrictions while members prefer implementing measures like qualification and licensing requirements, technical standards and qualification procedures, etc. The relevant disciplines are, however, rudimentary at present, except for the accountancy sector. For example, Article VI:4 merely contains a negotiating mandate to develop disciplines that seek to ensure, *inter alia*, that regulatory requirements are: based on objective and transparent criteria; not more burdensome than necessary to ensure the quality of services; and not in themselves a trade restriction (in the case of licensing procedures). Article VI:5 imposes some relatively soft, standstill obligations, such that the members should refrain from applying measures (qualifying and licensing requirements, etc.) that would nullify or impair a specific commitment, that are incompatible with the above set of criteria, and that could not reasonably have been expected of them at the time when they made commitment. Under the Article VI:4, disciplines apply to members that have undertaken specific commitments in accountancy, with focus on measures that neither fall under Article XVI (market access) nor are discriminatory within the meaning of article XVII.

GATS covered the following service sectors : Educational services as a tradeable sector and other eleven sectors, viz., business, communication, construction and engineering, distribution, environment, financial services, health services, tourism and travel, recreation, cultural activities, sports and transportation (along with sub-sectors in each sector. GATS defined measures as any law, regulation or practice from a national, regional or local government or a non-governmental body exercising authority delegated by government that affects covered service; these are referred to as "measures" affecting trade in services.

The different types of education service covered by GATS included : Cross-border supply (e.g. distance education), Consumption abroad of service by consumer traveling to supplier's country (e.g. student studying abroad), Commercial presence (e.g. : a campus abroad), Presence of natural person from supplying country in consuming country (e.g. : faculty, teaching abroad). The areas of services excluded, include (a) "Service supplied in the exercise of governmental authority", i.e., service not supplied on commercial basis or in competition with other supplier (social security) and other public service (health/education provide under non-market condition) in many countries, (b) Air transport service measures affecting air traffic rights and services related to these rights. GATS focuses on the following barriers on trade in education services : (i) legislation that discriminate against foreign provider; (ii) licensing requirement unique to external provider; (iii) accreditation or quality assurance standard that differ from those for local providers; (iv) custom duties for educational material that crosses borders; (v) taxes on earning or limitation on repatriation of profits; (vi) government red tape for foreign provider of services; (vii) subsidies for local provider, but not to foreign provider; (viii) citizenship requirement in order to teach/offer certain subjects of study; (ix) telecommunications restrictions on foreign access to the internet or phone services; and (x) visa and other travel restrictions on foreigners that affect education

Trade in services is defined as the supply of service through four modes of supply, namely, cross-border supply, consumption abroad, commercial presence and presence of natural persons. Developing countries apply traditional principle of trade in goods to trade in services, i.e. they consider only direct sale of services. On the other hand, developed countries support definition of trade in service that includes production and sale of service by non-residents in the country of the producer or consumer even if no cross-border transactions were involved, i.e. commercial presence. At Montreal-Mid-term Review, developing countries accepted temporary movement of factors of production. The definition finally included in GATS include movement of factors of production as well as consumer, but the spectrum of international service transactions include investment of capital and labour movements across borders. So this definition includes operations of foreign suppliers in domestic market in addition to import. This is clearly an innovation, of importance for developing countries. This wide definition of trade in service had led to future complications in determining the origin of service traded. The two major general obligations of the GATS are MFN and transparency :

1. Most favored nation (MFN) treatment is a general obligation applied to all service and important for achieving trade liberalization in multilateral trading system. Article II of GATS on MFN says, "with respect

to any measure covered by this Agreement, each Member shall accord immediately and unconditionally to service and service suppliers of any other Member treatment no less favourable than that it accords to like services and service suppliers of any other country."

2. Transparency is a key obligation of GATS given the importance of domestic regulations in relation to operation of service suppliers. Market operators are not able to access market without regulatory information. Article III of GATS prescribes transparency in terms of publication of all relevant measures of general application and international agreement, which affect operation of the Agreement. The member must notify new law, and regulation that affect trade in services covered by specific commitment and enquiry point. The overall structure of multilateral framework is of crucial importance and achieved separation in GATS between general obligations and specific commitment was essential for developing countries, because they could sequence liberalization by offering access commitment in negotiation and with respect to these sectors or sub-sectors or modes of supply with which liberalization is consistent and attach condition to Market Access and National Treatment.

Rules and Obligation of GATS

Market Access

When a Member undertakes *Market Access (MA)* commitment, it should not adopt the followings: (i) Limitation on number of service supplier (numerical quota, monopolies exclusive service supplier or requirement of economic need test); (ii) Limitation on total value of service transactions; (iii) Limitation on total number of service operation; (iv) Limitation on total number of natural person that may be employed in a particular service sector; (v) Measures which restrict or require specific type of legal entity or joint venture through which a service supplier may supply a service; (vi) Limitation on participation of foreign capital in term of a maximum percentage limit on foreign share holding; and (vii) Major trading partners are pressing developing countries to include economic needs test in their schedule as developed countries have already included it.

National Treatment

National Treatment (NT) is a result of Uruguay Round Negotiations on Specific Commitments. It is difficult to establish criteria and parameter for evaluation of value, impact of trade and impact of liberalization. The impact of specific commitment should be evaluated in overall term and sectoral basis. The objective of trade negotiation is to promoting economic growth of all trading partners and development of developing countries. The impact of specific commitment on market access and national treatment will be function of : (i) Service sectors and sub-sectors included in individual schedule; (ii) All modes of supply are bound; (iii) Market access and national treatment in the transaction list are limited; (iv) Economic needs tests; (v) Exemptions to MFN; and (vi) Additional commitment

A meaningful assessment would also require appropriate disaggregated statistical data on service trade through all modes of supply and a study of the impact of the barriers to entry. These disaggregated statistical data are not available, and even if they are available and comparable across countries, complexities associated with quantifying barriers and limitation on MA and NT are binding on different modes of supply, which preclude development of quantifiable criteria. In the absence of disaggregate statistical data on Maritime transport made horizontal commitment in movement of natural persons, became difficult to adhere to by the member-countries.

Sectoral Coverage

The specific commitment varies widely in sectoral coverage, extent of limitations to market access and national treatment and modes of supply coverage. The degree of development of the service sector is reflected by the coverage of sectors offered and the least developed countries could commit to only one sector—whether developed or developing. Most sectors as developing in these countries have a weaker service sector so they would prefer to include more number of limited sectors. The developed countries, on the other hand, exclude different services like the maritime services (USA), audiovisual services (EU), and specific sub sector in financial services and business services (Japan). In general, a high degree of coverage include tourism, business, financial service, communication, and transport, and the low degree of coverage includes construction, distribution, education, environment, health and recreational services. Most specific commitments of both developed and developing countries do provide a *status quo* on a wide range of sectors, which incorporate important qualifications and limitations. Even the consolidation of *status quo* through application of MFN clauses, and specific MA and NT commitments made in specific sectors and sub-sectors by guaranteeing security of access, had resulted in an expansion of trade and investment in service.

Modal Coverage

Under Mode 1 (cross border) and Mode 3 (commercial presence), there are full bindings on the commitments by member-countries, and full commitment on both market access and national treatment by most of the member-countries has been made. Mode 3 (commercial presence), and Mode 2 (consumption abroad) constitute most frequently covered mode in the schedule of commitment modes, and nearly half of commitments on these modes are without limitations, because of the difficulty to exercise regulatory control abroad. The mode of Cross Border trade has been left unbound, and the Commercial presence mode is preferred, since it leads to transfer of technology, employment and transfer of new management technique and allows country to exercise macro-economic management, jurisdiction and supervision. Emphasis of most commitments is on commercial presence and movement of persons in the form of intra-corporate transferees, and nearly 85% of these are partially binding commitments. Developing countries are not in a position to derive much benefits from commercial presence due high cost of establishment and other weakness in the developing countries. The movement of natural persons has been committed in nearly all schedules through "horizontal" concession in limited category of intra-corporate transferees and business visitors, which is linked to commercial presence but without sectoral specificity, and rarely have access to specific occupation categories. Business visitors allowed to stay upto 90 days and intra-corporate transferees for period between 2 to 5 years. Value of commitment determines connection with mode 3. The commitment do not provide for entry of "service supplier of a member", i.e. self-employed supplier who obtain their remuneration directly from customers. Some countries have committed for additional categories of natural person, e.g., Canada committed for "contract-related natural person" like engineer or agrologist, USA for recruitment and training of workers in speciality occupation, Japan committed for "unnatural person engaged in some specific activities" like legal, accounting, auditing, etc.

Most of the commitments in mode 4 are subject to economic need test (ENT). Specific commitments do not apply ENT to business visitor, but to intra-corporate transferees and independent contracted professionals. ENT acts as a quota restriction. The negotiations on movement of natural person were completed on 28 July 1995 and resulted in some limited improvement in schedule of commitment. Six countries included in the revised are Australia, Canada, EC, India, Norway and Switzerland. At the initiative of India, the committee on specific commitments has been established. The additional commitments related to natural persons engaged as part of a service contract granted by a juridical person and are limited to stay of up to 3 months in any 12 months period. Movement of persons other than managers, specialists, and executives is unbound in spite of including this mode of supply in the request of developing countries, as it provides some advantage to firms of few developing countries and greater benefits to developed country. This commitment does not provide any security of access for developing country service supplier, regardless of their skill to be recruited for specific assignment. These bindings only cover small proportion of various visa categories for temporary entry in developed countries.

Discussions in the Working Party on Domestic Regulations under Article VI:4 have revolved around four core elements and concepts: necessity in view of a specific legitimate objective, transparency of regulatory principles and processes; equivalence (including recognition of relevant foreign qualification); and international standards and their possible roles as benchmarks. Service trade under the four modes of supply may be affected by a multitude of measures—zoning laws, building regulations, shop opening hours, labour legislation, environmental standards, traffic rules, etc. that are normally contained in general economy-wide legislation. The impact and scope of such legislation are broader than the Article VI:4 mandate, which is confined to qualification requirements and procedures, licensing requirements, and technical standards. As regards measures of general application, the Article VI:1 of the GATS calls on members to ensure that such measures be administered in a "reasonable, objective, and impartial manner" in sectors where specific commitments exist. Notwithstanding the diversity of services sectors, there is similarity in the rationales for regulation and the reason for multilateral rules. The economic rationale for regulation arises essentially from market failure attributable to three kinds of problems—natural monopolies or oligopolies, asymmetric information, and externalities—and to Government obligations to pursue non-economic objectives. Because of its immediate impact on trade, market failure due to natural monopolies or oligopolies may need to be addressed directly by multilateral disciplines. However, the GATS provisions applying to monopolies, in Article VIII, deal with monopolistic and exclusive suppliers established or enabled under Government legislation, and only with resulting domestic distortions that are inconsistent with the MFN principle or specific commitments with relevant sectors. Other monopoly situations that may attributable, for example, to the existence of network effects (electricity grids, public transport, etc.) and/or economies of scale in market of limited size, are not covered. Nor could Article VIII be used to challenge competition-related access problems that effect all potential market entrants, whether domestic or foreign, to the same extent. The main question that remains to be addressed by WTO members, is whether there is a similar rationale for pro-competitive disciplines in other network services, including transport (terminals and infrastructure), environmental services (sewage), and energy services (distribution networks). In other cases of market failure, multilateral disciplines may not need to target the problem *per se*, but rather to ensure that any domestic regulatory response does not unduly restrict trade. Such trade-restrictive effects can arise from a variety of technical standards, including prudential regulations, and qualification and licensing requirements in professional, financial and numerous other services. They need be addressed in the negotiations mandated under Article VI:4.

Additional Transparency Obligations

Article III:3 requires members to inform the Services Council at least once a year of the introduction of new, or any change to existing laws, regulations, etc. that "significantly affect" trade in services covered by specific commitments. Like other notifications, these are circulated as WTO documents and accessible via the WTO website. About two-thirds of the 370-odd notifications made between January 1995 and April 2006 fall under Article III:3. Of these, some 12 percent are recognition measures covered by Article VII.

Competition Disciplines

Article VIII:1 calls on members to ensure that monopoly suppliers in their territories respect the MFN requirement and, if they compete outside their turn, extension of monopoly rights into these sectors must be notified to the Council for Trade in services and may result in the member being required to modify the relevant commitments against compensation. Similarly, the Annex on telecommunications specific commitments aims to ensure that the conditions governing access to and use of basic telecommunication networks and services are not biased against foreign suppliers. Again, this obligation applies only in sectors, possibly including other telecom services, that are covered by specific commitments.

Payments, Transfers and Capital Transactions

Apart from balance-of-payments difficulties referred to in Article XII, Article XI prohibits members from restricting payments and transfers for transactions falling under specific commitments. Similarly, any restrictions on capital transactions must be consistent with the access conditions that a Member has inscribed in its schedule of commitments.

Negotiations on Other GATS Rules

In addition to the negotiating mandate on regulatory disciplines under Article VI:4, the GATS contains three further rule-making mandates, namely on emergency safeguard measures (Article X), government procurement (Article XIII), and subsidies (Article XV). The fact that these issues were not solved during the Uruguay round may not only attributable to time constraints, but also to the structural peculiarities of the GATS (four modes of supply, right to operate quota-type and other limitations) and lack of empirical experience. The rule-making negotiations are some times referred to as the "built-in agenda", since the respective mandates are self-contained and not directly connected with the new round of services negotiations. A formal link was established only in the Negotiating Guidelines and procedures adopted by the Council for Trade in Services in March 2001, according to, members were to compete all rule-making negotiations, with the exceptions of those on safeguards, but including those mandated in Article VI:4, prior to concluding the negotiations on specific commitments. The safeguard negotiations were initially subject of an earlier deadline, which since has been revised several times. A council decision of 15 March 2004 now provides that, depending on the outcome, the results of the negotiations under Article X shall enter into force not later than the results of the current services round.

The New Service Round : The Mandate and (Slow) Initial Process

Unlike the GATT, the GATS explicitly provides for future trade negotiations. While the Uruguay Round proved a milestone in the history of services trade as it helped create a multilateral framework of rules and disciplines and the architecture for future rounds, it was certainly not a milestone in services liberalization, judging by the breadth and depth of most current commitments. Presently, virtually all current schedules offer significant scope for improvement even if members confine themselves to incorporating only the currently prevailing access conditions across a wider range of sector or extending the benefits exchanged in preferential agreements to all WTO members. According to Article XIX:1, WTO members are committed to enter into successive rounds of such negotiations "with a view to achieving a progressively higher level of liberalization". The first of such round was to start "not later than five years from the date of entry into force of the WTO agreement", that is January 1, 2000. The failure of the Seattle Ministerial Meeting in late 1999 did not prevent these negotiations from being launched. But, the overall climate had deteriorated, and it took more than one year until delegations in GENEVA were able to agree upon a negotiating mandate for services. In March 2001, the Council for Trade in Services, in Special Session, finally approved the "Guidelines and Procedures for the negotiations on Trade in Services". The two-page document, builds to a large extent on relevant GATS provisions, in particular Article IV ("Increasing Participation of Developing Countries") and Article XIX ("negotiation of Specific Commitments").

The guidelines' content is summarized as follows:

1. *Objectives and Principle.* Confirmation of the objective of progressive liberalization as enshrined in relevant GATS provisions; appropriate flexibility for developing countries, with special priority to be given to least-developed countries; reference to the needs of small and medium sized service suppliers, particularly of developing countries; and commitment to respect "the existing structure and principles of the GTS" (e.g. the bottom up approach to scheduling and the four modes of supply).
2. *Scope.* No sectors or modes are excluded *a priori;* special attention to be given to export interests of developing countries; (re-) negotiation of existing MFN exemptions.
3. *Modalities and Procedures.* Negotiations shall start from current schedules (rather than actual market conditions); request-offer approach as the main method; negotiating credit for autonomous liberalization based on common criteria; ongoing assessment of trade in services; mandate for the Service Council to evaluate the results of the negotiations prior to their completion in light of Article

IV. In keeping with another mandate under Article XIX:3, the Negotiating Guidelines were complemented later by the "Modalities for the Special Treatment for Least-developed Country Members". In view of the relatively detailed Negotiating Guidelines of March 2001, and Members' attention being absorbed by controversial other issues, the Doha Ministerial Declaration essentially confined itself to endorsing these guidelines and integrating the services negotiations, including the rule-making parts (Sections II.C.2(i) and II.D), into the framework of the Doha Development Agenda. The Doha Declaration contained target dates for the circulation of initial requests (June 30, 2002) and initial offers (March 31, 2003) of specific commitments, and envisaged all negotiations to be concluded not later than January 1, 2005.

However, the Ministerial Conference in Cancun, in November 2003 marked a serious setback. It was not until August 2004 that the negotiations were put back on track again. As far as services were concerned, the relevant decision of the General Council ("July Package") contained a relatively short Annex which essentially confirmed existing mandates and decisions and set a target date of May 2005 for the submission of revised offers. The initial offers of new or improved commitments were made known to all WTO members since everybody would be affected by their entry into force. Envisaged amendments were inscribed into the existing schedules and made commonly available via the WTO Secretariat. While the request-and-offer process advanced smoothly, at least in procedural terms, some qualifications may need to be made : (a) The overall momentum was not particularly impressive. At the target date of March 31st, 2004, only 12 offers were available, to be followed by 26 more submissions prior to the Cancun Ministerial Meeting in early September, 2004. Although this number had increased significantly since the mid-April 2006, when 70 initial and 30 revised offers were tabled—the geographic participation remained uneven. While a relatively large number of countries from Latin America and with some gaps, Asia had made contributions, Sub-Saharan Africa had remained largely on the sidelines; (b) More importantly, there was a sense of disappointment concerning the "quality" of offers, both in terms of new sector inclusions and improvements of existing commitments. On average for all members, if current offers entered into effect, the share of service sectors subject to commitments would increase by two or three percentage points to reach some 36%. The overall emphasis was on the services and modes that already dominated existing schedules, with relatively little innovation in "sensitive" areas (education, health and other social services, as well as mode 4); (c) The picture for MFN exemptions did certainly not look brighter either with less than 7% of the 480 odd exemptions were earmarked for removal. The situation was disappointing, in view of the fact that many of the proposed changes were only by-products of the Communities' enlargement to EC 25 and re-organization of preferential relations in Europe.

Hong Kong and a Renewed Impetus

The service-related sections of the Hong Kong Ministerial Declaration, of December 2005, set a new standard. The negotiating objectives contained in the relevant Annex were far more detailed than those listed in any earlier declarations. This was true not only for the definition of mode specific objectives, but also for the language of MFN exemptions and the proclaimed need to improve the technical quality and accuracy of the schedules. The gains in clarity and focus were combined, however, with relatively soft political language. Other new elements in the Declaration were provisions governing collecting exchanges of request and offers and an obligation to develop methods for the implementation of the LDC modalities. At the same time, the declarations exempted the LDCs, in recognition of their "particular economic situation", from the expectation to undertake new commitments. A second round of revised offers was due to be submitted by July 31, 2006, but fell victim to the suspension of the Doha Round negotiations, announced by the WTO's Director General on July 27, 2006 in view of the stalemate in agriculture. After the Hong Kong Ministerial Conference, many members were engaged intensively in the plurilateral request-offer process by the mid-April 2006, about 22 plurilateral requests were tabled and discussed in subsequent meetings with the targeted members.

The general response to the new element in this negotiating process had been positive. However, process must not be equated with substance. It is worth-noting that the services negotiations were part of a wider package. and, thus, intertwined with what happened in other areas of Doha Agenda. Table 3.2 below sums up the overview of mode-specific objectives as contained in the Hong Kong Ministerial Declaration.

TABLE 3.2

Overview of Mode-specific Objectives in the Hong Kong Ministerial Declaration

Mode 1:

(1) Commitments at existing levels of market access

(2) Removal of existing requirements of commercial presence

Mode 2:

(1) Commitments at existing levels of market access

(2) Commitments on mode 2 where commitments on mode 1 exists

Mode 3:

(1) Commitments on enhanced levels of foreign equity participation

(2) Removal or substantial reduction of economic needs tests

(3) Commitments allowing greater flexibility on the types of legal entity permitted

Mode 4:

(1) New or improved commitments on Contractual Services suppliers, Independent professional and others, delinked from commercial presence

(2) New or improved commitments on intra-corporate Transferees and Business visitors

These commitments are to reflect, *inter alia*:

— Removal or substantial reduction of economic needs tests

— Indication of prescribed duration of stay and possibility of renewal, if any.

Sources : Adapted from WTO.

Building on Hong Kong

Once the negotiations are re-launched at full throttle, further thought needs to be given to the negotiating methodology, including in areas of export interest to developing countries, and greater assistance be provided to these countries in the design and implementation of services reform.

Formulae *vs.* Request-and-Offer

As countries sought improved access for their exports, they needed to determine the appropriate approach to international negotiations, and choose between two alternatives of a conventional request-and-offer approach and the use of generally applicable negotiating formulae or model schedules. In the sphere of trade in commodities, governments sometimes agreed to a formula on the basis of which they cut tariffs across-the-board by a certain percentage. Barring a few notable exceptions, formulae have in general proved difficult to design for services negotiations because many different non-quantifiable instruments affected access to markets. Moreover, the developing nations often strongly supported the request-and-offer approach because it allowed considerable freedom in deciding on the intensity—by sector, mode and measure—of liberalization. More specifically, it may be possible to complement the traditional request-and-offer process with concerted or more co-ordinated approaches to liberalization on the following four grounds: (a) In a world of unequal bargaining power, multilaterally agreed formulae that can be deemed to be equitable and efficient are likely to produce a more favourable outcome for the weaker party (in terms of negotiating leverage or skills and expertise) than bilateral negotiations; (b) Formulae often help reduce the transaction costs of negotiations by avoiding the need to barter commitments sector-by-sector, country-by-country, and do not involve large negotiating costs; (c) Formulae can help overcome the free-rider problem that arises in negotiations conducted under an MFN-based system. The problem arises in bilateral negotiations because each of the beneficiaries of a concession from a trading partner may be tempted to understate their willingness to pay for it, hoping that offers of reciprocal concessions from other members will be sufficient to induce the concession anyway. If each member behaved accordingly, mutually beneficial deals might not be struck; (d) The use of multilaterally applied formulae is perhaps the only credible way of granting credit to unilateral liberalizers. It is much more difficult to ensure compensation for the loss of negotiating coinage caused by unilateral liberalization in a bilateral request-and-offer negotiation.

An analysis of the commitments indicates that very limited success in the liberalization of services has been realized under the GATS. For the most part, the commitments only bind the *status quo* or often backtrack on the *status quo*. Sectoral coverage of the commitments is poor: high-income countries have scheduled 45 percent of their service sectors and low and middle-income countries have scheduled only 12% of service sectors. Even when commitments have been made, the coverage of commitments in terms of liberalizing obligations is very low with many limitations on market access and national treatment. Only developed countries without expectations have scheduled an estimated 25 percent of all possible services while this coverage is as low as 7 percent in case of developing countries. (Hoekman, 1995). There are also lot of variations in the commitments across the sectors, reflecting the sensitivities with and political economy constraints associated with different services. In case of some service sectors, many countries have scheduled commitments and made quite liberal offers, while in many other services, agreement has been possible only after extended negotiations and moderate offers have been made, albeit with certain derogation and limitations. Yet in another group of service sectors, negotiations have failed to make any progress at all as fundamental differences in views and perceptions across member-countries have not been resolved. Overall, the commitments are biased towards sectors, which are relatively open, while major sectors which are subject to more restrictive measures, for the most part remain unscheduled, and even when scheduled, remain unbound for most of the models. Table 3.3 provides a summary of commitments by sectors.

It is evident from Table 3.3 that certain services have been subject to significantly more liberalization than others. The one sector where there is uniformly high coverage is in hotels/restaurants, that is, tourism and related services with 70 percent

TABLE 3.3
Commitments by Sectors

	Number of GATS Sector and modes of Supply	*Average Number of Commitments*		*Commitments/ GATS items per sector*	
		HIC	*LMIC*	*HIC*	*LMIC*
Construction	20	11.2	3.3	56.0	16.5
Motor vehicle repair	4	1.8	0.3	45.0	7.5
Wholesale trade	8	4.6	0.5	57.5	6.3
Retail trade	8	4.4	0.8	55.0	10.0
Hotel/restaurants	4	2.8	2.8	70.0	70.0
Land transport	40	9.4	2.3	23.5	5.8
Water transport	48	4.4	3.0	9.2	6.3
Air transport	20	3.7	1.5	18.5	7.5
Auxiliary transport	20	5.1	1.3	25.5	6.5
Postal services	4	1.3	0.6	32.5	15.0
Basic telecom	28	1.5	1.3	5.4	4.6
Value-added telecom	28	18.7	5.0	66.8	7.8
Financial services	60	31.3	12.4	52.2	20.6
Real estate services	8	3.5	0.3	43.8	3.8
Rental services	20	9.5	1.3	47.5	6.5
Computer-related services	20	15.5	4.2	77.5	21.0
R and D services	12	4.1	1.0	34.2	0.3
Business services	108	56.5	12.2	47.9	11.3
Refuse disposal	16	8.8	1.0	55.0	6.3
Education	20	4.7	1.3	23.5	6.5
Health and social	24	5.0	1.9	20.2	7.9
Recreation/culture	48	13.3	4.6	27.9	9.6

Source : Hoekman (1995), Table 8, p. 345.

of the sector being subject to commitments across both developed and developing countries. Sectors, which have been subject to the least commitments (less than 40 percent) across both groups of countries, include a variety of public services such as health, education, transport, postal, and basic telecom services. But across all sectors, developed countries have on average filed significantly more commitments than developing countries. Overall, commitments have been most forthcoming in the most open sectors such as tourism services and least forthcoming in public goods type of sectors where there are important social and economic considerations and where regulatory intervention and government monopoly are prevalent, for developed as well as developing countries. Sectors where there is wide variation in developed and developing country commitments are typically those falling under infrastructure services and selected business services where developed countries have a trade and investment interest. These are typically sectors where most low-income countries either do not have comparative advantage or where liberalization is politically sensitive and difficult and involves major domestic regulatory reforms and measures. Thus the sectoral distribution of the commitments closely reflects the regulatory characteristics of individual services, the political economy constraints in scheduling them, and the trade interests of different countries.

There is also major asymmetry in the distribution of both horizontal and specific commitments across the different modes of supply. Around 50 percent of unrestricted commitments are concentrated in consumption abroad, about 30 percent in cross border supply, 20 percent in commercial presence, and 0 percent in movement of natural persons. The absence of bound commitments in mode 4 clearly reflects the sensitive nature of this mode of supply since it impinges upon domestic migration and labour market regulations. The commitments are also more limited in the case of sectors, which are heavily regulated, and particularly in those modes, which are most important for these sectors. For instance, in sectors such as basic telecom and financial services, most commitments are subject to foreign equity ceilings and discriminatory treatments of foreign and domestic suppliers. In professional service sectors, limitations such as quantitative barriers to entry, licensing restrictions, nationality and residency conditions, and establishment restrictions are common. Moreover, countries have also taken MFN exemptions in many of the sensitive sectors, including financial services, basic telecommunication services, maritime, air transport, and audio-visual services, further limiting the significance of their commitments.

Overall, the GATS have been ineffective in liberalizing services trade and investment. The commitments are poor and uneven in sectoral coverage, mostly unbound or partial in nature, and have failed to liberalize the most sensitive and protected sectors and modes of supply. The wedge between the existing degree of openness to services trade and investment, and the level of binding gives countries the discretion to introduce and intensify barriers in future. Moreover, the commitments are often non-transparent, vague in wording and do not clearly specify terminology and criteria for their application. The conceptual framework and the commitment structure of GATS have several shortcomings which have contributed for their ineffectiveness. The first conceptual weakness of the GATS stems from the overlap between market access and national treatment commitments. For instance, quantitative limits on services are covered under market access, regardless of whether such limits are imposed on foreign services on a discriminatory or non-discriminatory basis, and conversely, measures relating to labour legislation, tax treatment, licensing, and regulation of monopolies listed under national treatment may limit contestability of markets and thus act as market access restrictions. Such overlap has been a source of confusion in scheduling commitments and the intermingling of commitments on discriminatory and non-discriminatory barriers has in turn led to the intermingling of trade liberalization and domestic regulatory reform objectives.

The second major shortcoming of the GATS concerns its modalities for negotiation. Given the positive list approach to commitments, negotiations are driven by concerns and interest of the main players and of certain sectors. This is reflected by the fact that an open sector such as tourism services has received the greatest number of bindings while restricted, social service type of sectors such as health and education have received only one-third the number of bindings as tourism services. The focus on sectoral reciprocity has further limited the scope for cross-sectoral tradeoffs and the possibility of a larger economy wide perspective in scheduling commitments. The mode-wise commitments have further biased liberalization towards certain modes of supply, which are less contentious to liberalize. There is therefore significant imbalance across the four modes. Finally, and more importantly, the main structural weaknesses of GATS has been the non-generality of its rules and disciplines, as many of the general principles are applicable only if specific commitments have been made and are conditional upon the nature of limitations specified in the schedules. The general principles such as MFN, market access, and national treatment do not extend to important areas such as government procurement and subsidies, which play a major role in the provision of many services and have a trade distorting impacts. The limited number and reach of generic rules, the sector-specificity of commitments, and the entire approach to scheduling commitments, have greatly diminished the liberalizing scope under the GATS.

An overview of information and statistics on service indicates *inter alia* the limitation of global data on trade in services for purpose of comparison, evaluation of the contribution of services to growth and employment creation in developing countries. Although the developing countries have made substantial commitments under GATS which are fully binding in market access under cross-border and commercial—presence modes of supply, they have not received concessions of any meaningful economic value under the movement of natural persons mode of supply. These data also show that : (a) the BOP statistics relate mainly to cross-border mode of supply; (b) most developing countries have deficit in services trade (except tourism, travel and workers' remittances); (c) for some developing countries growth in import of service is more important than export as it depends on import of professional and technical service; (d) since the adoption of GATS, developing countries' share of world services export has increased by 6% and this was mainly due to export competition of Asian countries; (e) the developed countries account for 75% of world export service and most of the top 20 exporters are from developed countries; (f) the infrastructural services (telecommunication, financial and transport service) have made important contributions to the competitiveness of goods and services; and (g) the social dimension of services, i.e., link between certain basic service sector and sustainable development and public welfare, need to be recognized. For many developing countries, export of services is their only means of diversification which make significant contributions to employment creation as they move from excessive dependence on export of primary commodities. But there is no clear empirical evidence of increase in FDI flows to developing countries. Most developing countries faces major supply constraint and do not satisfy the precondition for building a competitive service sector. Given their supply constraints and lack of market access, the implementation of Article IV on increasing participation of developing countries and its strengthening based on specific benchmarks would require a monitoring mechanism in these developing nations.

Developing countries face critical barriers to market access of their products in goods and services. In particular, the lack of commercially meaningful commitments in sector and modes of supply of natural person has created a major imbalances in trade in services by these developing nations. Services suppliers from developing countries face number of barriers, including: (a) prohibition of foreign access to service markets which are reserved for domestic suppliers; (b) price-based measures like entry and exit taxes, and visa fee for movement of natural persons, discriminatory airline landing fee and port charges, licensing fee, etc., (c) subsidies granted in developed countries as well as horizontal subsidies and investment incentives that can have trade distortive impact on export from developing countries. There are also financial constraints faced by the service suppliers from developing countries, and in the absence of support from their respective governments, they are placed at a disadvantage while facing competition from their much stronger counterparts in developed countries. The barrier to movement of Natural Persons have prevented developing countries to gaining benefits from trading opportunities and also technician and business person from participation in variety of activities that are essential to the penetration of world market for services. The developed countries have a greater number of higher level of personal linked to mode 3 on commercial presence such that they largely benefit from GATS commitment on movement of natural persons. Due to their discretionary nature, the economic needs tests represent a major barrier to trade in service, particularly with respect to the movement of natural persons. The measures affecting the presence of natural persons included general immigrating legislation, labour market regulations governing the issuance of work permit including wage parity requirement, and regulations defining foreign ability to work in individual activity, and differential treatment in the context of social security taxes and benefits and government subsidies which treat domestic and foreign service providers differently. Transparency with respect to measures affecting the movement of natural persons is critical for increasing the participation of developing countries in international trade. The movement of service provider could also be facilitated by GATS visas. To increase the competitiveness of developing countries, it would be essential that developed countries improve their commitments by including specific categories of natural persons without any economic need test. In case where economic need test is applied, effort should be made to reduce the restrictive impact of such test and ensure that would not nullify benefit of GATS, i.e. by: (i) criteria for such tests should be made transparent and specific and less discretionary through enquiry point and contact point and notification requirement; (ii) these criteria should be bound so that more stringent ones could not be introduced in future; (iii) rejections on the basis of such tests should be subject to review; (iv) reducing the scope of ENT by subjecting fewer categories of person to ENT; (v) the need for such tests could be removed through the negotiation of a safeguard provisions. According to Article XIX of GATS, the Council for Trade in Services is to make an assessment of trade in service in overall terms and on sectoral basis. At Singapore Ministerial Conference, the Ministers endorsed an information exchange programme, to facilitate negotiation of progressive liberalization dealing with the problems of the regulatory authorities, regarding transparency and restriction on market access or national treatment. The key issues of concern were : (a) the need to improve classification and definition of particular sector and activities; (b) Article VI type of measure and discipline ensuring that it would not raise any unnecessary barrier to trade in services; (c) presence of obstacles to movement of natural persons; (d) role of mutual recognition agreement (MRA); (e) non-transparent and discriminatory taxation; (f) the need for transfer of technology; (g) issues relating to electronic commerce; (h) subsidies granted by developed countries and the impact on developing countries' services; (i) the relation between services and goods sectors and need to remove barrier in complementary sector; and (j) need to further clarify the boundary between cross-border and consumption abroad.

3.4. MEASUREMENT OF BARRIERS TO SERVICE SECTOR OPENNESS

Trade Policy and the Service Sector

Government policies affect trade in goods through tariffs and non-tariff barriers. Tariffs are discriminatory taxes on trade. An import tax is a tax levied on foreign goods but not domestic goods. Tariffs are easy to measure and are very transparent instruments. Successive round of GATT negotiations were successful in achieving broad-based reductions in trade barriers via across-the-board reductions in trade taxes. Another feature of tariffs is that it is fairly clear what is meant by free-trade: zero tariffs. Non-tariff barriers (NTBs), on the other hand, are much more complex. An NTB is any government policy that has the effect of favouring local producers over foreign producers or which restricts or raises the cost of access to domestic markets by foreigners. NTB can include delays at the border, quantitative restrictions on foreign products, government purchasing policies that give preferences to local suppliers, subsidies, quality and certification requirements that favour local suppliers, etc. NTBs are more difficult to measure and are less transparent than tariff barriers. Furthermore, the trade-distorting effects of many policies are intertwined with other government policy objectives, such as protecting health and safety, encouraging regional development, etc.

Most trade barriers in the service sectors are NTBs, and tariffs (discriminatory taxes imposed on foreign service providers) are relatively uncommon. There are several reasons for this. First, cross border trade in services is often in intangible form, and this makes it difficult to monitor and tax. Second, the modes of supply for more services are different than for goods.

Many services are exclusively delivered via commercial presence or via temporary labour movement. Barriers to FDI and international labour mobility can therefore result in serious restrictions on service trade and obviate the need for additional discriminatory taxes. Finally, many services are highly regulated or are provided by public sector. Regulations that either intentionally or unintentionally make it relatively more costly for foreign suppliers to operate are major source of trade barriers in services.

The pervasiveness of NTBs in service sector trade is because of existence of market imperfection in service sectors. Many trade barriers in the service sector are a side effects of domestic regulations that have legitimate purpose. For example, because of asymmetric information, doctors must be certified to protect patients, engineers need certification to ensure that bridges they build do not collapse, and insurance companies have to be regulated to ensure their solvency. However, these same rules can be manipulated to protect local suppliers. For example, a rule requiring that an engineer graduate from a domestic university might ensure that quality standards are met, but would prevent consumers from having access to the services of highly qualified foreign engineers. The regulatory apparatus may therefore serve the dual purpose of responding to market failures and protecting local supplies at the expense of consumers. A challenge for trade-policy analysis is to isolate the protective effect of regulatory policy from the beneficial effects, and to suggest rules for liberalization that provide the benefits of increased trade while ensuring that other legitimate policy objectives are achieved. In many cases, trade liberalization may not be possible or viable unless it is accompanied by domestic regulatory reform.

Methods of Measurement of Service Barriers

Measurements in trade barriers, in markets for both goods and services, can be either direct or indirect. Direct measurements start from the observation of an explicit policy or practice, such as an import quota or a regulation of a foreign provider of services, and then attempt to measure its economic importance in some fashion. Indirect measurements, instead, try to infer the existence of barriers using observed discrepancies between actual economic performance and what would be expected if trade were free. Direct measurements have the advantage that one knows what one was measuring, and the disadvantage that they can only include those barriers that are in fact explicit and recognized. Indirect measurements have the advantage that their quantitative importance is known, at least in the dimension used to identify them, but the disadvantage that they may incorporate unrecognized frictions other than the policy impediments that one seeks to identify. In the case of trade in goods, direct measurements of NTBs typically take the form of inventories of identified trade restrictions, such as those complied in the United Nations Conference on Trade and Development (UNCTAD), Trade Analysis and Information System (TRAINS). Since NTBs usually cover only some industries or products, a first step in quantifying them is often to measure the fraction of trade that they cover in different sectors and countries. These fractions may then be used directly in empirical work, even though they do not themselves say anything about how effective the NTBs have been in restricting trade. Indirect measurements, on the other hand, can be fairly straightforward in the case of goods, based either on their observed prices before and after they cross an international border or on the quantities that cross it. Indirect measurements based on quantities are more difficult to quantify as they depend on a theoretical benchmark for comparability which is likely to be much less certain. For trade in services, direct measurements must be carefully done since regulation in service industries is so common that merely to document its presence would not be informative. Indirect measurements of restrictiveness are also possible with traded services, although simple price comparisons are seldom of much use. This is because many services are differentiated by location in a way that renders comparison of their prices inside and outside of a country meaningless. For example, the cost of providing telephone service to consumers on Texas side of the U.S.-Mexican border need bear no particular relationship to the cost, for the same firm, of providing it across the border in Mexico, where wages are much lower but costs of infrastructure may be much higher. So even if trade in the service were completely unimpeded, we would not except these prices to be the same, and we therefore cannot infer a trade barrier in either direction from the fact that they are not. Similar arguments can be made about most traded services. Indirect measurements of barriers to trade in services are therefore less common than for trade in goods, although they do exist. There have been some success using the so-called gravity models a benchmark for quantities of trade in services, and the results of these models have therefore been the basis for indirect measurement of barriers in the quantity dimension. Financial data have also often been the basis for inferring barriers from differences in the markups of price over cost.

Frequency Studies and Indexes of Restrictiveness

Studies of frequency-based measures identify the kinds of restrictions that apply to a particular service industry or to services in general. For particular industries, this requires considerable industry-specific knowledge, because each industry has its own terminology, and often also its own distinctive reasons for regulatory concern. Knowledge of the industry is necessary to distinguish such valid regulations such as for protecting health and safety from those that primarily offer protection. Thus, a frequency study is best carried out by an industry specialist, or it must draw upon documents that have been prepared by such specialists like the documentation provided by industry trade groups, such as the International Telecommunications Union in the case of telecoms, bilateral air service arrangements in the case of passenger air travel, or the Trade Port website in the case of maritime services.

For broader studies or restriction in services, covering multiple industries, an early approach was in studies by PECC (1995) and Hoekman (1995, 1996), which used information submitted by countries to the General Agreement on Trade in Services (GATS), as the basis for commitments to be made for services liberalization in the Uruguay Round negotiations. Such measures are not ideally suited for documenting trade barriers. Better information collected through the details of actual barriers and regulatory practices as in the data collected by Asia Pacific Economic Cooperation (APEC) and used by Hardin and Holmes (1997), contains information on the restrictiveness of these barriers in terms indicators such as the numbers of firms or countries to which they apply and other characteristics. This latter information is then used to construct an Index of Restrictiveness. Typically, each barrier is assigned a score between zero and one, with a score of one being the most restrictive and a score of zero being the less restrictive. These scores are then averaged, using weights that are intended to reflect the relative importance of each type of barrier. The weights on different barriers in a restrictiveness index may be assigned reflecting the importance of each type of barriers.

An alternative approach used by Nicoletti *et. al.* (2000) and subsequently by Doove *et. al.* (2001), applies the principal component analysis to the data assembled to distinguish those barriers that vary most independently among their data, and then to apply the largest weights to them. A third approach has been not to construct an index at all, but rather to use the sores or proxy measures for each type of barriers separately in an empirical analysis, with the advantage that it allows for the fact that barriers may differ in their importance for different aspects of economic performance, and it allows the weights in an index of restrictiveness to be estimated simultaneously with the importance of that index for a particular economic outcome. Thus the construction of the index would be interlinked with its use for estimating effects on prices and quantities.

Pecc (1995) and Hoekman (1995, 1996) have used information contained in the country schedules of the GATS, referring to all four modes of supply of services, to construct frequency ratios that measure the extent of liberalization promised by countries in the commitments to the GATS, as part of the Uruguay Round negotiations completed in 1993-94. The frequency ratios constructed are based on the number of commitments that were scheduled by individual countries designating sectors or sub-sectors as unrestricted or partially restricted. The calculated ratios are equal to the number of actual commitments in relation to the maximum possible number of commitments. Hoekman focused on commitments relating to market access and national treatment. As he notes (1996: 101), there were 155 sectors and sub-sectors and four modes of supply specified in the GATS. This yields 620×2=1,240 total commitments on market access and national treatment for each 97 countries. The frequency ratio for a country or a sector is then defined as the fraction of these possible commitments that were in fact made, implying an index of trade restrictiveness equal to one minus this fraction. There are, however, some important limitations to these calculations. Thus as Holmes and Hardin (2000: 58-9) noted, Hoekman's method might be misleading or biased because it assumes that the absence of positive country commitments in the GATS schedules can be interpreted as indicating the presence of restrictions, which may not be the case in fact. Also, the different types of restrictions are given equal weight.

Hardin and Holmes (1997) and Holmes and Hardin (2000) had attempted to build on and improve Hoekman's methodology, by focusing only on restrictions on FDI in services (mode 3). In particular, they used information on the actual FDI restrictions taken from Asia Pacific Cooperation (APEC), rather than just the GATS commitments. Rather than treating all restrictions equally, they devised a judgmental system of weighting that was designed, as in the case of the banking restrictions, to reflect efficiency costs of the different barriers. It is evident that communications and financial services were most subject to FDI restrictions, while business, distribution, environmental, and recreational services were less restricted. Korea, Indonesia, China, Thailand, and the Philippines had relatively high restrictiveness index, while the United States and Hong Kong had the lowest indexes. This is summarised in Tables 3.4 and 3.5.

McGuire and Schuele had used some restriction categories and weights applied to banking services in their study, which is based on a variety of data sources, including the GATS schedule of commitments and a number of other reports and documentation pertaining to actual financial-sector restrictions in 38 economies for the period 1995-98. McGuire and Schuele had assigned scores for different degrees of restriction, ranging between 0 (least restriction) and 1 (most restriction). The various categories were weighted judgmentally in terms of how great the costs involved were assumed to be with respect to the effect on economic efficiency. Thus it was found that restrictions on the licensing of banks were taken to be more burdensome than restrictions on the movement of people. Also the scores were given separately for the restrictions applicable to the foreign

TABLE 3.4
Components of an Index of FDI Restrictions

Type of Restriction	*Weights*
Foreign Equity limits on all firms	
No foreign equity permitted	1.000
Less than 50 percent foreign equity permitted	0.500
More than 50 percent and less than 100 percent foreign equity permitted	0.250
Foreign equity limits on existing firms, none on Greenfield	
No foreign equity permitted	0.500
Less than 50 percent foreign equity permitted	0.250
More than 50 percent and less than 100 percent foreign equity permitted	0.125
Screening and approval	
Investor required to demonstrate net economic benefits	0.100
Approval unless contrary to national interest	0.075
Notification (pre or post)	0.050
Control and management restrictions	
All firms	0.200
Existing firms, none for Greenfield	0.100
Input and operational restrictions	
All firms	0.200
Existing firms, none for Greenfield	0.100

Source : Adapted from Holmes and Hardin (200:62).

banks and the "domestic" restriction applicable to all banks. The differences between the domestic and foreign measures could be interpreted as indicating the discrimination imposed on foreign banks. Finally, it may be noted that the foreign scores summed to a maximum of 1 and the domestic scores to a maximum of 0.808, because some of the restrictions noted applied only to foreign banks and not to domestic banks.

Based on detailed information available, the scores for banking restrictions in individual countries could be constructed. Using the category weights, it is then possible to

Table 3.5
FDI Restrictiveness Indexes for Selected APEC Economies and Selected Sectors, 1996-98

(*Percentage*)

Sectors	*Australia*	*Canada*	*China*	*Hong Kong*	*Indonesia*	*Japan*	*Korea*	*Malaysia*
(1)	(2)	(3)	(4)	(5)	(6)	(7)	(8)	(9)
Business	0.183	0.225	0.360	0.015	0.560	0.062	0.565	0.316
Communications	0.443	0.514	0.819	0.350	0.644	0.350	0.685	0.416
Postal	1.000	1.000	1.000	1.000	1.000	1.000	1.000	1.000
Courier	0.175	0.200	0.275	0.000	0.525	0.050	0.550	0.075
Telecommunications	0.300	0.325	1.000	0.200	0.525	0.100	0.550	0.375
Audiovisual	0.295	0.530	1.000	0.200	0.525	0.250	0.640	0.215
Construction	0.175	0.200	0.400	0.000	0.525	0.050	0.750	0.775
Distribution	0.175	0.200	0.275	0.050	0.525	0.050	0.625	0.075
Education	0.175	0.200	0.525	0.000	0.525	0.200	0.550	0.075
Environmental	0.175	0.200	0.275	0.000	0.525	0.117	0.700	0.075
Financial	0.450	0.375	0.450	0.233	0.550	0.358	0.875	0.608
Insurance and related	0.275	0.425	0.475	0.400	0.575	0.450	0.838	0.600
Banking and other	0.625	0.325	0.425	0.067	0.525	0.267	0.913	0.617
Health	0.175	0.200	0.275	0.000	0.525	0.0505	0.550	0.317
Tourism	0.175	0.200	0.283	0.000	0.525	0.050	0.617	0.525
Recreation	0.175	0.200	0.275	0.000	0.525	0.050	0.550	0.175
Transport	0.204	0.235	0.455	0.093	0.525	0.114	0.573	0.122

(*Contd.*)

TABLE 3.5 (*Contd.*)

Sectors	*Mexico*	*New Zealand*	*Papua New Guinea*	*Philippines*	*Singapore*	*Thailand*	*United States*
(1)	(10)	(11)	(12)	(13)	(14)	(15)	(16)
Business	0.289	0.085	0.300	0.479	0.261	0.775	0.005
Communications	0.739	0.434	0.475	0.758	0.518	0.838	0.345
Postal	1.000	1.000	1.000	1.000	1.000	1.000	1.000
Courier	0.775	0.075	0.300	0.475	0.250	0.775	0.000
Telecommunications	0.705	0.425	0.300	0.975	0.571	0.804	0.200
Audiovisual	0.475	0.235	0.300	0.580	0.250	0.775	0.180
Construction	0.450	0.075	0.300	0.475	0.250	0.775	0.000
Distribution	0.325	0.075	0.300	0.475	0.250	0.775	0.000
Education	0.450	0.075	0.300	0.475	0.250	0.775	0.000
Environmental	0.075	0.075	0.300	0.475	0.250	0.775	0.000
Financial	0.554	0.200	0.300	0.954	0.378	0.375	0.200
Insurance and related	0.575	0.125	0.300	0.975	0.250	0.775	0.000
Banking and other	0.533	0.275	0.300	0.933	0.506	0.975	0.400
Health	0.408	0.075	0.300	0.475	0.250	0.775	0.000
Tourism	0.275	0.075	0.300	0.808	0.317	0.775	0.000
Recreation	0.075	0.075	0.300	0.475	0.250	0.775	0.000
Transport	0.283	0.131	0.300	0.975	0.250	0.780	0.025

Sources : Adapted from Holmes and Hardin (2000:63-4).

calculate "indexes of restrictiveness" of the foreign and domestic regulations by country. India, Indonesia, Malaysia, and the Philippines can be seen to have relatively high foreign index scores, Korea, Singapore, Thailand, and Turkey have moderate foreign index scores, and Australia, Hong Kong, Japan, New Zealand and South Africa have the lowest foreign index scores. The domestic index scores are indicative of the restrictions applied both to foreign and domestic banks, and it appears that the domestic index scores are highest for Japan, Korea, Malaysia, and the Philippines. While the absolute values of the foreign and domestic index scores are not reported, the differences in the scores can be interpreted as a measurement of the discrimination applied to foreign banks. McGuire and Schuele have also found that countries with less restricted banking sectors tended to have higher GNP per capita.

The frequency measures and indexes of restriction that we have discussed thus far are especially useful in identifying the types of barriers and the relative degrees of protection afforded to particular services sectors across countries. It is evident accordingly that there exists a considerable amount of information on barriers covering a wide variety of service sectors, including financial services, telecommunications, accountancy, distribution, air transport, and electricity supply. The compilation of such measurements and construction of such indexes are important first steps that can provide the basis for the next step, which involves using available methodologies to assess the economic affects of maintaining or eliminating the barriers.

Other Frequency Studies and Indexes of Restrictiveness

Several other studies on frequency studies and indexes of restrictiveness are also worth-noting. Mattoo (1998) analyzed market access commitments in financial services, covering direct insurance and banking. His results indicated that Latin America was the most restricted in direct insurance and Asia the most restricted in banking services. Marko (1998) constructed frequency measures for the basic telecommunications market, using Hoekman's (1995) methodology, and found that 58 percent of the basic telecommunications services was covered by partial or full GATS commitments. McGuire (1998) showed that Australia's impediments in financial services, including banking, securities, and insurance, were much lower as compared to other economies in Asia. Colecchia (2000) provided a methodological, pilot survey of the barriers on accountancy services for Australia, France, the United Kingdom, and the United States, using OECD information on regulatory regimes for 1997. The United Kingdom was found to be the most liberal, the United States the least liberal. Kalirajan (2000) constructed restrictiveness indexes for 38 economies, using GATS schedules and a variety of other information on barriers to distribution services as of June, 1999. The indexes covered the services of commission agents, wholesalers, retailers, and franchisers. His findings were that (a) Belgium, India, Indonesia, France, Korea, Malaysia, the Philippines, Switzerland, and Thailand were the most restrictive economies and Singapore and Hong Kong were the most open; and (b) the countries like Malaysia, the Philippines, Venezuela, Brazil, the United States and Greece were the most discriminatory against foreign firms. Kemp (2000) constructed restrictiveness indexes for the four modes of providing educational services, using GATS data on commitments for market access and natural treatment for the five sub-sectors of educational services and covering 29 countries. While only a quarter of GATS member-countries scheduled commitments, the evidence suggested the consumption abroad, which is the major mode of educational trade in terms of foreign-student tuition, fees, and expenditures, was comparatively the least restricted mode. McGuire, Schuele, and Smith (2000) also developed indexes for restrictions on foreign maritime service suppliers and all maritime service suppliers covering 35 economies during the period 1994-8, using a variety of GATS and other data sources. They found that (a) Brazil, Chile, India, Indonesia, Korea, Malaysia, the Philippines, and the United States had the most restricted markets against foreign maritime suppliers; and (b) Chile, Philippines, Thailand, Turkey, and the United States were the most discriminatory in favouring domestic suppliers. Nguyen-Hong (2000) constructed restrictiveness indexes for accountancy, architectural, and engineering services for 34 economies and legal services for 29 economies and found that : (i) legal and accounting were the most highly restricted services;

(ii) Indonesia, Malaysia, Austria, Mexico, and Turkey were the most restrictive for the four professions, and Finland, and the Netherlands most open; (iii) nationality requirements were the most extensive in legal and accountancy services; (iv) residency requirements were common in accountancy services; (v) partnership and practices between accountants and lawyer were commonly restricted; and (vi) recognition of foreign qualifications and licenses was subject to a variety of restrictions among countries.

Doove *et. al.* (2001) constructed restrictiveness indexes for international air passenger transport, telecommunications and electricity supply. The index for air transport was an average of the bilateral restrictiveness indexes applicable to pairs of countries. The data covered 875 airline routes for 35 economies and referred to the late 1990s. The bilateral restrictions included designations, capacity, fares, and charter services, with weights derived using factor analysis in an OECD study by Gonenc and Nicoletti (2001). The bilateral restrictions were generally not covered under the GATS, so that discriminatory restrictions on third countries may have been applied. The results are shown in column 2 of table and indicate substantial variation across countries as a consequence of the agreement-specific bilateral restrictions.

The restrictiveness index for telecommunications covered 24 OECD members-countries and 23 non-OECD countries, using data for 1997. In recent decades the telecom industry had undergone rapid technological change and there had been wide range of regulatory reform and structural reform undertaken in many countries. Doove *et al.* build upon the OECD study by Boylaud and Nicoletti (2000), who focused on the four major telecommunications sectors: trunk (domestic long distance); international (international long distance); mobile (cellular); and leased-line services. The regulatory measures covered include: market share of new entrants; index of governmental control of the public telecommunications operators (PTOs); degree of internationalization of domestic markets; time to liberalization; and time to privatization. These measurements were incorporated into an econometric framework for individual sectors in order to estimate the price impacts involved. Table 3.6 summarises the picture.

TABLE 3.6

Price Impact of Regulation on Telecommunications Prices, 1997

Economy	*Trunk*	*International*	*Mobile*	*Leasing*	*Industry-wide*
(1)	*(2)*	*(3)*	*(4)*	*(5)*	*(6)*
OECD					
Australia	21	33	23	4	19
Austria	10	51	17	11	20
Belgium	41	207	18	5	52
Canada	33	95	8	0	27
Denmark	63	12	15	3	39
Finland	5	34	50	17	22
France	41	95	16	9	34
Germany	40	176	17	8	38
Greece	37	35	10	19	27
Iceland	31	199	96	11	54
Ireland	17	56	16	10	22
Italy	32	41	10	3	21
Japan	39	34	14	5	23
Luxembourg	17	108	105	22	59
Netherlands	32	30	13	5	23
New Zealand	30	24	15	1	21
Norway	26	67	42	14	31
Portugal	22	15	8	6	15
Spain	28	30	7	4	18
Sweden	53	B	54	15	B
Switzerland	13	165	49	16	40
Turkey	35	B	17	24	B
U.K.	78	63	6	2	47
U.S.	61	32	8	1	38
Unweighted mean	34	73	26	9	31
Standard Deviation	17	61	27	7	13

(Contd.)

TABLE 3.6 (*Contd.*)

(1)	(2)	(3)	(4)	(5)	(6)
Additional OECD					
Czech Republic	36	20	6	Ne	22
Hungary	69	44	2	Ne	38
Korea	18	16	9	Ne	14
Mexico	54	16	7	Ne	40
Poland	18	30	9	Ne	17
Unweighted Mean	39	25	7	Ne	26
Standard Deviation	23	12	3	Ne	12
Non-OECD					
Argentina	64	21	6	Ne	45
Brazil	27	15	16	Ne	23
Chile	41	35	7	Ne	32
China	B	B	B	Ne	B
Columbia	28	22	20	Ne	25
Hong Kong	49	47	24	Ne	43
India	68	41	B	Ne	B
Indonesia	41	52	56	Ne	46
Malaysia	23	34	23	Ne	24
Peru	32	12	7	Ne	24
Philippines	30	23	8	Ne	23
Russia	63	B	B	Ne	B
Singapore	25	196	35	Ne	44
South Africa	35	26	B	Ne	B
Taiwan	25	54	40	Ne	32
Thailand	41	111	18	Ne	42
Uruguay	42	37	8	Ne	33
Vietnam	B	B	B	Ne	B
Unweighted Mean	40	48	21	Na	34
Standard Deviation	15	47	15	Na	9
All 47 Economies					
Minimum	5	12	2	0	14
Maximum	78	207	105	24	59
Unweighted Mean	36	58	22	9	31
Standard Deviation	17	54	22	7	12

Note : Ne : not estimated; Na : not applicable; b : excluded.
Source : Adapted from Doove *et al.*

Electricity supply had also undergone significant deregulation and structural reform. Building upon OECD work by Steiner (2000), Doove *et al.* assembled data for 50 economies for 1996. The regulatory measures covered were: unbundling of electricity generation from transition; third party access; presence of a wholesale electricity market; degree of private/public ownership; time to liberalization; and time to privatization. The price impacts of regulations were estimated and are presented in Table 3.7 below.

TABLE 3.7

Price Impacts of Regulation on Industrial Electricity Prices

Economies in Original Study	*Percent*	*Extended Coverage*	*Percent*
(1)	*(2)*	*(3)*	*(4)*
Australia	0.0	Argentina	0.0
Belgium	15.4	Austria	13.2
Canada	8.8	Bolivia	16.5
Denmark	8.5	Brazil	15.6
Finland	0.0	Chile	0.0
France	16.0	China	17.2
Germany	8.3	Columbia	0.0
Greece	16.6	Czech Republic	13.6
Ireland	13.9	Hong Kong	15.6
Italy	17.1	Hungary	13.3
Japan	10.2	Iceland	35.3
Netherlands	15.5	India	17.2
New Zealand	0.0	Indonesia	16.8
Norway	0.0	Korea	15.4
Portugal	17.9	Luxembourg	13.8
Spain	9.5	Malaysia	16.6
Sweden	0.0	Mexico	17.3
U.K.	0.0	Peru	0.0
U.S.	7.5	Philippines	17.6
		Poland	13.6

(Contd.)

TABLE 3.7 (*Contd.*)

(1)	(2)	(3)	(4)
		Russia	17.1
		Slovak Republic	14.8
		Singapore	15.6
		South Africa	15.6
		Switzerland	21.9
		Taiwan	16.1
		Thailand	16.3
		Turkey	20.7
		Uruguay	32.2
		Venezuela	27.2
		Vietnam	32.0

Source : Adapted from Doove *et. al.***

Price-Impact Measurement

In order to construct measurements of the price and/or quantity effects of barriers to trade in services, some other new approach is developed. The simplest one is just to make an informed guess. Having constructed a frequency ratio for offers to liberalize services trade in the GATS, Hoekman (1995, 1996) assumed that failure to liberalize in a sector would be equivalent to some particular tariff level that he selected using the knowledge of the sector. These maximum tariff equivalents ranged from a high of 200 percent for sectors in which market access was essentially prohibited in most countries (e.g. maritime cabotage, air transport, postal services, voice telecommunications, and life insurance) to 20-50 percent for sectors in which market access was less constrained. He then applied his frequency-ratio measurements of liberalization to these maximum tariffs to construct tariff equivalents that differed by country based on their offers in the GATS. Thus, assuming a benchmark tariff equivalent of, say, 200 percent of postal services, and a frequency ratio of 40 percent to reflect a country's scheduled market access commitments, the tariff equivalent for that sector and country is set at [200-0.4 (200)] = 120 percent. The resulting weighted-average tariff equivalent "guesstimates" for 1-digit International Standard Industrial Classification (ISIC) sectors were Australia, Austria, Canada, Chile, E.U., Hong Kong, Japan, Korea, Mexico, New Zealand, Sweden, Turkey, U.S., etc.

The tariff equivalents were found to be highest for ISIC 7, Transportation, Storage and Communication, reflecting the significant constraints applied within this sector. It may be noted that Hoekman's measurements were designed to indicate only the relative degree of restrictions, which should not to be taken literally as indicators of absolute *ad valorem* tariff equivalents. Table 3.8 portrays Hoekman's guesstimates.

An alternative and perhaps improved approach has been to combine other data together with an index of proxy measures of restrictiveness in order to estimate econometrically the effects of barriers. For example, suppose that an index of restrictiveness has been constructed for a group of countries, and that price data are also available for the services involved in this same group. Using knowledge and data on the economic determinants of these prices, an econometric model can be formulated where the restrictiveness index and/or proxy measures of restrictiveness are included in the estimable equation as additional explanatory variables, and the estimated coefficients will measure the effect of trade restrictions on prices, controlling for the other determinants of prices. Such an econometric method would require data on more than just the barriers themselves, including prices and other relevant determinants of prices, for the subset of the countries, assuming that the effects of restrictions may be common across countries. The estimated coefficients can then be applied to the other countries as well. Such an approach had been used by Doove *et. al.* (2001: Chapter 2) for the study of the international air passenger.

They built on work by Gonenc and Nicolleti (2001), who had constructed an index of restrictiveness for this industry, and who had also used an econometric model to estimate the effects of restrictiveness for a group of 13 OECD countries. Doove *et. al.* extended the index of restrictiveness to a larger set of 35 OECD and non-OECD countries and applied this estimated coefficient to calculate price effects.

TABLE 3.8

Constructed Ad Valorem Tariff Equivalent 'Guesstimates' by 1-digit ISIC Services Sectors for Selected Countries

Country	*ISIC 5 Construction*	*ISIC 6 Wholesale and Retail Distr.*	*ISIC 7 Transp., Storage and Communic*	*ISIC 8 Business and Fin. Services*	*ISIC 9 Social and personal Services*
(1)	(2)	(3)	(4)	(5)	(6)
Australia	12.0	7.4	183.4	24.8	25.4
Austria	5.0	4.6	98.7	20.1	13.9
Canada	6.0	9.0	117.7	25.9	40.2
Chile	40.0	34.4	182.2	45.2	42.9
E.U.	10.0	10.0	182.0	27.2	23.6
Finland	19.0	14.6	181.0	23.8	31.7
Hong Kong	32.0	31.5	149.8	39.0	42.9
Japan	5.0	4.6	142.0	28.9	32.3
Korea	16.0	21.4	164.9	36.3	40.7
Mexico	24.0	21.3	152.3	40.9	29.8
New Zealand	5.0	13.4	181.5	30.5	36.1
Norway	5.0	13.4	122.2	25.7	24.0
Singapore	12.0	34.4	138.8	35.9	33.7
Sweden	12.0	13.4	184.2	22.5	26.9
Switzerland	5.0	8.0	178.1	27.7	32.3
Turkey	5.0	34.4	31.6	35.4	35.9
U.S.	5.0	4.6	111.4	21.7	31.7

Source : Adapted from Hoekman (1995: 355-6).

The estimating equation used for this was the following:

$$\dot{p} = \alpha + \beta BRI + \gamma E + \varepsilon \quad (1)$$

where $\dot{p}$ represents the price of air travel over a particular route, BRI is the index of representatives for that route, and E is a vector of variables for the determinants of prices, including indexes of market structure both for the route and the route ends, measurements of airport conditions, government control and propensity for air travel.

The coefficients a, b, and g were estimated econometrically, while e was the disturbance term. The price variable $\dot{p}$ in this equation demonstrated the common need to model particular features of a service industry. Based on a separate analysis of international airfares, relating them to distance and to other route-specific variables, the price variable in equation (1) provides information regarding the percentage that the actual airfare lies above the price predicted from this analysis. By holding this predicted price constant as unaffected by a particular trade restriction, the estimated coefficient measures the percentage by which the price of airfare in this case, increased by a restrictiveness of one, compared to the price at a restrictiveness of zero.

Applying this estimated coefficient to the values of the index of restrictiveness for larger set of countries, Doove *et. al.* (2001) produced the price effect estimates, which happened to be largest for developing economies and for the business travel. Table 3.9 summarises their results.

Other studies, which used variations on this technique, included the use of separate indexes of restrictiveness or proxy measures for different type of trade barriers, including individual modes of supply. A number of similar studies covered several sectors, including international air services, wholesale and retail food distributors, banks, maritime services, engineering service, telecommunications, and industrial electricity supply in both developed and developing countries. These various sectors are evidently distinctive in terms of their economic characteristics and the regulatory measures that affect their operations. Specialized knowledge of these sectors is thus essential in designing the conceptual framework and adapting

TABLE 3.9

International Air Passenger Transport: Bilateral Restriction Indexes and Price Impacts

	Number of agreements/ routes	*Bilateral Restriction Index*	*Price Impacts*		
			Business	*Economy*	*Discount*
(1)	*(2)*	*(3)*	*(4)*	*(5)*	*(6)*
		Asia Pacific Economies			
Australia	24	0.62	146.0	54.8	14.6
India	20	0.77	164.4	81.3	21.8
Indonesia	16	0.73	139.7	53.0	20.4
Japan	29	0.73	121.1	41.4	18.1
Korea	18	0.72	181.5	89.9	20.4
Malaysia	22	0.71	199.1	95.6	18.4
New Zealand	15	0.39	82.1	66.8	11.7
Philippines	20	0.79	207.5	70.1	20.9
Singapore	30	0.70	141.5	57.5	16.8
Thailand	25	0.68	124.5	71.3	16.2
		American Economies			
Argentina	12	0.74	161.7	62.0	17.5
Brazil	19	0.70	195.5	63.9	15.5
Canada	29	0.60	114.5	56.9	11.4
Chile	17	0.61	125.2	49.5	12.9

Mexico	19	0.82	224.7	92.2	18.4
Uruguay	32	0.52	96.9	38.5	12.3
U.S.	32	0.40	52.9	33.2	8.9
		European Economies			
Austria	28	0.32	47.2	20.6	6.1
Belgium	31	0.36	63.3	22.0	6.9
Denmark	30	0.34	53.1	21.1	7.0
Finland	22	0.23	33.6	11.5	3.8
France	32	0.35	57.0	20.8	8.3
Germany	32	0.37	56.5	20.3	8.1
Greece	26	0.31	72.1	24.9	7.2
Ireland	23	0.21	32.2	20.1	4.5
Italy	25	0.29	49.9	18.5	6.4
Luxembourg	23	0.24	36.9	15.0	4.2
Netherlands	31	0.39	104.0	20.0	10.0
Norway	28	0.32	62.1	16.4	4.4
Portugal	21	0.14	45.5	20.3	6.1
Spain	31	0.36	68.0	25.4	8.9
Sweden	29	0.32	45.5	20.3	6.1
Switzerland	32	0.75	102.5	42.6	13.8
Turkey	20	0.56	98.8	32.2	10.7
U.K.	32	0.30	46.3	21.5	7.6

Source : Adapted from Doove *et al.*

the available data to calculate the price impacts of the regulatory measure involved.

Quantity Impact Measurements

Another approach, appropriate for some service industries, has been to model the determinations of quantity rather than price, and then to include the trade restrictiveness index in a quantity equation. The result, analogous to that for prices above, was an estimate of effects of trade barriers on quantities. This can in turn be converted into an effect on prices with an assumed or an estimated price elasticity of demand. Warren (2000b) had assessed the quantitative impact of barriers in telecommunication services, chiefly mobile telephony and fixed network services, for 136 countries. For this purpose he estimated the following equation for the mobile telephony sector :

$$Q_i^m = \alpha + \beta_1 Y_i + \beta_2 Y_i^2 + \beta_3 PD_i + \beta_4 [P_i^m] + \varepsilon_I \qquad (2)$$

In equation (2) for each country I, Q_i^m is the number of cellular telephone subscribers per 100 inhabitants, Y_i is GDP per capita, and PD_i is population density. $[P^m{}_i]$ is a policy variable, which for mobile telephony took two forms: an index of market accesses for investment in the industry based on number of competitors, privatizations, and policies towards competition; and a broader average of several trade and investment-related indexes. Combining these quantitative estimates of the effects of removing existing barriers with an estimate of the price elasticity of demand for the telecommunications services involved, tariff equivalents in the form of price wedges were calculated. The estimates for the advanced industrialized countries are relatively low in comparison to the much higher estimates for the newly industrializing countries. There were cases of developing countries that in some cases have very large tariff equivalents, including some with several hundred percent, e.g. China (804, and 1000 percent), Columbia (11 and 24 percent), India (861 and 1000 percent), Indonesia (71 and 128 percent), South Africa (14 and 21 percent) and Venezuela (10 and 15 percent). Table 3.10 summarises his estimates.

Table 3.10

Tariff Equivalents of Barriers to Telecommunication Services in Major Nations

(Percentage)

	Domestic	*Foreign*
Australia	0.31	0.31
Austria	0.85	0.85
Belgium	0.65	1.31
Brazil	3.81	5.68
Canada	1.07	3.37
Chile	1.68	1.68
Hong Kong	1.26	1.26
Colombia	10.55	24.2
Denmark	0.20	0.20
Finland	0.00	0.00
France	0.34	1.43
Germany	0.32	0.32
Ireland	1.46	2.67
Italy	1.00	1.00
Japan	0.26	0.26
Korea	4.30	8.43
Mexico	6.24	14.43
Netherlands	0.20	0.20
New Zealand	0.27	0.27
Singapore	2.10	2.72
Spain	2.03	3.93
Sweden	0.65	0.65
Switzerland	1.23	1.23
Turkey	19.59	33.53
U.K.	0.00	0.00
U.S.	0.20	0.20

Sources : Adapted from Warren (2000b).

Nguyen-Hong (2000) had estimated the influences of restrictions on the price-cost margins of 84 engineering service firms in 20 economies, using 1996 company accounting data complied from a variety of private and official sources. He developed a linear model of of firm behaviour to include the determinants of the observed price-cost margins, and used ordinary least squares method to cross-section data and estimated the coefficients, and the sample means of the independent variables. The index of foreign barriers to establishment was found to have a negative and significant Impact, while the price and cost impacts of the restrictions were found to exceed 10 percent for Austria, Mexico, Malaysia, Indonesia, and Germany. His estimates of cost impacts were relatively small, ranging between 0.7 and 6.8 percent, as is reported in Table 3.11. Trewin (2000) used time-series data on the total costs of providing telecommunications services for 37 countries obtained from the International Telecommuni-cations Union (ITU) for the period 1982-92. He used a frontier cost method as a means of estimating the minimum possible costs that were expended from a given combination of inputs, using measurement of restrictiveness calculated by Marko (1998) and Warren (2000a). His results suggested that countries that provided higher levels of FDI faced lower costs, after making allowance for the quality-cost aspects of telecommunication services When the sample was divided between low and high income countries, the average efficiency of the high income set was found to be more than three times better than low income set. The results are listed in Table 3.12. It can be seen, in the high income set, that Luxembourg is close to the efficiency frontier whereas Portugal and Korea were relatively high cost countries.

Doove *et al.* (2001) constructed restrictiveness indexes and estimates of price impacts for international air passenger transport, telecommunications, and electricity supply. Their indexes of bilateral restrictions on international air passenger transport referred to 35 economies in the Asia-Pacific, Americas, and European regions. Focusing on the discount segment of the air passenger market, they implement a procedure for estimating the price effects of the applicable restrictions, using fare data primarily for the end years of 1990s. The results, indicated that the higher price effects range from 12 to 22 percent in the Asia-pacific economies, 9 to 18 percent in the Americas, and generally below 10 percent in the European economies. The price impacts for business and economy airfares were considerably higher but should be interpreted tentatively due to data constraints.

TABLE 3.11

Estimated Price and Cost Impacts of Restrictions on Engineering Services

(*Percent*)

Economies	*Price Impacts*			*Cost Impact*
	Foreign Barriers to Establishment	*Foreign Barriers to Ongoing Operations*	*All Foreign Barriers*	*Domestic Barriers to Establishment*
Austria	11.1	3.5	14.5	6.8
Mexico	13.9	0.2	14.2	1.9
Malaysia	11.3	0.7	12.0	5.3
Indonesia	9.9	0.3	10.2	3.2
Germany	4.7	5.5	10.2	2.9
Spain	5.1	3.7	8.7	3.9
U.S.	5.1	2.2	7.4	3.8
Sweden	5.9	0.9	6.8	0.7
Japan	3.1	3.4	6.6	2.2
Canada	3.1	2.2	5.3	2.7
Singapore	4.9	0.2	5.0	0.8
Hong Kong	3.6	1.5	5.1	2.3
South Africa	3.5	0.2	3.7	0.7
Netherlands	3.5	0.2	3.7	5.2
Australia	2.1	0.7	2.8	2.1
U.K.	2.3	0.2	2.5	1.4
Finland	1.8	0.5	2.3	0.7
Denmark	0.3	0.8	1.1	0.7
France	0.3	0.6	0.9	0.7
Belgium	0.3	0.2	0.5	0.7

Source : Adapted from Nguyen Hong (2000: 63).

TABLE 3.12
Coefficient Estimates of Technical Efficiency in Telecommunications Services

Low Income	*Technical Efficiency*	*High Income*	*Technical Efficiency*
(1)	*(2)*	*(3)*	*(4)*
Chile	3.82	Australia	1.67
China	6.31	Austria	1.31
Hungary	2.61	Belgium	1.55
Iceland	1.16	Canada	1.34
Indonesia	11.96	Denmark	1.43
Ireland	3.22	Finland	1.24
Malaysia	4.31	France	1.74
Mexico	15.41	Germany	1.66
PNG	7.75	Greece	1.11
Philippines	3.06	Hong Kong	1.44
Poland	2.30	Italy	1.71
Thailand	5.25	Japan	1.21
Turkey	4.07	Korea	1.98
		Luxembourg	1.03
		Netherlands	1.43
		New Zealand	1.83
		Norway	1.75
		Portugal	2.08
		Singapore	1.57
		Spain	1.75
		Sweden	1.40
		Switzerland	1.42
		U.K.	1.67
		U.S.	1.48
Mean	5.48	Mean	1.54

Source : Adapted from Trewin (2000:112).

Gravity Model Estimates

Because of the sector specific nature of prices that are needed to estimate a price effect, the above methods often are not useful for comparing the overall levels of service trade barriers across countries. We need a more general model of trade as a benchmark, and the natural choice is so-called gravity model, which relates bilateral trade volumes positively to the incomes of both trading partners, and also negatively distance between them. François (1999) had fit a Gravity model to bilateral services trade for the United States and its major trading partners, taking Hong Kong and Singapore to be free trade benchmarks. The independent variables, in addition to distance between trading partners, included per capita income, gross domestic product (GDP), and a Western Hemisphere dummy variable. The differences between actual and predicted imports were taken to be indicative of trade barriers and were then normalized relative to the free trade benchmarks for Hong Kong and Singapore. Combining this with an assumed demand elasticity of 4, tariff equivalents were estimated, which were found to be considerably higher for construction services, in the 40-60 percentage for China, South Asia, Brazil, Turkey, Central Europe, Russia and South Africa, and in the 10-30 percent range for industrialized countries. Table 3.13 summarises his estimates.

TABLE 3.13

Estimated Tariff Equivalents in Trades Services : Gravity-Model-based Regression Method

(Percentage)

Countries/ Regions	*Business/ Financial Services*	*Construction*
(1)	*(2)*	*(3)*
North America	8.2	9.8
Western Europe	8.5	18.3
Australia and New Zealand	6.9	24.4
Japan	19.7	29.7
China	18.8	40.9

(Contd.)

TABLE 3.13 (*Contd.*)

(1)	(2)	(3)
Taiwan	2.6	5.3
Other Newly Industrialized Countries	2.1	10.3
Indonesia	6.8	9.6
Other South East Asia	5.0	17.7
India	13.1	61.6
Other South East Asia	20.4	46.3
Brazil	35.7	57.2
Other Latin America	4.7	26.0
Turkey	20.4	46.3
Other Middle East and North America	4.0	9.5
CEECS and Russia	18.4	51.9
South Africa	15.7	42.1
Other Sub-Saharan Africa	0.3	11.1
Rest of World (ROW)	20.4	46.3

Sources : Adapted from Francois (1999).

Deardorff and Stern (1998:24) have noted that measurements based on the gravity model are useful mainly in identifying relative levels of protection across sectors and countries. But gravity models have some important drawbacks. A problem arises when this technique is used to infer barriers for separate industries. The theoretical basis for the gravity equation, as in Anderson (1979) and Deardorff (1998), applies to total trade, not to trade in individual sectors. The gravity equation makes sense at the sectoral level only if all countries are equal in their capacity to produce in a sector, which of course would be a denial of the role of comparative advantage. Thus, if a country were in fact to have a comparative advantage in a particular service sector, so that its output would be high and its cost of serving its domestic market itself would be low, then it would import less from abroad than would be expected based on income and distance alone. Thus comparative advantage may show up as an implicit barrier to trade, when in fact none exists.

The above discussions portray the use of a wide variety of approaches to study the effects of service barriers, which are varied. Such wide variety of measurement of service barriers need to be incorporated into an explicit economic modeling framework in order to determine how the existence or removal of the barriers actually affect conditions of competition, productivity, the allocation of resources, and economic welfare within or between sectors and countries. The computable general equilibrium (CGE) modeling may be used for individual sectors or on an economy-wide basis to estimate such effects. Fink *et. al.* (2003) provided such a sectoral modeling to analyze the impact of policy reform in basic telecommunications, covering 86 developing countries globally for the period of 1985-99. They addressed three questions, covering the impact of: (1) policy changes relating to ownership, competition, and regulation; (2) any one policy reform coupled with the implementation of complementary reforms; and (3) the sequencing of the reforms. Their findings were: (1) privatization and the introduction of competition significantly increased labour productivity and the density of telecommunication mainlines; (2) privatization and competition worked best through their interactions; and (3) there were more favourable effects from introducing competition before privatization. They further concluded that autonomous technological progress outweighed the effects of policy reforms in increasing the growth of teledensity. What is especially noteworthy about this type of study is its focus on both the policy and the market structure of the sector and the econometric framework that is designed to measure the determinants of teledensity and telecommuni-cations productivity. The assessment of particular services barriers may therefore be most effectively addressed when incorporated into a sectoral-modeling framework.

In contrast, CGE modeling provides a framework for multisectoral and multi-country analysis, of the economic effects of services barriers and related policies. Most CGE modeling research to date had been focused on barriers to international trade in goods rather than trade in services and FDI. The reasons for this arises from the lack of comprehensive data on cross-border services trade and FDI and the associated barriers, together with the difficult conceptual problems of modeling that are encountered. Some indications of pertinent CGE modeling work relating to services is provided in Hardin and Holmes (1997), Brown and Stern (2001: 272-4), and Stern (2002: 254-6). The approaches of modeling can be divided as follows: (a) analysis of cross-border services trade liberalization in response to reductions in service barriers; (b) modeling in which FDI is assumed to result from trade liberalization or other exogenous changes that generate international capital flows in the form if FDI in response to changes in rates of return; and (c) modeling of links between multinational corporations' (MNCs) parents and affiliates and distinctions between foreign and domestic firms in a given country or region. The third variety of CGE modeling comes closest to capturing the important role played especially by MNCs and their foreign affiliates in providing mode-3 type services. This, for example, is the focus of the study by Brown and Stern (2001). Brown and Stern analyzed the effects of removal of services barriers under alternative conditions of international capital mobility and changes in the world capital stock due to increased investment. Their results suggested that the welfare effects of removing services barriers were sizable and vary across countries depending on how international capital movements and changes in domestic investment respond to changes in rates of return. The largest potential benefits were realized for all of the major developed and developing countries when allowance was made for changes in investment that augmented the stock of. capital. Their results on welfare effects of removal of barriers in services under alternative scenarios are presented in Table 3.14.

It is evident that these welfare effects associated with an increase in the world's capital stock in response to an increase in the rate of return to capital are considerably larger than what is commonly seen in CGE models in which capital is assumed to be internationally immobile. This may not be surprising because it has been apparent from previous CGE analysis of trade liberalization that have made allowance for international capital flows that the largest welfare gains stem from these flows rather than from the removal of tariffs and other trade barriers that distort consumer choice in good trade. The understanding of consequences of liberalizing services barriers thus is enhanced

TABLE 3.14

Welfare Effects of Elimination of Services

(percent and billion of dollars)

Country	Scenario A: Perfect international capital mobility and fixed world capital stock		Scenario B : Risk Premium elasticity = 0.1 and fixed world capital stock		Scenario C : Risk Premium elasticity = 0.1 and world capital stock increased by 3%	
	% GNP	$ Bill	% GNP	$ Bill	% GNP	$ Bill
(1)	(2)	(3)	(4)	(5)	(6)	(7)
Industrialized Countries						
Australia	1.8	6.0	1.5	5.0	4.9	16.8
Canada	14.8	84.0	12.9	73.7	14.9	85.0
E.U.	0.5	42.4	0.5	38.0	2.5	202.4
Japan	-2.0	-103.7	-1.7	-88.4	0.5	25.7
New Zealand	9.1	5.2	7.5	4.3	10.5	6.0
U.S.	0.5	35.0	0.3	23.2	3.1	222.5
Developing Countries						
Asia						
China	3.8	26.9	3.2	22.9	6.0	42.8
Hong Kong	6.6	6.6	5.4	5.5	13.4	13.5
Indonesia	15.6	30.8	13.1	25.8	16.9	33.3

(Contd.)

TABLE 3.14 (*Contd.*)

(1)	(2)	(3)	(4)	(5)	(6)	(7)
Korea	-2.8	-12.3	-2.3	-10.1	1.4	6.4
Malaysia	2.3	2.1	1.9	1.8	4.7	4.4
Philippines	2.3	1.6	1.9	1.3	8.3	5.7
Singapore	1.7	1.0	1.3	0.7	4.3	2.5
Taiwan	7.6	20.7	6.8	18.5	7.7	21.2
Thailand	-2.2	-3.6	-1.8	-2.9	4.4	7.1
			Other			
Chile	-2.0	-1.3	-1.6	-1.0	2.7	1.7
Mexico	-4.3	-11.7	-3.2	-8.8	0.2	0.5
Rest of Cairns	-3.7	-39.6	-3.2	-34.1	0.6	6.2
Total	90.3		75.6		703.7	

Source : Adapted from Brown and Stern (2001: 277-78).

when allowance is made for the behaviour of multinational firms whose foreign affiliates are already located in or attracted to host countries. When services liberalization occurs and the real return to capital is increased, so that there are FDI (mode 3) international capital flows and the world capital stock expands, most countries stand to gain significantly in terms of economic welfare.

3.5. GATS AND TRADE IN EDUCATIONAL SERVICES

The discussions on trade in education services began in 1994 when the GATS was signed by the members of WTO, which aimed at liberalization of trade in services. Since then there has been frank and open discussions on Trade in Education Services (TES) as simple goods trade. Trade in services is more varied phenomenon than simple goods trade, and trade in education sector services includes study abroad, education delivered by foreign teachers, long distance learning between countries, and creation of foreign establishment and this global trade in educational service is in rapid growth path, accelerated by development of new information technology. For teacher, student and majority of citizens, the term "education" connotes public services whose aim is primarily non-commercial in nature. In fact, it was considered primarily a non-tradeable merit good with the objective of improving the welfare and empowerment of the population. The GATS framework has considered the educational services as internationally traded commodity, for which private sector's participation is emphasized. Education is divided into five categories: (a) Primary education; (b) Secondary education; (c) Higher education; (d) Adult education; and (e) Other education services, i.e, new teaching-related activities which are difficult to classify like testing and certification. Although education acts as a promoter of economic growth, WTO points out that in last 10 years proportion of public spending assigned to education remained more or less stable as percentage of GNP. Although there are inter-country variations in the percentage of public spending on education, and there are inter-temporal variations in these figures, primarily in developing countries, public sector remained the main source of funding on education, even though private sector's roles varied from a country to another. In certain cases it is often difficult to distinguish between the funding of private and public sector (specially in case of secondary and primary education).

Although educational services were not considered as a tradable sector for long by different countries, the GATS treaty has opened up the scope for expanding educational trade among nations. At the same time, it may be noted that international mobility of students, teachers' education and training programs have been happening for a very long time, and therefore the renewed enthusiasm in the prospect of expanding import/export of education services hinges on the fact that while cross-border education was an important aspect of the internationalization of higher education, it was not subject to international trade rules, and until recently, has not really been described as commercial trade. Education has been largely absent from the debate on globalization because it was thought to be essentially a non-traded service. But now trade in educational services are a major business in some countries, e.g. in Australia, Canada, New Zealand, the United Kingdom and the United States. Students traveling to study abroad are the largest component of international trade in educational services. This trade has been established over many years, but a newer prospect is the widespread provision of courses and qualifications by providers originating from, and in some cases operating the country of a student who stays at home. Internet, the new communication system is creating rapidly the conditions that could allow such trade to flourish in the future. International Trade in education services experienced steady growth especially in tertiary (higher education) sector, implying thereby an increase in number of students going abroad for study, exchange and linkage among faculties and researchers, increased international market for educated manpower, and academic programmes, opening of branches/campuses abroad, etc. By the early 1990, 1.5 million tertiary students were going abroad. In the United States, during the period 1989-93, foreign student enrolments increased by 3% which went up to by 6% in 1996-97. In 1996 USA exported $ 7 billon worth of higher education, making higher education country's fifth largest services sector export item. The major export market of USA were in Asia, with Japan, China, Republic of Korea, Chinese Taipei, India, Malaysia and Indonesia accounting for 58% of its export of education, followed by Europe and Latin America. USA faces major competition from Australia, and UK (mainly for Asian students). About 2/3 of US students study abroad in Western Europe (UK, France, Spain and Italy) and in Latin America. The main aims of GATS regarding the higher education was to removing restriction to market access and barrier to competition in higher education, i.e. to liberalized the higher education sector.

The GATS definition of services excludes those services which are provided by the government authority without a commercial purpose from the ambit of trade in services. Education service is fully financed and administered by state and without commercial purpose. So most, if not all, of the education sector falls in the scope of the GATS agreement. In a mixed economy like India, courses offered by public, required the payment, so fall within category of "commercial activity" and hence under Agreement. According to the GATS Agreement, WTO classifies four forms of trade in services :

(a) Cross-border supply—from territory of a member country to another Country, e.g., distance education. When country A provides distance course to country B, then A is exporting education service to country B.

(b) Consumption abroad—by citizens of member country on territory of another member country, e.g., courses taught abroad. When a student of country A takes a course from B, then A exports education services to B.

(c) Commercial presence—supplier from a member country on the territory of another member country, enabling the supplier in question to provide a service on that territory, e.g., activity carried out by foreign university or foreign educational enterprise. When an institution from country A is implanted to country B's territory to perform education activities, then A exports to B.

(d) Presence of natural person, i.e., mobility of people from one member country which supply a given service in another country; e.g., courses offered by foreign teacher. When a teacher from country A teaches in B, then A is exporting educational services to country B.

The development of the system of higher education and the polices for higher education has varied across the countries over a long period of time. So, some countries have evolved specific comparative advantage, which have developed when higher education was not part of trade negotiations. These comparative advantages are the resultant of multiple factor like prior and current educational policies, allocation of resources, concentration of academic weight, and so on, so that the nations put their proposal according to the comparative advantage in different modes of the supply under GATS. The commitments of different countries to higher education under the GATS varied with countries like Congo, Lesotho, Sierra Leone and Jamaica making full unconditional commitments in higher education perhaps with the intention of encouraging foreign providers to help develop their education system. Australia's commitment for higher education covers provision of private tertiary education services, while the European union has included higher education in their schedule with clear limitations on all modes of trade except "consumption abroad", which means foreign tuition paying students.

The four modes of supply mentioned by GATS are useful not only from the viewpoint of their location, but also with respect to their importance. Consumption abroad has been the prime factor of internationalization of higher education. In the past few decades consumption abroad has witnessed enormous growth because of the large numbers of student traveling from developing countries to the advanced developed countries in the West, resulting in the creation of the basic ground for non-tradable education to be considering as tradable sector. This led to creation of new modes, more specially, distance education and commercial presence. So, it can be said that the modes such as distance education, commercial presence and movement of professionals has its origin in the recent past, but the mode II, i.e. consumption abroad has originated in the traditional period.

In the education sector, the student is the consumer or "recipient" of education and education is traded as a tradable service. This phenomenon is known as *trade creep*. The growth of number of students going abroad has increased in the recent times, mainly due to the fact that the education provided by the country abroad, i.e., mainly advanced countries were based on better technology and more job-orientated. When the colonized world was introduced to the western form of education, there was also a flow of students from developing countries to the western world. This trend continued and became stronger throughout the post-colonial period and in the recent time mode II, i.e. student moving abroad occupied the market. This had shown the clear picture of education provider and recipients and shows that due technological development in abroad countries, they have developed comparative advantage in the Mode II. We now move on to different modes of educational services in some details.

Mode I—Cross Border Supply

Mode I include process of learning in which the receiver receives the education without moving to any place. Different forms of distance education mainly e-learning and also correspondence courses through postal delivery system, are covered in this mode. Every mode of supply of services has associated restrictions imposed along with it, and the barrier along with this mode is the electronic transmission of course materials and validity of the awarded degree and certifications.

Distance education is perceived as an increasingly effective method of instruction, and the educational researchers have examined the purpose and situation for which distance education is best suited—which is mainly to provide technological assistance. In the USA, the increased use of personal computers by public, the spread of user-friendly online learning softwares allow colleges to launch new distance courses on demand from the consumer. Again in the USA, people are in general computer literate, and they can easily access the computer of their own. USA has the maximum internet penetration level of 68.7% in world, compared to 3.65% in India, 68.2% in Australia, 10.9% in Japan. As a technologically advanced nation, the USA has comparative advantage in this mode of supply compared to many countries in the world. USA is leading exporter of higher education in this mode followed by France, Germany and UK. Although in developing countries with low internet penetration, on campus education enrolment dominates that of distance education, there has been increasing tendency in developing countries like India to expand distance education mode, and there is a strong possibility that the student of the developing world may view distance education offered by western universities as a better substitute than domestic mainstream education—as many students now-a-days moving to the foreign land for higher education and also opting for distance education. The preference of developing countrys' students in favour of distance education in the USA may be due to the "brand name", and available studies reveal that an American university has largest comparative advantage in mode I. The US proposal to WTO includes the use of the "knowledge economy" concept in higher education along with the use of internet and improving the country through liberalization of "educational testing services". To meet in the increasing demand in developing countries for distance education, it is required to increase the penetration level of internet services in these countries.

Mode II—Consumption Abroad

In this mode the process of learning takes place through the movement of consumer or student or recipient to the other countries. Presently, this is the most convenient way of acquiring higher education i.e., the student enrol themselves in the universities or institution of higher education abroad to acquire higher education. There are also barriers to this mode—visa requirement and costs, recognition of new qualification by other countries, quotas on number of international students in total and at a particular institution, restrictions on employment while studying, etc.

In this mode the movement of student reflects a growing competition among the developed nations. USA is the leading exporters of educational services followed by France, UK, and Australia. The export market of USA are Asia (Japan, China, Republic of Korea, Chinese Taipei, India, Malaysia and Indonesia), which roughly account for 58% of its export of education, and Europe and Latin America. And USA also imports educational services as 2/3 of US students study abroad mainly in countries of Western Europe. In 1954-55, there were an estimated 34,232 foreign students in institutions within American territory, of whom 30% were from Asian countries. By year 2001, the number of Asian students to the US universities was a phenomenal 2,94,230, while total number of students from Asia going to all OECD countries stood at 6,56,832. International students mobility to OECD countries had doubled over the past 20 years, and these countries host currently about 1.5 millions foreign higher-level students. In the period between 1998-2001 the total number of foreign students increased more rapidly than the total number of students in OECD countries. OECD countries receives about 85% of the world foreign students movement. This reflects that the growing demand for higher education is not met in the domestic market of Asian countries. This also reflects that Asian countries do have comparative advantage in mode III, which again are concentrated in the OECD countries and the USA. The brand name or product quality is also an important factor driving student movements abroad. Many students from Asia seek migration to countries in Western Europe and particularly USA for higher studies because of perceived superiority of education provided there, thereby creating comparative advantage of mode II in developed world. USA, which has developed infrastructure base to absorb larger capacity of students, do not get sufficient applications from US citizens for graduate programmes in science, engineering and advanced areas of research, and are dependent on international applicants. Enrolments in mathematics and computer science in the USA grew by about 13% from 2000-01 to 2001-02, perhaps reflecting the increases in Indian and Chinese enrolments. On the other hand, as the Australia and New Zealand had acceptance of English language, they were able to corner a share of international students in spite of being late entrants in the GATS negotiation. The four leading English-speaking countries account for 56% of all foreign students, and non-English speaking countries like Vietnam and Indonesia had to make special effort to attract the international students.

Mode III—Commercial Presence

Commercial Presence is one of the most difficult modes of supply under GATS, as it involves both market access and market presence. In this mode, foreign university establishes branches in a country (other than its own country) or joint venture in another country. There exists a big controversy on how to set international rules on these foreign universities. Like in the other modes of supply, this mode also has barriers with it, i.e., obstacles for establishment of a foreign owned institutions and moreover, not granting permission to issue qualification and refusal of national authorities to recognize the foreign institutions. During the last decade, international higher educational institutions have been aggressively promoting courses offered by them to overseas students including students of both metropolis and non-metros. These have resulted in the increase in availability and diversity of higher education abroad, but the high cost of higher education abroad has limited the number of offering students, particularly only those who could afford it or could take educational loans to study abroad. Many universities abroad were facing non-utilisation of capacities due to slack of students and were induced to open up local branches of foreign universities franchises and even joint ventures.

Indian market for higher education has witnessed a high growth rate in exclusive profit-oriented areas in recent year due to their orientation towards immediate employment. It is possible that expansion of foreign branches may take the same growth path. The socio-economic inequalities inherent in a developing country can be seen from the regional disparities, cost and access to higher education.

In its proposal to the WTO, the USA had mentioned intra-corporate movement resulting in commercial presence in the developing country. It also reflected the interest shown by the multinational companies in providing training services and they were extremely keen on removal of barrier on Mode III. The US proposal mainly requested on removing the barrier to mode III on the education service provided by foreign companies and organizations and many others. Australia and New Zealand, the two new entrants, put different proposals on mode III. Australia proposed to establish Australian Universities in the overseas area, and New Zealand's proposal involved new agencies to recruit oversea students. It may be noted that while the United States pressurises for opening up of educational markets in other countries by removing barriers to the mode of commercial presence, US federal and state laws do not allow establishment of branches in the USA by universities and institutions of other countries. Like the practice of free trade, which the USA always preaches for other countries to pursue, but itself violates always, in this case of liberalization of educational services too, the USA's role is asymmetrical and runs counter to the interests of many developing countries.

Mode IV—Presence Natural Persons

The last or the fourth mode of supply, provided by GATS, says that a persons can travel to a country (other than its own) on a temporary basis to provide education services in that country. In this mode the person traveling may be teachers/ professors or researchers. In trade in educational service under the mode IV, the service provider moves to other country, and not the service recipient, i.e. the opposite of mode II, consumption abroad. This mode is also not free from restrictions. The restrictions on this mode are immigration requirement—tight immigration policy followed by developed countries and requirement of nationality and issue of recognition of qualification of people from developing countries. The fact is that globalization has created a link between the movement of capital (mode 3 or commercial presence) and natural persons (mode 4), and developed countries simply cannot expect to have one without the other. Many developing countries have put pressure on developed nations on relaxation of immigration laws so that the developing countries that have a comparative advantage in human capital can benefit from liberalization of higher education in this mode. The Indian response to WTO negotiations on mode IV clearly expresses concern regarding the sluggishness of response in liberalizing this mode and states that horizontal commitments in mode IV are subject to limitation in the case of 100 countries as opposed to only four countries for mode II. The existing commitments are largely linked to commercial presence, which is of very limited use to developing countries that are interested primarily in movement of independent professional and other persons.Fourteen developing countries including India, China and Mexico have jointly put forward proposals for liberalization of mode IV through amendments in immigration laws in the developed countries including the USA. Among the developed countries, the USA, European Union, Japan and Canada have also put forth the proposal regarding the mode IV, which is focused on the transparency and to the general obligation for developing and developed countries, but no specific commitments of allowing labour mobility along the mode IV, for which many developing countries have comparative advantage in skilled manpower export or educational trade in mode IV. For the benefits of developing nations, having comparative advantage in mode IV, the issues of policy reforms and further openness of the markets are of crucial importance. If the costs of labour movements from LDCs could be minimized and the skill and educational qualifications are accepted by the other developed countries, then the benefits of labour migration and export of educational services through mode IV could bè enormous for many developing countries like India.

Effects on Adjustment Costs

Different modes of supply have different effects on factor markets. Cross border trade and consumption abroad resemble goods trade in their implications. The impact of the movement of the factors depends critically on whether they are substitutes or compliments for domestic factor services. Given the structure of factor prices in poor countries, we would typically expect liberalization to lead to an inflow of capital and skilled workers. Such inflows would tend to be to the advantage of the unskilled poor-increasing employment opportunities and wages. Interestingly, even when foreigners compete with local skilled workers in a service sector, the productivity boost to the sector from allowing foreigner access could lead to an increase in the demand for skilled workers—the scale effect could outweigh the substitution effect. But the skepticism about the benefits of liberalization emanates from the possible contraction in employment in formerly public monopolies that have frequently employed surplus labour. Evidence, however, suggests that such pessimism may not always be justified, as a number of developing countries have managed to maintain or even increase employment in their liberalized telecommunications sectors.

Even though international migration offers potentially large benefits to sending and receiving countries, the developed industrial countries had have shown little interest in liberalizing the inward flow of the unskilled while being relatively open to the entry of the skilled. A development-friendly migration policy would strive to ensure temporariness. On the one hand, industrial countries may be willing to accept a higher level of unskilled immigration if they could be certain that it was temporary. On the other hand, concerns about brain drain in developing countries would be greatly alleviated if emigration was temporary. The problem is that host countries cannot unilaterally ensure temporariness of unskilled migration because repatriation cannot be accomplished without the cooperation of the sources. And source countries cannot unilaterally ensure temporariness of skilled because repatriation cannot be accomplished without the cooperation of the host—today most temporary migration schemes in the OECD countries are in fact stepping stones to permanent migration.

Negotiations on the "temporary presence of natural persons" (mode 4) under the GATS have not been particularly successful in the past and prospects in the current Doha round are not bright. The negotiations under the GATS have failed to do better because only host countries are induced to make commitments to allow entry. Such an approach is ill-suited to unskilled migration because there is no provision for source countries undertaking binding commitments on screening, selection and facilitation repatriation. The approach is also ill-suited for skilled migration because it does not enable host countries to undertake binding commitments to ensure temporariness of skilled personnel from developing countries. In the absence of a dramatic change in the multilateral framework, a development-friendly approach to manage migration is more easily developed in a bilateral context.

Temporary *vs.* Permanent Migration

The official statistical distinction between temporary and

permanent migration is usually between stays of less than or more than one year. This is the threshold at which for many purposes residence is held to have changed. Many permanent, or at least very long-lived, migrations start at ostensibly short term temporary movements and some comprise solely a sequence of such contracts. On the other hand some migrations of over one year are nonetheless explicitly intended to be temporary, as, for example, when managers move to some of their firms' off-shore branches, with diplomatic postings and the U.S. H-1B visa for highly skilled workers. Hence inevitably there is only a relatively weak associations between what is reported (if temporary mobility is reported at all) and what one would really like to know. The distinction between temporary and permanent migration is potentially important in a number of ways. Thus a stream of, say, ten one-year migrants is likely to be less productive in the host country than a single ten-year migrant, not primarily because there will be ten "somewhat skilled" rather than one "very skilled" worker (if the long-term migrant returns at all). Relatively temporary migrants tend to remit a higher percentage of their incomes to their home countries than do permanent ones. Local attitudes toward temporary and permanent migrants may differ, although not necessarily in the same way in all countries. The two principal fears of migration are the displacement of local workers from (premium) employment and the threat of cultural dilution. Often, cultural and displacement fears can influence host countries' preferences between temporary and permanent migration. In Europe, intense cultural xenophobia coupled with relatively benign policies for displaced workers favoured TM. In the U.S., on the other hand, with a disposition towards migration and a relatively harsh labour market, the labour unions (and hence, to some extent, policy in general) favour permanent immigrants who can be unionized and incorporated into "the system" to potential "hit-and-run" competition from temporary migrants, especially if they are delivered by overseas firms which have the right to bring in their own workers.

In addition to strong natural barriers like home attachment, problems of language and cultural barriers as well as the loss of the functional social networks at home, migrants, both permanent and temporary, face a host of official and regulatory restrictions. Most obvious are the migration regulations embodied in visa policies. Temporary migrants are typically processed in exactly the same way as potential permanent migrants with very high levels of screening and delay, which strongly discourages temporary migration. In many countries visa regulations permit entry to foreign workers provided that their services are held to be necessary to the local economy via so called "economic-needs" tests. In some cases, these are operationalised by arbitrary decisions by the immigration services. In most, they entail the potential employers undertaking extensive bureaucratic processes to prove their needs. Even when visa regulations do not prevent mobility, other regulations can. For example, many professions are licensed, and licenses are hard to acquire for people with foreign qualifications or foreign experience. In some cases, nationality is a qualification, e.g. for the CEOs of financial institutions in some countries. Practical issues such as the transfer of pension rights or access to health facilities can make mobility expensive and unattractive.

The Temporary Movement of Natural persons, as the GATS calls temporary mobility (TM), can be visualized under two analytical paradigms. At one extreme it can be viewed as no different from cross-border services trade (mode 1), which, in turn, is often argued to be analytically no different from ordinary goods trade. For example, a consultant traveling to Brussels to deliver a course module in person is analytically close to a paper being sent in hard copy form, electronic form or even delivered by video-link. Hence one part of the "mode 4 story" is the familiar trade story. At the other extreme, TM has much in common with "traditional" long-term migration, whereby workers actually relocate from one country to another. This is particularly true where periods of stay are long or where a particular job in country B is filled by a circulating flow of temporary workers from country A, each being replaced by another as her contract expires. While such a "revolving door" provision differs from permanent migration in terms of its implications for social integration, network formation and the inter-generational spill-over from education, the basic fact that country B gains a worker while country a loses one is common to both. The "revolving door" provision differs from permanent migration in terms of its implications for social integration, network formation and the inter-generational spill-overs from education, the basic fact that country B gains a worker while country A loses one is common to both. The "revolving door" model could be particularly relevant to agency provided flows of middle-level professional workers such as nurses and teachers. Hence a second strand of thought about TM is based on the economics of factor mobility. Neither of the polar models—trade or migration—of course, captures the full character of TM.

The real economic issue pertaining to trade in educational services through mode 4 is the temporary mobility of persons across borders. Such temporary mobility (TM) can be thought about under two analytical paradigms. The duration of temporariness—one year or more—has not been properly defined by GATS, and immigration laws of different developed countries including the USA have put a brake on the developing countries' ability to export educational services and skills through this mode.

Growth in international trade in educational services has profound impact on higher education and economics of education sector in developing countries like India. The institutions for higher education are looking for new partners to become more market-orientated so as make higher education profitable for private investors without public subsidies Access to international education market increases human capacities in domestic institutions, promote their development, increases flow of people, and creates exposure of new idea having impact on societies. The main issues that need focused attention by GATS are : (a) growing importance of the mode of consumption abroad; (b) increased opening of education market to private traders in domestic and foreign countries; and (c) prevention of the problem of non-recognition of diplomas/degree granted by foreign providers. In order to increase domestic capabilities in higher education as well as reduce foreign exchange cost from outflow of student many Asia Pacific countries are allowing establishment of local branch campuses of foreign university.

This type of trade is taking place through partnership. Other Commercial Presence is twinning arrangement (TA) frequent in S.E. Asia, consist of domestic private college offering course leading to degree at overseas universities, it adopted partner abroad to validate in country course, validating instructional method and examination standard. Thus TA led to franchising of individual courses and programmes.

4

GATS and Higher Education in India

4.1 INTRODUCTION

The Indian economy has been exposed to the forces of globalisation, and following the GATS agreement, India's higher education system has also been opened up for service trade as per the different modes of supply specified in the Agreement. To study the impact of such globalisation on the country's education system, we need to understand the complexity of the scenario, as India exhibits the duality of the presence of modern high quality excellent education together with the low quality, weak and inefficient education services, that affect the resource allocation within the education sector. The hierarchial pattern that evolved over the years, and the interesting mix of public-private partnership in the field educational services, now face the forces of globalisation in an era of reforms, the rhetoric of inclusive growth notwithstanding. Internationalisation of education through inflow and outflow of students and teachers, and entry of foreign enterprises on education, with investment and technology, would be affecting the present structure of educational system in our country with long-term consequences on its human resource development.

Despite the low level of spread of higher education at the time of independence, India could make remarkable progress in the field of higher education during the post-independence period. We have been able to create a large base of higher educational institutions, and some of them are known to be excellent by world standards. Importance of education (higher education) has been constantly growing in India, and knowledge-based industries are now occupying the center stage in the development of a nation. Modern higher education system in India is almost 135 years old and it has grown faster after independence. India inherited a system of higher education in 1947, which was small and was characterized by persistence of large intra/inter-regional imbalances. Over the past *sixty* years, there has been significant growth in number of new universities and institutions of higher learning in specialized area, with more than 300 university level institutions (single and dual mode universities that include central and state universities, deemed to be universities, institutions of nation importance, open universities), 14000 colleges, 9 million students and 0.4 million teachers. The figures have still expanded beyond 2001, with the different state governments trying to expand the university system by establishing new universities and new colleges, and the central government also following suit by establishing new central universities and institutes in distant parts of India for spreading higher education as well as to pacify the local electorate in an era of coalition-based politics at the center. As a consequence, India has been able to create one of the largest trained and educated manpower in the world with considerable scientific and technical capabilities. Our research in agricultural sciences has contributed significantly to our food security. Our engineers have constructed huge dams, seaports, aerodromes, and power houses. We have made significant strides in nuclear and space research. We have produced excellent scientists in a number of other fields. We have produced fine practitioners of medicine and surgery. Good advances are made in biotechnology, genetics, and material sciences. We have developed comparative advantages in knowledge-based industries such as pharmaceuticals and IT. We have also been able to develop entrepreneurial and managerial skills for our educated youth. All these are by no means small achievements within a span of sixty years. But the capacity and capabilities in higher education in the country are still grossly inadequate to meet the needs of fast growing, knowledge-based economy of 21st century, on the one hand, and the demand from the youth aspiring to enter and be part of this dynamic world of growth and progress, on the other. The growth of facilities for higher education has been very slow and the quality has been uneven. Within the domestic economy, severe capacity constraints have emerged, particularly in those segments of higher education which are most in demand. Given the structure of income and asset distribution in the country, access to the existing capacities are also unequally distributed. All these have been compounded by the relatively niggardly allocation of public resources to higher education in India compared to its main Asian competitors, especially China but also Singapore, Taiwan and South Korea. They are providing access to large number of students at the bottom of the academic system while at the same time building some research-based universities that are able to compete with world's best institutions (Altbach, 2005). Due to our international compulsions in the GATS Treaty, India has exposed its inadequate, yet large system of higher education to the forces of globalisation.

The chapter is organized as follows. In section 4.2, we discuss the overall growth and spread of demand and supply of higher education in India, and argue that in spite of tremendous growth of higher education system in India during the post-independence period, there remains serious gaps, disparities and inadequacies of educational facilities between states, groups, and across rural and urban areas in India. Section 4.3 presents some recent trends in educational budgets in India and the implications of such expansion of expenditure on higher education. Section 4.4 outlines the patterns of enrolments between different types of educational institutions and the gender gap across the states of India. Section 4.5 discusses the participation of higher education in India in international trade through different modes of supply as indicated by the WTO and the participation of foreign students from different parts of the world in various institutions of higher learning in India. The implications of globalisation of educational services are discussed in section 4.6.

4.2. GROWTH OF DEMAND AND SUPPLY OF HIGHER EDUCATION IN INDIA

Demand

There has been sharp increase in the demand for higher education in India in recent years due to: (a) the acceleration of growth rates during the post-reforms period, whose sustenance requires inputs from higher education, (b) larger number of students completing school education, (c) the relative return from skilled-based earning continued to be higher than the alternative legal sources of earnings, and (d) an increase in the income levels and its distribution tilted in the middle, so as to expand the base of middle-income population whose only source of entry to the gateway of high growth and economic security lies in the field of higher education. The high growth experienced by the Indian economy during the post-reform era was driven mainly by growth in the service sector and a few segments of manufacturing such as motor vehicles, etc. This growth is manifested in fast modernizing metro-towns, growth in a variety of 'service' activities, bullish trends in stock exchanges, pervading growth and influence of IT, boom in the construction industry, globalization of retail trade, and very high income in certain segments of the fast growing economy. This growth is largely urban-oriented and is contributing to a fast expansion of urban middle class, which has created large demand for higher education.

The relationship between the levels of education and long run earnings of households has been studied by the NCAER's MIMAP India Survey Report, (2003), based on a survey of 5000 households for the reference period July 1994 to June 1995. The report has found a positive correlation between average household income and the education level of the head of the household for both rural and urban households. Lack of education is found to be more disadvantageous to earnings in urban households compared to those in rural areas—while some education below undergraduate level could help improving the earning levels in rural areas, in urban areas, only education at graduate and higher levels could make a real difference in earning levels (Table 4.1).

TABLE 4.1

Percentage Distribution of Households and Income by Education Level of the Head of the Household

Education Level of Head	*Rural*		*Urban*	
	HHS	*Income*	*HHS*	*Income*
No formal education	50.81	42.34	15.69	9.72
Below primary	11.41	11.08	4.93	4.45
Below middle	14.39	15.64	12.15	8.34
Below secondary	8.50	9.99	10.40	7.53
Below higher secondary	10.14	13.41	21.88	22.31
Undergraduate	2.43	3.61	9.22	9.13
Graduate and above	2.43	3.93	25.74	38.52

Source : MIMAP (2003).

The data also reveal that experience, as reflected in age, matters for earnings only if the educational level is high enough (Table 4.2). While earnings of illiterates and those with lower than secondary level of education initially decline with age,

TABLE 4.2

Per Household Income (Rs. per annum) by Head's Education and Age

Age group in years	*Education Level of Head*		
	Illiterate	*Below Secondary*	*Above secondary*
Below 30	20,134	28,422	32,871
30-9	18,323	23,755	46,729
40-9	21,749	29,898	54,065
50-9	26,710	37,972	76,085
60 and Above	29,950	42,202	80,974

Source : MIMAP (2003).

picking up only at later stages though at slow rate, earnings of the better educated rise sharply with age or experience. Higher education is, therefore, is seen as the more enduring basis of economic security and social status.

The perceptions of households regarding the value of education has also undergone change as are reflected in the in the pattern of household consumption expenditure on education. Household expenditure on education as per NSS has been generally low since large segments of population have been traditionally dependent on education provided by the government. However, household expenditure on education has gone up sharply as income rises as is indicated in the high income elasticity of expenditure on education (worked out across 12 expenditure classes) for both urban and rural areas (Table 4.3).

TABLE 4.3
Income Elasticity of Household Expenditure on Education

Year	*Rural*	*Urban*
1993-94	1.685	1.834
1999-2000	1.821	1.617

Source : Calculated from Household Consumption Expenditure data from NSS 50th and 55th rounds.

When we look at the educated youth (in age group of 15-29 years) in the labour force (Table 4.4), educated being defined as those having completed middle level of schooling and more, we find that the urban areas, as expected, have a significantly higher proportion of educated youth in the labour force than the rural areas—the percentage of all educated persons in labour force in urban areas is 70.3 while the corresponding percentage for rural areas is 43.4. It is interesting to note that the proportion of educated youth in labour force has increased over the five year period 1993-94 and 1999-2000 in all the sub-groups of age and sex in rural areas and female in both rural and urban areas, have shown a faster rate of growth of 'educated' in the labour force.

TABLE 4.4

Educated Youth in Labour Force, Middle Level of Schooling and Above (as Percentage of Labor Force in Relevant Age Group)

Sex	*Age Groups*	*Rural*		*Urban*		*All*	
		1993-4	1999-2000	1993-4	1999-2000	1993-4	1999-2000
(1)	(2)	(3)	(4)	(5)	(6)	(7)	(8)
Male	15-29	44.2	50.9	66.7	72.1	49.8	56.4
	15-19	49.5	55.1	67.4	71.9	52.1	58.7
	20-4	47.4	23.8	69.7	73.8	53.1	59.2
	25-9	36.6	45.2	63.5	70.7	44.0	52.3
Female	15-29	21.7	29.0	54.5	62.5	26.5	33.5
	15-19	30.6	40.6	63.6	69.7	34.7	44.3
	20-4	21.1	28.9	56.0	64.6	26.2	33.9
	25-9	14.2	21.3	47.0	55.9	19.6	25.9
Persons	15-29	36.6	43.4	64.1	70.3	42.5	49.3
	15-19	43.1	50.2	66.5	71.4	47.2	54.2
	20-4	38.0	45.3	66.7	72.1	44.3	51.5
	25-9	29.4	36.7	60.2	68.0	36.9	44.1

Notes : Data pertain to the 50th and 55th Rounds of NSS. The original table has been re-cast here.

Source : Planning Commission (2003).

It is worthnoting that although higher education in India has been the single most potent means of social mobility, that is, for moving from the rural poor, and the downtrodden sections of population to respectable status in society, the growth in facilities for higher education has, however, not kept pace with the need and demand for higher education in recent years, and rationing the access to it, particularly for the less privileged part of the population.

Supply

The long tradition in higher education and learning in ancient India, imparted mostly through family lines or gurukul traditions, had continued through the formal institutions of learning such as Pathshalas, Vihars, and Madrasas developed during the middle ages and flourished at various points in history, particularly during the pre-British period. However, 'barring a few exceptions' higher education had remained monopoly of the few. In fact, in ancient and in Mughal times, education for general masses were considered as antithetical to the interests of the maintenance of law and order by the rulers. In 1835, Lord Macaulay propounded the British education policy, which favoured educating the 'elite' and made a vigorous plea for spreading western learning through English language. Although the British, at times, appeared to show concern for the education of masses, education, particularly higher education, remained, by and large, the preserve of the 'elite'. The involvement of the British in the Indian Education System, particularly from the middle of the nineteenth century led to a rapid growth of schools, colleges, and Universities established by the Government as well as by Missionaries and other private agencies for spreading the western system of education. Universities of Bombay, Madras and Calcutta were established in 1857 and Universities of Allahabad and Punjab (at Lahore) in 1887. During the period, 1880-1900, three different agencies came forward to spread education: (i) mission schools and colleges, (ii) educational institutions made by government, and (iii) private institutions. Thus a westernized education system (through English Language) came to be established. The nationalist movement raised the question of education for the masses, and the need for a nationalist education policy with education in the native language and holistic development of education through technical and vocational education was emphasized by the nationalist leaders which led to the establishment of Bengal Engineering College in 1906, which was later transformed into Jadavpur University. However, the overall provision of educational facilities remained extremely inadequate. There was just a little over one person per thousand of population enrolled in higher educational institutions in 1951.

The main thrust of the education policy after independence had been to spread education for the masses, which was quite natural given the woeful state of literacy and elementary education among the people. Recognizing that economic development made growing demands on human resources, and in a democratic set-up, it called for values and attitudes for which the quality of education was an important element, the Second Five Year Plan provided for a larger emphasis on basic education, expansion of elementary education, diversification of secondary education, improvements of standards of college and university education, extension of facilities for technical and vocational education, and the implementation of social education and cultural development programmes. The Second Plan document stipulated a number of measures for improving the quality of university and college education and for reducing wastage and stagnation of students who were unable to qualify. These included the institutions of three-year degree courses and improvement in the overall environment and infrastructure, etc. The plan had a enthusiastic approach toward higher technical education—the IIT at Kharagpur was established during the First Five Year Plan and the establishment of other technological institutions, in a phased manner, was envisaged for different regions of the country. Over the years after independence, a large number of teaching and research institutions/universities and IITs and IIMs were established, covering almost all the major disciplines in technology sciences, social sciences, management and arts. By the year 1991, we had 5.8 persons per thousand population enrolled in institutions of higher education and by the year 1998-99—this number had reached 7.5 persons per thousand, making an almost 11-fold increase over the base of 1951. The number of colleges increased from 750 in 1950-51 to 11,089 in 1998-9, a 15-fold increase. The number of universities increased from 30 to 238 over the same period. The number of students increased from 263,000 to 7,417,000 over the same period, an increase of 28 times. The number of teachers went up from 24,000 to 342,000, that is, 14 times. Thus, over this period, the student-teacher ratio had doubled. In 2004, there were 300 universities/or deemed universities including 18 medical universities and 40 agricultural universities and more than 15,000 colleges, of which over 5000 were in rural areas (approximate numbers). Enrolment in higher education rose from less than half a million in 1950-1 to over 9 million in 2003.

Table 4.5 gives the growth rate of enrolment from 1982-83 to 2001-02. It can be seen that the growth of enrolment has slowed down since 1991-92. Table 4.6 indicates the inter-state disparities in gross enrolment ratio in higher education, with states like Bihar, Madhya Pradesh, Rajasthan, UP, and Tripura are lagging far behind that of other states. Thus, even with the great strides in the expansion of education, the enrolment in higher education today would be less than nine persons per thousand population. Table 4.7A gives alternative estimates of gross enrolment of students in the field of higher education. In fact, a large number of aspiring youth do not have access to higher education (Table 4.7B). There are also gender disparities, rural-urban disparities and disparities across socio-economic-religious groups and across occupations, which indicate that access to higher education are extremely skewed and inadequate compared to the aspirants of higher education. In fact, despite tremendous in the post-independence period, the facilities for higher education have not grown in proportion to the demand and in proportions to the growing aspirations among the people for a higher degree or for real higher education. In such an environment of scarcity, the poor are more deprived of access while the unscrupulous private providers flourish extorting huge rentals from the scarcity. Quality of supply too suffers under scarcity. In countries where job opportunities are good and rates of earning are not so widely different between jobs requiring higher education and other jobs requiring somewhat lower education but particular skills, many young people voluntarily branch-off towards skilled jobs requiring school education and vocational skills. However, even in international comparison, the current enrolment ratio in

TABLE 4.5

All India Growth of Student Enrolment (Higher Education) 1982-83 to 2001-02

Year	*Total Enrolment (in thousand)*	*Percentage Increase*
1982-83	3133	6.1
1983-84	3308	5.6
1984-85	3404	2.9
1985-86	3605	5.9
1986-87	3757	4.2
1987-88	4020	7.0
1988-89	4285	6.6
1989-90	4603	7.4
1990-91	4925	7.0
1991-92	5266	6.9
1992-93	5535	5.1
1993-94	5817	5.1
1994-95	6114	5.1
1995-96	6574	7.5
1996-97	6843	4.1
1997-98	7260	6.1
1998-99	7706	6.1
1999-2000	8051	4.5
2000-01	8399	4.3
2001-02	8821	5.0

Source : Kaur (2003).

higher education in India is less than the average for lower-middle income countries in the world. The gross enrolment ration is around nine percent in India, while it is 15 percent in China, more than 20 percent in many developing countries like Mexico, Malaysia, Thailand, Chile, and Brazil, and 40 to 50 percent in most of the developed countries.

When we look to the distribution of colleges and universities by type of management in India, we find that there have been sharp rise in private institutions and enrolments therein which are much higher compared to those under the

Table 4.6
Higher Education : Regional Imbalances (2001-02)

	State	*Enrolment/Million*
National Average:	AP	9297
8589/Million	Delhi	12049
	Goa	14319
	Gujarat	9647
	Haryana	10971
	Karnataka	10184
	Maharashtra	12611
	Orissa	9310
	Punjab	9624
	Arunachal Pradesh	5346
	Assam	7292
	Bihar	5780
	Kerala	7539
	MP	7465
	Rajasthan	6402
	Sikkim	7039
	Tripura	6022
	UP	6611
	West Bengal	7733

Table 4.7A
Gross Enrolment Ratio in Higher Education in India (Different Estimates)

Years	*SES*	*NSS*	*Census*
1983	4.04	7.67	NA
1987-88	4.69	8.57	NA
1991	4.63	NA	10.95
1993-94	4.80	8.85	11.74
1999-00	7.22	10.08	13.19
2001	7.85	10.00	13.82
2003-04	9.01	13.22 (1.61 Cr)	14.48
2006-07*	9.70 (1.28 Cr)	NA	15.60 (2.07 Cr)

Source : S.K. Throat, Keynote Address, Chennai, March 10, 2007.
*Ravi Srivastava, *EPW*, March 10, 2007.

TABLE 4.7B

Gross Enroment Ratio in Higher Education in India (Age Group 18-24 Years)

Decade	*GER*
1950-51	1.0
1960-61	2.0
1970-71	3.9
1980-81	5.4
1990-91	4.3
2000-01	7.9
2003-04	9.2

Source : J. Tilak, *EPW*, Feb. 24, 2007.

public aid and ownership, which indicates that although educational investments has become relatively attractive to private players, the government sector's expansion has been rather sluggish (Table 4.8). Table 4.9 indicates the state-wise distribution of existing facilities in higher education and it is clear that backward states have higher enrolment per university indicating lack of facilities so that the existing universities and colleges have to cater to much larger intake of students than are warranted for quality education. Table 4.10 indicates the state-wise targeted improvement in gross enrolment ratio in the states during the 11th Five Year Plan—a task that appears gigantic given the paucity of resources flow that are estimated in the field of higher education in the states by the central and state governments.

Investment in Higher Education

The main constraint to the expansion of higher educational facilities India has been the meagre public resources allocated to education. Priority within the available resources naturally goes to primary and secondary education (Table 4.11). The Education Commission (1964-66) had recommended that at least 6 percent of GDP should be spent on education. However, we find that in recent years public expenditure on education as a percentage of GDP has declined, and it was only 3.49 percent in 2004-05. (Table 4.12)

TABLE 4.8

Higher Education Institution and Enrolment (By Type of Management)

Type (by management or/Funding)		*Universities*		*Colleges*		*Higher Education Institutions*		*Enrolment (in Thousand)*	
		2000-01	*2005-06*	*2000-01*	*2005-06*	*2000-01*	*2005-06*	*2000-01*	*2005-06*
(1)	*(2)*	*(3)*	*(4)*	*(5)*	*(6)*	*(7)*	*(8)*	*(9)*	*(10)*
Public	Govt.	245	268	4097	4225	4342	4493	3443	3752
	Private Aided	#	10	5507	5750	5507	5760	3134	3510
Private	Private Un-aided	21	70	3202	7650	3223	7720	1822	3219
	Total	266	348	12806	17625	13702	17973	8399	10481

Source : UGC.

TABLE 4.9
Existing Institutional Capacity

State	Higher Education Institution			Total Enrolment	Enrolment per University	Enrolment Per College
	Colleges for General Education	Colleges for Professional Education	Univ/Deemed Univ./Institute of national Importance			
(1)	(2)	(3)	(4)	(5)	(6)	(7)
Arunachal Pradesh	10	4	1	6745	6745	482
Assam	317	50	7	214342	30620	584
Bihar	743	45	19	553693	29142	703
Jharkhand	117	22	8	209176	26147	1505
Manipur	58	5	2	38679	19340	614
Meghalaya	54	2	1	30716	30716	549
Mizoram	26	2	1	12180	12180	435
Nagaland	37	1	1	13644	13644	359
Orissa	700	80	15	367187	24479	471
Sikkim	2	4	2	6596	3298	1099
Tripura	14	3	1	22447	22447	1320
W.B.	374	139	26	746509	28712	1455
Total	2452	357	84	2221914	26451	791
India	10377	3201	407	11777296	28937	867

Source : UGC.

TABLE 4.10

Enrolment Target in 11Th Plan

State	Total Enrolment 2005	GER 2005	Projected Enrolment 2012	Projected GER 2012	Additional Enrolment during 11th Plan
Arunachal Pradesh	6745	5.62	12113	9	5368
Assam	214342	6.80	384927	10	170585
Bihar	553693	5.99	994353	9	440660
Jharkhand	209176	7.02	375650	11	166474
Manipur	38679	13.11	69462	20	30783
Meghalaya	30716	11.38	55162	17	24446
Mizoram	12180	9.98	21874	15	9694
Nagaland	13644	4.58	24503	7	10859
Orissa	367187	8.55	659415	13	292228
Sikkim	6596	9.04	11845	14	5249
Tripura	22447	6.02	40312	9	17865
W.B	746509	8.02	1340623	12	594114
Total	2221914	7.28	3990238	11	1768324
India	11777296	9.65	21150332	15	9373036

Source : Planning Commission.

TABLE 4.11

Expenditure on Education in Five Year Plans

Five Year Plan	Total Education	Elementary Education	Secondary	Higher
Fifth Plan	3.27	0.8	0.4	0.5
Sixth Plan	2.70	0.8	0.7	0.5
Seventh Plan	3.55	1.3	0.8	0.5
Eighth Plan	4.50	2.1	0.8	0.3
Ninth Plan	6.23	3.2	1.1	0.5

Note : Other level and type of education are included in Total Education.
Source : Tilak (2006).

TABLE 4.12

Growth of Public Expenditure on Higher Education in India

Year	*Percentage of GDP*	*Percentage of Budget*	*Per capita (Rs.) (1993-94 prices)*
1990-1	4.07	13.97	329
2000-1	4.26	12.23	509
2001-2	3.82	10.80	470
2002-3	3.97	12.60	495
2003-4	3.74	12.31	498
2004-5	3.49	12.27	—

Source : Tilak (2006).

Table 4.13A and B provides some recent data on public expenditure on higher education, and its projections over time.

TABLE 4.13A

Public Expenditure on Higher Education

Total Public Expenditure on higher education (2005-06 B)	Rs. 10688 Cr
Central Public Expenditure on higher education (2005-06 B)	Rs. 2018 Cr
State Public Expenditure on higher education (2005-06 B)	Rs. 8580 Cr
Public Expenditure on Higher education as % of GDP	0.35%
Public Expenditure Required to achieve 1% of GDP in 2012	Rs. 66905 Cr
Public Expenditure Required to achieve 2% of GDP in 2012	Rs. 133811 Cr
Public Expenditure by State Required to Achieve 1% of GDP in 2012	Rs. 53524 Cr
Public Expenditure by State Required to Achieve 2% of GDP in 2012	Rs. 107049 Cr
Compound Rate of Growth of state public expenditure required to achieve 1% of GDP	35%
Compound Rate of Growth of state public expenditure required to achieve 2% of GDP	52%

Source : UGC.

Thus, we find that although there have been acceleration in

TABLE 4.13B

Projected State Expenditure on Higher Education during 11th Plan to Achieve 1% of GDP

States	*2005-06 Budget*			*Moderate Target*	*Required Target*
	Plan	*Non-Plan*	*Total*	*Total state expenditure on higher education by 2012 (Assuming 20% rate of growth)*	*Total state expenditure on higher education by 2012 (Assuming 35% rate of growth) to achieve 1% of GDP target*
(1)	*(2)*	*(3)*	*(4) (5)*	*(6) (7)*	*(8) (9)*
Arunachal Pradesh	6.4	13.6	20	60	121
Assam	24	226	250	746	1513
Bihar	3	667	670	2001	4056
Jharkhand	24	246	271	809	1640
Manipur	58	44	102	305	617
Meghalaya	4	26	30	90	182
Mizoram	11	13	24	72	145
Nagaland	7	11	18	54	109
Orissa	72	224	297	887	1798
Sikkim	3	1	4	12	24
Tripura	1	25	26	78	157
West Bengal	6	668	674	2013	4080
Total	219.4	2164.6	2386	7125	14444
India	1346	9342	10688		

Source : Planning Commission.

the overall growth rate of the economy during the post-reform period, our knowledge base which has largely contributed to this high growth achieved with poor infrastructure and acute shortage of energy, our per capita public expenditure on higher education, in real terms, has not increased much. Since public expenditure, in spite of its frugality, has almost entirely been the source of our knowledge base and expansion of infrastructure on higher education, we need to step up the public expenditure on higher education, if we need to survive the onslaught of global competition and maintain and upgrade the quality in higher education, and at the same time distribute the access and facility across different regions and socio-economic groups in a more inclusive manner.

The recently released Planning Commissions' Paper on approach to the XIth Plan has shown a promising awareness of the issue. The approach paper states 'It (the 11th Plan) must address simultaneously the issues of increasing enrolment in universities and colleges especially the high end institutions like the IITs and IIMs, the problems of varying standards, outdated syllabi, inadequate facilities, and most of all need to create an environment that will attract top class faculty'. The 'approach' further says, 'Achievement of these objectives will require a substantial increase in resources devoted to this sector and successive annual plans will have to provide rising levels of budgetary support. However, this must be accompanied by internal resource generation by duly and realistically raising fees. Simultaneously, efforts will be made to develop wide merit-*cum*-means-based loan and scholarship programmes through the banking system and other agencies' (Planning Commission, 2006).

Participation of private providers in higher education has gone up in recent times—today they almost account for about one-third of all the higher education institutions, majority of them being 'for-profit' type. 'For-profit' considerations raise the costs enormously and do not necessarily pay due attention to quality. A well thought out regulatory framework detailing the system of grading, accreditation, and regular monitoring of quality of teaching and academic standards are to be in place for private and foreign providers. Their participation in the system should, however, be welcome in order to ease capacity constraints. Entry of foreign providers of repute (A-grade universities/institutions) may even have a positive impact on the quality of education.

4.3. STATE EXPENDITURE ON HIGHER EDUCATION

There is a general euphoria that the outlay for education has been hiked very significantly in the Eleventh Five-Year Plan and that the days of underfunding of education are a thing of the past. The allocation to education in the Eleventh Plan is likely to be Rs. 2,87,000 crore, which is five times the allocation made in the Tenth Plan in nominal terms. This is also expected to constitute nearly 20 per cent of total plan expenditure, compared to 7.7 per cent in the Tenth Plan. This is considered as an "unprecedented increase in financial support for education in India. Does the treatment of the education sector in the Union Budget 2008-09, the "crucial" second annual budget of the Eleventh Plan, fit in the grand scheme of the five-year plan, which is proclaimed as a "national education plan" which recognises education as a "centered (central) instrument for achieving rapid and inclusive growth".

The finance minister allocated in the budget for 2008-09 an amount of Rs. 34,400 crore for education, compared to the revised estimate of Rs. 28,674 crore in 2007-08. A close examination of the budget allocation shows that the increase is not particularly high, besides indicating marked shifts in education priorities of the government: from elementary to secondary and more importantly to higher education, from mass expansion to expansion of some kind of elite institutions, from a system of funding out of general budgetary support to funding out of earmarked taxes/cess, and to a system of delivery that relies more on public-private partnership.

First, at the national level. The total expenditure on education incurred by the union and state governments increased from Rs. 67,000 crore in 2000-01 to Rs. 1,33,000 crore in 2007-08. The nearly two-fold increase in a period of eight years, though in nominal prices, seems to be impressive. However, according to the *Economic Survey, 2007-08*, the allocations to education made by the union and the state governments together, as a proportion of GDP, have not been satisfactorily progressing during the last few years. The ratio was above 3 per cent in 2000-01, and ever since it has steadily declined to reach a low level of 2.69 per cent in 2005-06. It is only in the last couple of years that the declining trend seems to have been reversed, according to the revised estimates for 2006-07. However, even according to the revised estimates, the proportion allocated to education in 2007-08 is much less than the 2000-01 level! Further, we often note substantial differences between budget estimates, revised estimates and actual levels of expenditure. So one cannot be certain that the downward trend has been actually reversed in the recent years.

These figures refer to the expenditure on education incurred by the departments of education (school and higher education), and do not seem to include the expenditure incurred by other departments on education, which also seem to be significant. For example, the total expenditure on education incurred by the departments of education and other departments on education together constituted 3.7 per cent of GDP in 2005-06, *Budget Analysis of Expenditure on Education,* 2003-04 to 2005-06 while as shown in Table 3.14, the expenditure of the departments of education accounted for only 2.7 per cent.

Further, these figures in Table 4.14 also mark a declining trend in the relative priority given to education. The shares of education in total government expenditure on all sectors declined from 11.3 per cent in 2000-01 to 10 per cent in 2005-06. Even within the total social sector expenditure, the share of education declined from above 50 per cent to 47.2 per cent in 2005-06 and further to 45.3 per cent in 2007-08 (revised estimates). The total budget expenditure on education consists of education incurred by the union and the state government. That about 80 per cent of the government expenditure on education is met by the states, and that the expenditure of the union government is relatively small is well known. The states meet a substantial, nearly all of the non-plan expenditure on education, while in case of plan expenditure, the centre meets a good proportion of it.

TABLE 4.14
Government (Centre + State) Expenditure in Education
(in current prices)

Years	*Rs. Crore*	*Per Cent of GDP*	*Per Cent of Total Expenditure*	*Per Cent of Social Sector Expenditure*
2000-01	67,000	3.19	11.3	50.8
2001-02	68,071	2.99	10.6	49.4
2002-03	71,298	2.96	10.3	50.3
2003-04	75,607	2.74	9.6	49.3
2004-05	84,111	2.67	9.8	48.7
2005-06	96,365	2.69	10.0	47.2
2006-07RE	119,199	2.88	10.4	46.5
2007-08RE	133,284	2.84	10.2	45.3

RE : Revised estimate.
Source : *Economic Survey*, 2007-08 and earlier years.

Education in Union Budgets

Though the expenditure of the union government on education is small, it may assume much significance as it can set new directions for development, induce state governments to take up new programmes, mobilise more resources to take advantage of central schemes that require matching shares by the state governments, and on the whole, contribute significantly to education development in the country. From Table 4.15, it is clear that there has been a significant increase in the union government's budget expenditure on education.

The total plan plus non-plan increased from Rs. 7,900 crore in 2000-01 to 38,700 crore in 2008-09, as per the budget estimates. This, as an proportion of GDP also increased, particularly in the recent years. It is estimated to be 0.7 per cent in 2008-09, compared to 0.4 per cent in 2000-01. But given the long-pending goal of allocating 6 per cent of GDP to education by the union and state governments together, the current level does seem to be far less from satisfactory. Apart from the Union Government, the states have to increase their allocations to education substantially to reach the goal. While non-plan

TABLE 4.15

Expenditure on Education Incurred by the Union Government (Plan and Non-Plan)

Years	*Rs. Crore*	*Per Cent of GDP*	*Per Cent of Total Budget*
2000-01	7,925.2	0.377	2.43
2001-02	8,037.0	0.353	2.22
2002-03	9,089.3	0.370	2.20
2003-04	10,177.5	0.369	2.1
2004-05	13,228.7	0.420	2.66
2005-06	17,809.6	0.497	3.52
2006-07	23,809.6	0.574	4.09
2007-08RE	29,588.7	0.630	4.35
2008-09RE	38,702.9	0.730	5.15

RE : Revised estimates; BE: budget estimates (in all tables henceforth).
Source : Based on *Union Budget, 2008-09* and related budget documents of previous years and *Economic Survey, 2007-08* and earlier years.

expenditure is also important as it is required for the maintenance and upkeep of the system, it is plan expenditure that sets new directions for development. During the last five years, one notices a significant increase in plan allocations to education in the union budgets. The expenditure increased by 3.4 times from Rs. 10,224 crore in 2004-05 to Rs. 34,394 crore in 2008-09. Compared to the average annual increase during the last five years, the nearly 20 per cent increase in the 2008-09 budget seems to be the smallest, and the 35 per cent increase over the previous year's revised estimate the second lowest. In 2005-06, this increased by 47 per cent over the preceding year's revised estimate; the corresponding ratio was 38 per cent in 2007-08. Further, education sector also accounts for less than 10 per cent of the total plan expenditure of the union government, though the ratios increased marginally over the years.

Expenditure by Levels

Plan allocations to every level of education have been raised in the union budgets during the last five years in nominal prices. Significant hikes in allocation to elementary education took place in 2005-06 and later; those to secondary and higher education in 2006-07 and later; and those to adult education and technical education only in 2008-09. During the Tenth Plan, allocation to elementary education was raised, but the relative shares of all other levels including secondary, higher general and higher technical, and adult education were reduced. On the whole, in the Tenth Plan 78 per cent of the total plan expenditure on education was devoted to elementary education, a meager 6.4 per cent to secondary education, 7.1 per cent to higher education and 5.8 per cent to technical education. Against this background, the allocations in the 2008-09 annual Union budget mark a clear shift: allocation to elementary education has been reduced to 63 per cent from around 80 per cent of the total in 2006-07 and 2007-08; allocation to secondary education was doubled from 6.4 per cent in 2007-08 (and the average of the Tenth Plan); the share of higher education was increased by 50 per cent to above 10 per cent, and a similar increase was made in technical education. Table 4.16 summarises the plan allocations by the Union government over the years.

TABLE 4.16

Plan Expenditure on Education of the Union Government

Years	*Rs. Crore*	*Per Cent Increase over the Preceding years*	*Per Cent of All Sectors*
2004-05RE	10,244.2	—	7.73
2005-06RE	15,041.7	47.1	7.32
2006-07RE	20,745.5	37.9	8.49
2007-08RE	25,452.4	22.7	8.17
2007-08RE	28,671.5	38.2	8.97
2008-09RE	34,393.5	35.1* (20.0**)	9.16

* Over the revised estimate of the preceding year.
** Over the budget estimate of the preceding year.
Source : Union Budget, 2008-09 and earlier years.

Further, annual increases have not been even across all levels of education nor are they steady and smooth over the years at any level of education. For example, there was a negative rate of growth in expenditure on higher education in 2003-04 over the preceding year, followed by a 45 per cent increase in the following year, which in turn was followed by a modest increase by 4 per cent only in 2005-06. Similar fluctuating trends can be noted at all levels of education, but secondary, higher and technical education suffered more, with occasional negative or very low rates of increase. The increase in the allocation to elementary education in the 2008-09 Union budget has been the lowest. If the current year's budget allocations are an indication of the trends to come during the Eleventh Plan, one can say that there is going to be a significant shift in relative priorities in education. The pattern of allocation may shift in favour of secondary and higher technical education and away from elementary education.

There is a significant hike in the allocations to higher education in 2008-09 compared to the revised estimates for 2007-08. In last year's budget an allocation was made for Rs. 6,483 crore for higher education. It is important to note that both general higher education and technical higher education have been assigned substantially increased allocations in the current budget, as shown in Table 4.17. Plan allocation to the University Grants Commission has been nearly doubled; allocation to the All India Council for Technical Education has been raised by 2.4 times; the allocation for the Indian Institutes of Management doubled and for the Indian Institutes of Technology and also the Indian Institutes of Sciences trebled.

These hikes are over the revised estimates for 2007-08. In fact, if we compare the allocations in the current year with the budget estimates of the allocations made in 2007-08, we note that the increase has been made only in case of allocation for UGC (and total general higher education); and allocations to technical education have been considerably less than the budget allocations made in the previous year. A substantial proportion of the increase in the plan allocation to the UGC is perhaps meant for establishing 16 new central universities in each of the states where there exists no central university as of now. An amount of Rs. 50 crore is allocated for setting up three new Indian Institutes of Technology (IITS)—one each in Andhra Pradesh, Bihar and Rajasthan. Increased allocation for technical

TABLE 4.17

Allocations to Selected Institutions/Programmes in Higher Education in the Union Budget

(*Rs. crore*)

	Plan			*Non-Plan*			*Total*		
	2007-08BE	*2007-08RE*	*2008-09BE*	*2007-08BE*	*2007-08RE*	*2008-09BE*	*2007-08BE*	*2007-08RE*	*2008-09BE*
(1)	*(2)*	*(3)*	*(4)*	*(5)*	*(6)*	*(7)*	*(8)*	*(9)*	*(10)*
UGC	2,124.8	1,633.1	3,095.5	1,638.8	1,948.9	2,009.4	3,763.5	3,581.9	5,104.9
IITs	1,111.7	335.3	1,020.7	442.0	490.0	525.0	1,553.7	825.3	1,545.7
New IITs	80.0	0.[illegible]	50.0	—	—	—	80.0	0.0	50.0
IIMs	103.0	43.[illegible]	88.0	41.0	42.2	27.0	144.0	85.2	115.0
IISc	196.0	40.[illegible]	130.0	87.2	86.0	91.0	283.2	126.0	221.0
AICTE	892.0	297.4	718.0	234.1	263.0	285.0	1,126.1	560.4	1,003.0
Total General	2,910.0	1,958.4	3,946.0	1,755.0	2,072.7	2,137.7	4,665.1	4031.1	6,083.7
Total Technical	2,929.0	981.5	2,888.5	941.0	1,020.4	1,074.7	3,870.0	2001.9	3,963.3
Grand Total (Dept. of higher education)	6,483.0	3,262.0	7,600.0	2,729.0	3,136.0	3,259.4	9,212.0	6,398.0	10,859.4

Source : Union Budget, 2008-09 : Expenditure Budget, Vol. II.

education includes allocation for two Indian Institutes of Sciences for Education and Research (IISER) at Bhopal and Thiruvanantapuram and two Schools of Planning and Architecture at Bhopal and Vijaywada. During the Eleventh Plan, in all, it is planned to establish 30 new central universities, as many as eight new IITs, seven new Indian Institutes of Management, 10 new National Institutes of Technology, three IISER, 20 Indian Institutes of Information Technology and two Schools of Planning and Architecture. This indeed marks a massive expansion.

Although expansion to higher education system is a welcome move by the Union government, the expansion of both general as well as technical higher education needs to be carefully planned. There is a real shortage of high quality faculty in the existing institutions, and with the establishment of private, foreign institutions and central universities the shortage will be severely felt. Long periods of under-funding of higher education, virtual ban on recruitment of faculty and other similar measures have resulted in accumulation of such problems. All of a sudden, when funds are made available, it may be possible to set-up some central universities and technical institutes with higher quality faculty, unless new and innovative methods are thought of to attract good faculty. Otherwise there is a danger of planning and designing these new institutions on a very small scale, with a very small number of faculty and student numbers, offering a few specialized, if not market-oriented, programmes, as a result of which they may turn out to be privileged and elite institutions. Alternatively, these institutions will be allowed to grow into large size in terms of student numbers but with small faculty, or large number of low quality faculty. Both are serious dangers that need to be avoided. The question of sustainability or their "viability" assumes importance, as the location of the central universities and other institutes, including world class universities, it appears, is being decided more on political considerations, rather than on educational and other relevant scientific and objective considerations. Further, public-private partnership models are being thought of in setting up some of these institutions, but such modes do not necessarily work in the area of education for the benefit of the larger society. With the opening up of higher education sector to global competition, there is a danger that the paucity of good quality manpower in higher education will act as a constraint on the development of technical manpower though the mode of higher education sector. Moreover, when allocations to good quality higher educational institutions like the IIMs and IITs reduced, the costs of higher education in these institutions would rise, making the process more exclusionary in nature.

4.4. ENROLMENT TRENDS IN HIGHER EDUCATION

The phenomenal expansion in the field of higher education in India during the post-independence period, was reflected in the increase in number of colleges and universities to meet the rising demand of higher education. The number of the higher educational institutions has increased from 27 in 1950-51 to 159 in 1986-87 to 304 in 2002-04 (universities/deemed universities/ institution of national importance). Arts, Science and Commerce colleges increased from 4135 in 1986-87 to 9166 in 2002-03 engineering technical and architecture colleges increased from 258 to 978 during the same period. The number of medical students rose from 367 to 756 and teacher-training colleges grew from 442 to 873. So it can be concluded that from 1950 till the present time there is a significant growth in number in number of institutions. Table 4.18 summarises the picture. This was accompanied by rise in enrolments in higher education, and diversification of students enrolled into different disciplines and subjects and degrees. The enrolment of women students had made a steady progress over the years, and across disciplines as are shown in Tables 4.19 and 4.20. Interestingly, the growth in the number of arts and science colleges were far greater than the growth of medical and engineering colleges, and despite impressive growth in overall and women enrolment rates over the years, the achieved gross enrolment ratio is far below the required ratio at the national level, with substantial variations across the states.

TABLE 4.18

Number of Institutions for Higher Education (Degree Level and Above) in (1986-87, 1990-91, 1996-97 to 2002-03)

Year	*Universities/ Deemed Universities Institutions of National importance*	*Research Institutions*	*Arts, Science and Commerce Colleges*	*Engg. Tech. and Arch. Colleges*	*Medical College (allop/ayur/ homeo/unani/ Nurs/pharm, etc.*	*Teacher Training Colleges*	*Others*	*Total*
(1)	(2)	(3)	(4)	(5)	(6)	(7)	(8)	(9)
1986-87	159	47	4135	258	367	442	780	6188
1990-91	184	49	4862	282	130	474	780	6761
1996-97	228	65	6759	418	655	697	1411	10233
1997-98	229	65	7199	458	769	848	1404	10972
1998-99	237	71	7494	540	755	818	1790	11705
1999-2000	244	71	7782	635	685	804	1959	12180
2000-01	254	77	7926	680	709	834	2657	13137
2001-02	272	79	8737	838	725	846	2004	13501
2002-03	304	81	9166	978	759	873	1982	14143

Source : Selected Educational Statistics, 2002-03 (as on 30th September, 2002), Department of Secondary and Higher Education, Ministry of Human Resources Development, Government of India and Past Issues.

TABLE 4.19
Growth of Student Enrolment (Total and Women) in India (1950-1951 to 2000-02)

Year	Total enrolment	Annual growth rate	Women enrolment	Annual growth rate
(1)	(2)	(3)	(4)	(5)
1950-51	396745	—	43126	—
1951-52	459024	15.7	49195	14.1
1952-53	512853	11.7	56522	14.9
1953-54	580218	13.1	67681	19.7
1954-55	651479	12.2	79415	17.3
1955-56	712697	9.3	91893	15.0
1956-57	769468	7.9	106781	16.2
1957-58	827341	7.6	118379	10.9
1958-59	928622	12.2	139873	18.2
1959-60	997137	7.4	154745	10.6
1960-61	1049864	5.3	170455	10.1
1961-62	1155380	10.1	190627	11.8
1962-63	1272666	10.2	223408	17.2
1963-64	1384697	8.8	258513	15.8
1964-65	1528227	10.4	297276	14.9
1965-66	1728773	13.1	255476	-14
1966-67	1949012	12.7	405306	58.6
1967-68	2218972	13.9	465523	14.9
1968-69	2473264	11.5	526659	13.1
1969-70	1792780	-27.5	394594	-25.1
1970-71	1953700	8.9	430822	9.1
1971-72	2065041	5.7	468696	8.9
1972-73	2168107	4.9	500832	6.9
1973-74	2234385	3.1	520825	3.9
1974-75	2366541	5.9	553009	6.2
1975-76	2426109	2.5	595162	7.6
1976-77	2431563	0.2	627346	5.4
1977-78	2564972	5.5	359457	-42.7

(*Contd.*)

TABLE 4.19 (*Contd.*)

(1)	(2)	(3)	(4)	(5)
1978-79	2618228	2.1	673942	87.5
1979-80	2648579	1.2	689042	2.2
1980-81	2752437	3.9	748525	8.6
1981-82	2952066	7.3	816704	9.1
1982-83	3133093	6.1	880156	7.8
1983-84	3307649	5.6	940253	6.8
1984-85	3404096	2.9	992139	5.5
1985-86	3605029	5.9	1067484	7.6
1986-87	3757158	4.2	1148849	7.6
1987-88	4020159	6.9	1224089	6.5
1988-89	4285489	6.6	1319931	7.8
1989-90	4602680	7.4	1436036	8.8
1990-91	4924868	7.0	1556258	8.4
1991-92	5265886	6.9	1685926	8.3
1992-93	5534966	5.1	1811115	7.4
1993-94	5817249	5.0	1931327	6.7
1994-95	6113929	5.1	2064982	6.9
1995-96	6574005	7.5	2363607	14.5
1996-97	6842598	4.1	2514511	6.4
1997-98	7260418	6.1	2722062	8.3
1998-99	7705520	6.1	2932993	7.7
1999-2000	8050607	4.5	3112090	6.1
2000-01	8399443	4.3	3306410	6.2
2000-02	8821095	5.0	3514450	6.3

Source : University Development in India, (1995-96 to 2000-01), University Grant Commission.

Barring the year 1969-70, when there was a sharp fall in enrolment rates to negative rates, there had been steady progress in total enrolment. Annual growth rates of enrolment showed steady but uneven patterns

When we concentrate on the period between 1995-2001, we find that annual growth rate of total student enrolment between

TABLE 4.20
Enrolment of Students by Level of Education (University Teaching Department/University College and Affiliated Colleges) in India (2001-1995)

Level	*Total enrolment*	*Women enrolment*	*Percentage of women*	*% of level*
(1)	*(2)*	*(3)*	*(4)*	*(5)*
		2000-01		
Graduate	7488736	2943807	39.31	89.16
Post-graduate	775303	315236	40.66	9.23
M.Phil.	11964	5359	44.79	0.14
Ph.D.	45447	15277	33.61	0.54
Diploma/certificate	77993	26731	34.27	0.93
Total	8399443	3306410	39.36	100
		1999-2000		
Graduate	7183557	2774380	38.62	89.23
Post-graduate	733410	291823	39.79	9.11
M.Phil.	11271	4932	43.76	0.14
Ph.D.	45888	15243	33.22	0.57
Diploma/certificate	76481	25712	3.26	0.95
Total	8050607	3112090	38.66	100
		1998-1999		
Graduate	6883341	2619931	38.06	89.33
Post-graduate	692726	269608	38.92	8.99
M.Phil.	11558	4834	41.82	0.15
Ph.D.	44692	14676	32.84	0.58
Diploma/certificate	73203	23944	32.71	0.95
Total	7705520	2932993	38.06	100
		1997-1998		
Graduate	6491540	2335083	37.51	89.41
Post-graduate	642547	245444	38.2	8.85
M.Phil.	10891	4555	41.72	0.15

(Contd.)

TABLE 4.20 (*Contd.*)

(1)	(2)	(3)	(4)	(5)
Ph.D.	45014	14589	32.41	0.62
Diploma/certificate	70426	22402	31.18	0.97
Total	7260418	2722062	37.49	100
		1996-97		
Graduate	6124125	2249916	36.74	89.5
Post-graduate	597358	225456	37.74	8.73
M.Phil	10948	4449	40.64	0.16
Ph.D.	43792	14048	32.08	0.64
Diploma/certificate	66375	20642	31.1	0.97
Total	6842598	2514511	36.75	100
		1995-96		
Graduate	5890755	2120629	36	89.61
Post-graduate	565465	205694	36.38	8.6
M.Phil.	10421	4122	39.55	0.16
Ph.D.	42772	13593	31.78	0.65
Diploma/certificate	64592	19569	30.3	0.98
Total	6574005	2263607	35.95	100

Source : University Development in India (1995-96 to 2000-01), University Grant Commission.

1995-2001 shows first a decreasing then increasing and remaining stable and again decreasing and remaining stable trend. It decreased to a minimum level in 1996-97 to 4%, thereafter increased to be stable around 6% in 1997-99, and again decreased and settled around 5% in 2001. We further see that along with the increase in total enrolment of students in higher education, total number of women students enrolled in higher education also increased barring few years. Since 1950-51, total enrolment of women increased slowly, and fell in 1965-66, 1969-70 and 1977-78 but then again increased sharply. The percentage of women enrolment in total enrolment increased slowly, and during the period 1995-2001, women enrolment ratio was found to be quite stable. In 1995-96 it was 2363607 and in 2000-01, 3306410. The annual growth rate of women enrolments was first decreasing, then increasing and remaining stable, and again was decreasing and remaining stable. It was high in 1995-96 and decreased to a minimum level at 6.4% in 1996-97 and increased in 1997-98 again, but thereafter slowly decreasing and remaining stable. The annual growth rate of total enrolment as well as women enrolment exhibited a non-linear trend, although the level of enrolments showed a linear trend.

Enrolment in Different Discipline

When we look to the total enrolment of students by level of education, and here we include Graduate, Post-graduate, M.Phil., Ph.D., Diploma/Certificate level of education, we find that for all levels of higher education in India as a whole, there is an increasing tendency for enrolment, excepting that in 2000-01, enrolment in Ph.D. registered a decline. The total number of students enrolled in graduate level increased from 5890755 in 1995-96 to 7488736 in 2000-01, and in case of post-graduate level of education, it increased from 56565 to 775303, in M.Phil. from 102421 to 11964, diploma/certificate from 64592 to 77993 during the same period. When we include the Ph.D. enrolments, the total enrolment of student in 1995-96 was 6574005 and it increased to 8399443 in 2000-01. Thus, about 89.16% of total enrolment was occupied by graduate level of education. Other level of enrolment in the year 2000-01 covered the remaining 10.84%. The percentage of level of education remain almost similar during 1995-2001, even if the total enrolment increased continuously during these period. But on the other hand, the total enrolment and percentage of enrolment of women increased steadily but slowly during this period. In each level of education, the number of women students increased during 1995-2001. It is interesting to note that the percentage of women was slightly higher at the post-graduate and M.Phil. level (40.66% and 44.79% respectively) than at the undergraduate and Ph.D. level and this was higher than the enrolment in the diploma level (34.87%) in 2000-01. Table 4.20 above corroborates this.

Faculty-wise Enrolment

When we look to the faculty-wise enrolment of students in higher education in India (Table 4.21) we find that above eighty percentage (83.8%) of such enrolments were concentrated in three faculties—Arts, Science and Commerce and the remaining 16.2%) was in other professional faculties like education, engineering/technical, medicine, agriculture, vet. science, law and others in the year 2000-01. Each of these three faculties covered 46.1%, 19.9%, and 17.8% in arts, science, commerce respectively in 2000-01. These concentration decreased by 0.1% in 2000-01 as compared to 1995-96. In 1995-96 these distribution was 83.9% comprising of three faculties and remaining 16.1% by other professional courses. Data on faculty-wise enrolment of women shows that of all the women enrolled in higher education in the year 2000-01, the largest percentage (44.20% and 51.20%) were in the faculty of arts and education, and 39.40% in commerce and 21.50% in engineering, and about 44% in medicine. The similar trend was also observed for earlier years, and the total number of enrolment in each of these above faculties had increased continuously and reached this level in 2000-01, comparing from 1995-96 as is shown from Table 4.21. Table 4.22 indicates the enrolment pattern for students belonging to backward classes, particularly those belonging to SCs and STs. Given the government's social objective of bringing such backward students into the mainstream of higher education and knowledge, statutory reservation of seats were made for students belonging to SC and ST categories of students in every educational institutions, universities (central, state, deemed) and colleges. And in recent years, with emphasis on inclusive growth in the XI Plan, more and more scholarships are also being sanctioned for students belonging to SC, ST and OBC students. Table 4.22 indicates that there were about 628558 students of schedule castes and 134016 students of schedule tribes categories, who were enrolled in higher education out of 8399443 total enrolments in 2000-01. In the year 1999-2000 there were 737445 schedule caste students and 237812 schedule tribe students. Thus, in 2000-01, 7.4% of schedule caste students and 1.6% of schedule tribe students were enrolled in higher education, as compared to 9.2% of schedule caste students and 2.9% of schedule tribe students enrolled in 1999-2000, indicating

TABLE 4.21

Faculty-wise Enrolment of Students (University Teaching Departments/University Colleges and Affiliated Colleges) in India (1995-2001)

Faculty	*Total enrolment*	*Women enrolment*	*% of women*	*% of faculty*
(1)	(2)	(3)	(4)	(5)
		2000-01		
Arts	3875102	1712010	44.2	46.1
Science	1670263	658769	39.4	19.9
Commerce/mgt.	1500609	547342	36.5	17.8
Education	109196	55923	51.2	1.3
Engg./Tech.	576649	123992	21.5	6.9
Medicine	262753	115557	44	3.1
Agriculture	50308	8773	17.4	0.6
Vet. Science	13588	2838	20.9	0.2
Law	267043	53337	20	3.2
Others	73932	27869	37.7	0.9
Total	8399443	3306410	39.4	100
		1999-2000		
Arts	3743532	1628988	43.5	46.5
Science	1581944	614432	38.8	19.6
Commerce/mgt.	1426568	507284	35.6	17.7
Education	107878	54241	50.3	1.4
Engg./Tech.	537781	110083	20.5	6.7
Medicine	247959	106820	43.1	3.1
Agriculture	49108	8161	16.6	0.6
Vet. Science	13686	2767	20.2	0.2
Law	268085	51740	19.3	3.3
Others	74066	27574	37.2	0.9
Total	8050607	3112090	38.7	100
		1998-99		
Arts	3613888	1549527	42.9	46.9

(Contd.)

TABLE 4.21 (*Contd.*)

(1)	*(2)*	*(3)*	*(4)*	*(5)*
Science	1492559	574933	38.5	19.4
Commerce/mgt.	1352319	471553	34.9	17.5
Education	107877	53107	49.2	1.4
Engg./tech.	500088	96917	19.4	6.5
Medicine	233477	98807	42.3	3
Agriculture	46233	7420	16	0.6
Vet. Science	13870	2728	19.7	0.2
Law	270466	50631	18.7	3.5
Others	74743	27370	36.6	1
Total	7705520	2932993	38.1	100
		1997-98		
Arts	3434903	1452191	42.3	47.3
Science	1390370	531201	38.2	19.1
Commerce/mgt.	1263313	432789	34.3	17.4
Education	103823	50208	48.4	1.4
Engg./tech.	456680	83207	18.2	6.3
Medicine	215634	89229	41.4	3
Agriculture	45018	6923	15.4	0.6
Vet. Science	13068	2499	19.1	0.2
Law	265731	47911	18	3.7
Others	71878	25904	36	1
Total	7260418	2722062	37.5	100
		1996-97		
Arts	3264603	1353210	41.5	47.7
Science	1293251	486710	37.6	18.9
Commerce/mgt.	1180348	394938	33.5	17.3
Education	101270	48012	47.4	1.5
Engg./tech.	416029	71141	17.1	6.1
Medicine	199119	80922	40.6	2.9
Agriculture	42424	6330	14.9	0.6
Vet. Science	13002	2416	18.6	0.2

Law	261389	45541	17.4	3.8
Others	71163	25291	35.5	1
Total	6842598	2514511	36.7	100
		1995-96		
Arts	3162582	1283522	40.6	48.1
Science	1227359	454710	37	18.7
Commerce/mgt.	1123633	365242	32.5	17.1
Education	100602	46746	46.5	1.5
Engg./tech.	386879	61914	16	5.9
Medicine	188187	74838	39.8	2.9
Agriculture	40505	5795	14.3	0.6
Vet. Science	12340	2217	18	0.2
Law	261130	43870	16.8	4
Others	70788	24753	35	1
Total	6574005	2363607	36	100

Source : University Development in India (1995-96 to 2000-01), University Grant Commission.

declining tendency for these categories for enrolment in spheres of higher learning, with large interstate variations.

Enrolment of Teaching Staff

As there is a high demand for higher level of education, which becomes clear by the fact that total enrolment and women enrolment increased from during 1995-2001, even if growth rate was non-linear. As a consequence, the demand for educated manpower or teachers also rose. The number of teaching staff increased from 343420 in 1995-96 to 411628 in 2000-01, against the total enrolment of 8399443 students in 2000-01. The teacher-student ratio remained quite stable 1995-96 to 2000-01 (i.e. 1:19 to 1:20). The annual growth rate of teaching staff showed firstly an increasing path, then stable and thereafter decreasing and again increasing. It was low in 1996-97, then increased and remained stable in 1997-99 and once again decreased in 1999-00 and increases in 2000-01.

TABLE 4.22

State-wise Enrolment of Schedule Caste and Schedule Tribe Students

	Schedule Caste		*Schedule Tribe*	
	1999-2000	*2000-01*	*1999-2000*	*2000-01*
State	*Total*	*Total*	*Total*	*Total*
Andhra Pradesh	78482	91840	19147	22866
Arunachal Pradesh	269	407	3234	4048
Assam	18130	Na	26107	Na
Bihar	20540	0	12382	Na
Goa	129	146	1	25
Gujarat	28693	Na	26410	Na
Haryana	13644	15418	0	Na
Himachal Pradesh	8245	8945	2724	2941
Jammu & Kashmir	1496	Na	11	Na
Karnataka	78194	82308	21172	23374
Kerala	26060	24069	1542	1521
Madhya Pradesh	30789	Na	25049	Na
Maharashtra	107672	110149	23322	25158
Manipur	716	714	5460	5518
Meghalaya	444	455	11484	11677
Mizoram	0	0	8132	7109
Nagaland	118	116	7384	7612
Orissa	11464	Na	8067	Na
Punjab	19053	Na	0	Na
Rajasthan	26310	Na	18304	Na
Sikkim	77	103	351	471
Tamil Nadu	66727	65409	1424	6048
Tripura	3031	3194	1370	143
Uttar Pradesh	105630	141707	3189	3841
West Bengal	82696	80011	9830	9685
Andaman & Nicobar Islands	0	0	58	74
Chandigarh	1390	2003	281	459
Dadra & Nagar Havelli	0	0	0	Na
Daman and Diu	33	32	75	77
Delhi	5940	Na	1302	Na
Lakshadweep	0	0	0	0
Pondicherry	1473	1532	0	78
India	737445	628558	237812	134016

Na : Not available.
Source : Ministry of Human Resource Development, Government of India.

TABLE 4.23
Enrolment of Students, Teaching Staff and Teacher-Student Ratio During 1995-96 to 2000-01

Years	*Total Student Enrolment*	*Women Enrolment*	*Percentage*	*Teaching Staff*	*Annual growth rate*	*Teacher-Student Ratio*
1995-96	6574005	2363607	(35.9)	343420	3.7	1:19
1996-97	6842598	2514511	(36.7)	354430	3.2	1:19
1997-98	7260418	2722062	(37.5)	370352	4.5	1:20
1998-99	7705520	2932993	(38.1)	386620	4.4	1:20
1999-2000	8050607	3112090	(38.6)	397721	2.9	1:20
2000-01	8399443	3306410	(39.4)	411628	3.5	1:20

Source : University Grants Commission, Govt. of India.

Technical Education

In the field of technical education, there have been rapid expansion during the last four decades. A wide network of technical institutions developed in India, which offer different types of programmes: craftsman courses, technician course, graduate and post-graduate course etc., catering to the various level of knowledge, skills and competences required by the economy. Technical education in India is imparted at three different levels: (a) Industrial training institutes; (b) Polytechnic institutes; and (c) Engineering colleges and universities. There are engineering institutes and also a large number of private engineering colleges and institutes that provide technical education in India. The enrolment of students in polytechnic institution numerically increased except for the year 1999-2000 till 2000-01. The growth rate showed a decreasing trend with a negative growth rate in 1999-2000. The growth rate showed first a decreasing, and then a highly increasing trend. The decreasing rate reached a negative level and the growth rate of enrolment of students in engineering showed almost increasing trend, with slightly decreasing in 1999-2000.

Premiers among the training institutes offering technical education in India are the Indian institutes of technology (IITs), Indian institutes of science, regional engineering colleges, school of planning and architecture and international center for science and technology. Internationally renowned engineering institutions known as Indian institutes of technology (IITs) are providing science and engineering education in our country. There are six IITs located in India at Kharagpur (near Kolkata), Madras, Bombay, Kanpur, Delhi and Guwahati, and six more are coming up during the XI Plan. The number of polytechnic institutions and technical, industry, arts and craft schools and engineering, technical and architecture colleges had increased during 1995-2001. In polytechnic, the number of institutions was 1110 in 1995-96 and it increased to 1155 in 2000-01. The number of technical, industry, arts, crafts school increased to 4417 in 2000-01. And, the number of engineering technical and Architecture Colleges were 458 in 1997-98 and 680 in 2000-01. Tables 4.24, 3.25 and 4.26 provide a summary of the technical institutes, polytechnics and engineering colleges and their enrolments during 1995 to 2000.

Despite impressive growth of formal education in India, the gap between the demand for and supply of higher education in India through formal mode of enrolment into colleges, institutes and universities remained quite large and non-formal education through open universities and correspondence courses have developed to cater to these needs. There have been increase in enrolment through open universities over the last one decade, and the number of teachers have also grown, but there have been concentration of spread of this open system of education in some states like Andhra Pradesh, Tamil Nadu and Delhi, but in other states the spread of open university system have been rather thin. Due to the entry of foreign education provider through the GATS mode, there is increasing hurdles faced by this system. Table 4.27 provides a summary picture of growth of enrolment of students and engagements of teachers in India through the open university system.

Foreign Students

There have been increasing tendency for foreign students to take part in Indian universities and institutes, and the trend has increased in recent years. The cluster is still biased in favour of central universities and institutes, which is unevenly distributed across the states of India. Indian students, on the

TABLE 4.24

State-wise Enrolment in Polytechnic and Technical Industry, Arts and Crafts School

State	1995-96		1996-97		1997-98		1999-2000		2000-01	
	Poly-technic Insti-tution	*Technical Industry, Arts, Crafts School*	*Poly-technic Insti-tution*	*Technical Industry, Arts, Crafts School*	*Poly-technic Insti-tution*	*Technical Industry, Arts, Crafts School*	*Poly-technic Insti-tution*	*Technical Industry, Arts, Crafts School*	*Poly-technic Insti-tution*	*Technical Industry, Arts, Crafts School*
(1)	(2)	(3)	(4)	(5)	(6)	(7)	(8)	(9)	(10)	(11)
Andhra Pradesh	37960	36384	39654	36384	39694	36384	36487	42470	52951	43063
Arunachal Pradesh	0	195	0	221	0	259	250	300	513	238
Assam	4407	4321	4424	4389	443	4399	4482	4513	4494	4544
Bihar	4075	11152	2833	7049	2833	7049	2833	7049	3772	4239
Goa	1554	2362	1449	1369	1879	1865	2110	3866	2110	2514
Gujarat	24187	7135	26503	7283	27617	6613	30534	58421	30508	64721
Haryana	8298	24133	7330	24133	10151	15975	10151	15975	12069	15975
Himachal Pradesh	1056	3535	1169	3625	1185	3484	1235	3347	863	3475
Jammu and Kashmir	668	4541	935	4821	935	4821	935	4821	375	4455
Karnataka	44284	3613	45809	3618	45809	3618	23965	3618	24315	3618
Kerala	10517	44337	13776	44402	16610	37461	20286	56996	24769	58895
Madhya Pradesh	12731	16808	12690	16808	15234	16808	16134	16751	16134	6737
Maharashtra	41324	126175	65309	126176	65309	126176	82082	134575	83819	134575
Manipur	421	603	309	301	408	364	424	420	433	431

(*Contd.*)

TABLE 4.24 (*Contd.*)

(1)	(2)	(3)	(4)	(5)	(6)	(7)	(8)	(9)	(10)	(11)
Meghalaya	306	277	221	278	224	283	320	237	240	237
Mizoram	179	165	179	165	107	165	157	252	160	223
Nagaland	338	271	343	278	343	278	293	305	293	305
Orissa	670	5841	7031	10443	7031	10443	860	7430	900	7300
Punjab	5205	18364	5956	18514	7570	18512	8153	18762	8649	19161
Rajasthan	5977	8959	4864	9085	5283	9219	4885	10957	4885	11158
Sikkim	0	65	0	88	0	91	0	111	78	113
Tamil Nadu	65900	17611	66100	19942	82290	22356	82290	22356	82290	22356
Tripura	237	426	171	268	253	361	286	373	289	154
Uttar Pradesh	24077	50160	24077	50160	24338	50211	25310	50236	25569	50513
West Bengal	19343	12555	19343	12555	19343	12555	19343	12555	5490	12641
Andaman and Nicobar Islands	170	151	376	156	320	167	289	99	378	147
Chandigarh	1254	1474	1291	1074	1351	1120	1390	2516	1261	1034
Dadra & Nagar Havelli	66	0	230	0	271	0	350	0	426	0
Daman and Diu	191	250	181	351	257	355	278	355	260	411
Delhi	3894	8343	3894	8343	4672	2028	4672	2028	4909	2129
Lakshadweep	0	16	0	16	0	57	0	0	0	0
Pondicherry	1177	308	1404	502	1687	462	1795	324	1755	320
India	320466	410546	357851	412797	383447	393939	382579	482018	394957	475362

Source : Selected Educational Statistics from 1983-95 and 2001-03, Ministry of Human Resource Development, Govt. of India.

TABLE 4.25

Number of Polytechnic Institutions and Technical Industry, Arts and Crafts School

Year	*Polytechnic Institution*	*Technical Industry, Arts Crafts School*	*Engineering Technical and Architecture Colleges*
2000-01	1155	4417	680
1999-2000	1082	4161	635
1997-98	1051	4159	458
1995-96	1110	4192	—
1994-95	1107	3835	—

Source : Ministry of Human Resource Development, Govt. of India.

TABLE 4.26A

Enrolment in Science and Engineering in India

Year	*Science/Engineering*		*Growth Rate*
1995-96	1880		
1996-97	1979.3	5.281915	5.3
1997-98	2073.9	4.779467	4.8
1998-99	2173.5	4.802546	4.9
1999-2000	2241.2	3.114792	3.1
2000-01	2443.6	9.030876	9

TABLE 4.26B

Polytechnic Institution

Year	*Student enrolment*		*Growth rate*
1995-96	320466		
1996-97	357851	11.66582	11.7
1997-98	383447	7.152698	7.1
1999-2000	382579	-0.22637	-0.2
2000-01	394957	3.23541	3.2

TABLE 4.26C

Technical/Industry

Year	*Student enrolment*		*Growth rate*
1995-96	410546		
1996-97	412797	0.548294	0.5
1997-98	393939	-4.56835	-4.6
1999-2000	482018	22.35854	22.3
2000-01	475362	-1.38086	-1.4

TABLE 4.27

Enrolment and Teachers in Open Universities in India (2001-02 and 2002-03)

Open University	*2001-02*				*2002-03*			
	Enrolment		*Teacher*		*Enrolment*		*Teacher*	
	Total	*Girls*	*Total*	*Female*	*Total*	*Girls*	*Total*	*Female*
(1)	(2)	(3)	(4)	(5)	(6)	(7)	(8)	(9)
Indira Gandhi National Open University, New Delhi	298987	—	307	100	316547	—	265	—
Dr. B.R. Ambedkar Open University, Hyderabad, Andhra Pradesh	95469	—	98	8	172846	31038	55	12
Vardhaman Mahaveer Open University, Kota, Rajasthan	9125	—	36	—	13296	3407	20	—
Nalanda Open University, Patna, Bihar	2098	—	4	—	1805	437	2	—
Yashwantrao Chavan Maharasthra Open University, Nashik, Maharashtra	112000	—	64	12	113934	36894	32	9
Dr. Babasaheb Ambedkar Open University, Ahmedabad, Gujarat	11015	—	39	—	13824	4468	10	0
Karnataka State Open University, Mysore, Karnataka	35825	—	68	14	33172	17301	17	5

Netaji Subhash Open University, Kolkata, West Bengal	5000	—	19	—	25244	6604	4	0
Madhya Pradesh Bhoj Open University, Bhopal, Madhya Pradesh	57436	—	49	—	57436	—	49	0
Uttar Pradesh Rajarshi Tandon Open University, Allahabad, Uttar Pradesh	5259	—	46	—	8024	2210	11	4
Tamil Nadu Open University, Chennai	—	—	—	—	9361	3632	20	4
Total	532214		730	134	765489	105991	485	34

Source : Selected Educational Statistics, 2002-03 (as on 30th September, 2002), Department of Secondary and Higher Education, Ministry of Human Resource Development, Govt. of India and Past Issues.

other hand, are going to foreign universities and institutes, primarily to the USA and Europe, and in recent years to universities in South East Asia too, on a variety of subjects, including technological and management studies. Table 4.28 indicates the Region/Country-wise enrolment of foreign students in Indian Universities during 2001-02 to 2003-04. It is clear that maximum number of foreign students are coming to study in India from Asian and African countries.

TABLE 4.28

Region/Country-wise Enrolment of Foreign Students in Indian Universities (2001-02 to 2003-04)

Country	*2001-02*	*2002-03*	*2003-04*
(1)	*(2)*	*(3)*	*(4)*
ASIA			
Eastern Asia			
China (Including Hong Kong)	16	19	31
Japan	65	51	45
North Korea	94	108	84
South Korea	38	14	29
Mongolia	29	25	20
Taiwan	6	6	9
Western Asia	248	223	218
Bahrain	108	59	160
Iraq	24	15	12
Israel	0	6	7
Jordan	92	40	51
Kuwait	30	23	85
Lebanon	2	1	0
Oman	216	94	183
Qatar	9	13	21
Saudi Arabia	31	36	108
Syria	25	32	26
Turkey	4	6	8
United Arab Emirate	58	68	233

Yemen	349	242	222
South and Central Asia			
Afghanistan	33	24	24
Bangladesh	545	372	372
Bhutan	254	227	227
Iran	245	336	336
Kazakhstan	8	9	9
Kirgizistan	14	12	12
Maldives	14	34	34
Nepal	873	801	801
Pakistan	3	3	3
Sri Lanka	504	391	391
Tajikistan	16	14	14
Turkmenistan	1	1	1
Uzbekistan	9	7	7
Southeast Asia	2519	2231	2231
Brunei	0	1	3
Cambodia	11	20	23
Indonesia	62	58	54
Laos	5	3	2
Malaysia	92	788	806
Myanmar	27	47	32
Philippines	0	1	0
Singapore	5	10	20
Thailand	307	293	244
Vietnam	88	142	202
Australasia (Oceania)	597	1363	1386
Australia	21	11	17
Fiji	13	23	19
New Zealand	9	4	1
Papua New Guinea	0	1	0
Samoa	0	0	3
Tonga	2	1	2
AFRICA	45	40	42
North Africa			
Algeria	1	1	1

(Contd.)

TABLE 4.28 (*Contd.*)

(1)	*(2)*	*(3)*	*(4)*
Egypt	3	2	3
Libya	4	8	4
Morocco	0	3	2
Sudan	301	186	188
Western Africa	309	200	198
Cote D'Ivoire (Ivory Coast)	1	1	2
Ghana	6	9	55
Guinea	1	1	0
Liberia	18	6	6
Mali	0	1	0
Nigeria	23	16	17
Sierra Leone	2	1	0
Middle Africa	1951	1602	1465
Angola	0	6	2
Cameroon	0	0	1
Congo	3	1	5
Zaire	4	2	2
EUROPE	35	58	65
Northern Europe			
Denmark	3	0	2
Finland	0	2	0
Ireland	1	0	1
Lithuania	1	0	2
Norway	1	0	0
Sweden	1	1	2
United Kingdom	96	54	55
Western Europe	103	57	62
Austria	1	4	3
Belgium	4	5	2
France	49	15	12
Germany	19	12	10
Netherlands (Holland)	7	1	1
Switzerland	13	0	3

Eastern Europe	93	37	31
Armenia	2	2	0
Bulgaria	10	1	1
Czech (Czech Republic)	1	2	1
Hungary	2	0	1
Poland	7	13	7
Romania	1	2	3
Russia	10	7	5
Slovakia	2	1	1
Ukraine	2	5	2
Southern Europe	37	33	21
Bosania-Herzegoniva	0	1	0
Croatia	0	0	1
Greece	6	5	3
Italy	4	4	8
Portugal	1	1	0
Slovenia	0	2	1
Spain	6	5	2
Yugoslavia	1	0	0
North America	18	18	15
Canada	80	81	99
USA	331	244	354
Central America & Caribbean	411	343	468
Jamaica	0	12	10
Mexico	4	2	3
St. Lucia	1	0	0
Trinidad & Tobago	2	4	2
South America			
Brazil	5	6	4
Columbia	1	0	0
Guyana	5	2	1
Surinam	0	1	1
Venezuela	3	1	1

(*Contd.*)

TABLE 4.28 (*Contd.*)

(1)	*(2)*	*(3)*	*(4)*
Miscellaneous*	734	862	544
Eastern Africa	51	35	80
Djibouti	9	28	27
Eritrea	73	74	49
Ethiopia	281	225	351
Kenya	548	521	454
Malawi	0	5	4
Mauritius	550	366	370
Mozambique	0	2	1
Reunion	1	1	1
Rwanda	128	45	2
Seychelles	1	11	26
Somalia	143	146	54
Tanzania	78	68	56
Uganda	132	93	53
Zambia	7	7	8
Zimbabwe	10	10	9
Southern Africa	7	9	10
Botswana	1	4	3
Lesotho	1	13	10
Namibia	1	11	22
South Africa	31	25	25
Swaziland	1	5	5
Total	8145	7738	7830

Note : * Palestine, Gazastrip, PLO and Tibet.
Data for 2002-03 and 2003-04, Includes information from only Universities that are members of AIU.

Source : Lok Sabha Unstarred Question No. 40, dated 1.3.2005.

Indian students who study abroad go mainly to the USA upto 1997-99, but from 1999-2000, Indian students are migrating mainly to countries in European Union, as are indicated from Table 4.29.

TABLE 4.29

Region-wise Distribution of International Students in Indian Universities (1988-89 to 1999-2000)

Region	Year													
	1988-89	1989-90	1990-91	1992-93	1993-94	1994-95	1995-96	1996-97	1997-98	1998-99	1999-2000	2001-02	2002-03	2003-04
(1)	(2)	(3)	(4)	(5)	(6)	(7)	(8)	(9)	(10)	(11)	(12)	(13)	(14)	(15)
East Asia	47	81	104	108	114	182	168	168	202	153	147	248	223	218
Western Asia	1730	2200	2130	1747	1378	1222	645	359	662	377	579	948	635	1116
South Asia	2408	2416	2239	2392	2667	2070	2850	1838	2261	1735	2203	2519	2231	2231
Southeast Asia	1195	1225	1268	836	1703	1537	1168	370	480	468	563	597	1363	1386
Australia	46	35	35	28	36	49	40	28	35	32	31	45	40	42
Northern Africa	1733	1684	1562	1698	1341	1031	471	388	367	254	305	309	200	198
Western Africa	355	251	158	117	98	73	52	28	38	34	44	51	35	80
Eastern Africa	3565	3825	4497	5143	5572	4674	3496	2238	2104	1766	2164	1961	1602	1465
Middle Africa	21	40	37	31	10	14	3	15	7	7	10	7	9	10
Southern Africa	127	14	64	35	88	60	59	11	20	24	35	35	58	65
Northern Europe	120	79	75	51	66	50	60	30	39	36	43	103	57	62
Western Europe	45	61	49	60	66	30	28	22	27	29	38	93	37	28
Eastern Europe	32	36	24	24	32	21	20	29	60	26	34	37	33	21

(Contd.)

TABLE 4.29 (*Contd.*)

(1)	(2)	(3)	(4)	(5)	(6)	(7)	(8)	(9)	(10)	(11)	(12)	(13)	(14)	(15)
Southern Europe	15	16	25	18	23	19	19	10	25	20	5	18	18	15
North America	157	160	234	134	247	418	299	161	132	117	270	411	325	453
Central America and Caribbean	18	14	16	12	8	3	9	1	4	4	5	21	28	22
South America	17	16	13	5	5	5	1	1	4	3	0			
Miscellaneous	231	310	369	326	253	430	699	144	234	238	512	734	862	544
Total	11844	12463	12899	12765	13707	11888	10087	5841	6701	5323	6988	8137	7756	7956

Notes : I : No data available for 1991-92.

II : The figures can be a little higher as a few universities have not submitted information.

The data of Region-wise Distribution of International Students in Indian Universities suggest that students from Eastern Africa mainly concentrate in Indian University. Number of students from Eastern Africa increases and reached a maximum level in 1993-94, then continuously decreases, but number of students is high compare to other countries in each year. Foreign students of large number from South Asia came to India to study in Indian University. Also a quite high number of students from Southeast Asia and Northern Africa.

Source : Association of Indian Universities, New Delhi.

4.5. GATS AND HIGHER EDUCATION IN INDIA

The General Agreement on Trade in Services (GATS) is one of the crucial agreements signed under the purview of WTO (world trade organization) with a view to ensure progressive liberalization of trade in commercial services to promote economic growth of the WTO members. It covers 12 sectors (161 sub-sections) including education with 5 sub-sectors. GATS consider education as a tradable service, because in the field of education, there are already many private institutions operating in India, which are in direct competition with government-run institutions. Per capita total government expenditure on education for 1995 is less than $ 10 per year in India, but in US it is $ 1400, and the share of higher education in total planned resources had decreased over the years.

Trade in education is organized into five categories or sub-sector of service: (a) Primary education; (b) Secondary education; (c) Higher education; (d) Adult education; and (e) Other education. In case of higher education, we have (i) Post-secondary technical and vocational education service, and (ii) Other higher education services leading to university degree or equivalent.

According to GATS, trade in educational services are classified trade in *four* modes:

(a) *Cross-border supply* which includes Distance education, online courses through Internet, educational testing service, Cds. etc., (b) *Consumption abroad* which involves movement of consumers/students to other country for pursuing education e.g.: studying abroad; (c) *Commercial presence* which implies presence of an educational service provider for a country in another country; and (d) *Movement of natural presence* which involves people moving between countries to provide educational service, e.g. Indian teachers going abroad to teach in high school in US.

In case of educational testing service through the cross border supply mode, the Indian experience of conducting tests such as CAT of IIMs, JEE of IITS, GATE, can be used with computerization and internet to obtain gains from liberalization. In the case *students on foreign campuses*, we find that about 6734 Indian students had enrolled for courses in foreign lands in 1997-98, i.e. significant import of service, and export of educational service took place as about 6706 international students from neighbouring developing countries and developed countries got enrolled in Indian universities, and institutes/colleges. India can also establish schools or educational institutions abroad, for which there are increasing demand, but there are restrictions and limitations of their entry in some advanced developed countries. There is also an increasing demand for trained teachers and researchers working abroad, there is a sufficient supply of trained teachers in India, particularly at secondary and higher education levels. In the new regime under WTO, it is possible that country should exploit its excellent potential in higher education and training facilities and prepare itself to export Indian brand of education to foreign. In recent years, there is pressure of large number of foreign students to get enrolled in Indian institutions of higher education, which poses new challenges of management and regulation faced by these institutions in both the public and private sectors.

The *Mode I (cross border supply)* presents prospect for distance education, tele-education in management and executive training and experience with distance learning use of new technologies. Distance education is becoming increasingly popular as economic forces encourage and new technologies facilitate, traditional education institution join with businesses, foreign government and international organizations to offer and use it, all these facilitate its spread. Technology is a major contributor to the dramatic transformation of distance learning. Radio, television effectively used for 40 years and now opportunities to access knowledge and increase their human capital. Realizing the need for distance education, Government of India opened the prestigious Indira Gandhi National Open University (IGNOU) in 1985. IGNOU had expanded its regional education council (DEC) to act as nodal agency at tertiary level and adopted as instruction strategy through print material and audio-video programmes, with the help of a 24-hours satellite TV channel (Gyan Darshan) and a 40 FM educational radio channel (Gyan Vani). Similarly, most universities of India have started to impart distance education to meet the growing demand. Presently, there are 11 Open Universities and 68 institutions of Correspondence Course and distance education in India. In these non-formal systems of education, total enrolment in open universities was about 765489, in correspondence course about 1012779 and in Open School and Patracher Vidyalya system about 280446 in the year 2002-03. Number of teachers in open universities were 485, and in correspondence course were about 1629 in 2002-03. This mode provides the potential for expansion of higher education under the GATS, provided the competition from foreign players are suitably regulated, and export of education services through this mode could be ensured through technological support and networking.

Under the *Consumption abroad (mode II)*, Indian students are going abroad for further higher studies in foreign countries and also the foreign students come to India to study in Indian universities. Available information shows that, number of foreign students coming to India from the neighbouring developed and developing countries had increased from 1997 to 2004. In 1998, the number of international students studying in Indian universities (i.e. export of services) went down to 5233, and but it rose as high as 8137 in 2001-02. These foreign students mainly came from African and Asian countries—Nepal, Bangladesh, Sri Lanka, Mauritius and Kenya were the main supplier of international students to India, and there were some international students from the developed countries as well. Regarding the import of educational services, i.e. Indian students going abroad, available information indicated a sharp increase in number of female students from 887 to 112 over a period of 1991 to 1999, and the number of male students had increased by only by 452 (i.e. from 6466 to 6918). The maximum number of Indian students going abroad were in the field of engineering and architecture and commerce business administration/business management, and in sciences. From 1997-99 Indian students showed a tendency to move to American countries, but since 1999-02 the students mainly opted for the European universities. The enrolment of international students in Indian universities during 1998-2000, indicated that enrolment of foreign students were concentrated mainly in Aligarh Muslim University, University of Delhi, Dr. Babasahed Ambedkar Marathwada University, Manipal Academy of Higher Education, University of Mumbai, University of Mysore, Osmania University, Punjab University and Pune University, apart from IITs, IISC, Bangalore, and a small number in IIMs.

Under the mode III of *Commercial Presence, there is scope for* establishment of local branch of foreign campus in India and *vice verse.* At present, there are over 100 Indian CBSE system of secondary education, catering to diaspora, and demand of these CBSE school are increasing in UK-USA and FIJI and other parts of the world. In the field of higher education, although the Indian presence abroad under this mode is limited at present, a notable exception is establishment of Central Institute Of English And Foreign Language (CIEFL), Hyderabad, which had successfully launched English language teaching (ELT) programme in Kirgizistan. In recent times, there are examples of some reputed private university level institutions (deemed universities) in India that had ventured abroad and set-up campuses in foreign countries e.g., Birla Institute of Technology And Science in Dubai, Birla Institute of Technology, Ranchi in Oman, and Manipal Education And Medical group (parent organization of Manipal Academy of Higher Education, MAHE) in Dubai and Nepal and looking to expand to Malaysia and the USA. There are also few examples of the establishment of foreign branch campuses, like Institution Of Hotel Management Maulana Azad Educational Campus under University of Hudders-Field, UK, and the Asia Pacific Institute Of Information Technology under Stafford Shire University, UK.

In Natural Presence (mode IV), there is temporary presence in the export market of an individual (not a legal person as in the case of commercial presence) for the purpose of supplying a service, and this person could be the service supplier. In both cases, the GATS definition covers only the temporary stay of such person, but not a situation where a person is seeking citizenship, residency or employment on a permanent basis. The temporary movement of teachers, lecturers and education personnel to provide education services overseas are considered under this mode. Available data on migration from India suggests that a shift had occurred from Indian teachers and entrepreneurs to the teachers, and dearth of educators in foreign countries (mainly UK and US) had created global market for Indian teachers, particularly in schools in Nigeria, Uganda and South Africa, Zambia, and some Asian countries, especially in Mathematics, Science and English.

International trade in the field of higher education as per the GATS provisions has opened up scope for expansion of educational services in India through different modes as outlined above. But careful regulatory and quality control mechanisms need be evolved to ensure high quality in the field of higher education. The inflow of foreign students to Indian universities/institutes is likely to rise in coming years, and the scope for infrastructural support to these students would warrant further investment, which would require additional funding by the states to these universities and institutes. The importance of regulation and accreditation would be very much increase when foreign universities and institutes start setting up branches in India, and offer degrees on subjects of emerging nature. The accreditation of these universities, and regulation of their activities, including fixing of tuition fees for Indian students are also necessary so that the Indian students opting for such degrees do not face discrimination in job markets in India and abroad. This task can be taken up by bodies like the UGC. Perhaps the most important part of globalisation of educational services for India would be in the realm of migration laws in many developed WTO member-countries, where educational visa granting system is far from liberalized, as a result of which there exist restrictions on mobility of educated manpower from India to many countries. Further, despite GATS commitments, there are restrictions on establishment of branches of Indian educational institutions in foreign countries, particularly in the USA, where state laws do not permit such an entry by foreign institutions for educational purposes. These need to be taken up at the WTO level so that Indian exporters of higher education do not face asymmetry of treatment in foreign countries.

4.6. POLICY CHALLENGES

Globalisation of educational services have opened up new challenges for the Indian higher education sector. This differentiated sector has not been able to total domestic needs, despite impressive growth in enrolment of students in different streams and spread of distance education mode. The enrolment of foreign students in increasing numbers in Indian Universities and institutes indicates growing demand for Indian Higher Education, while the outflow of Indian students to foreign universities and institutes for higher degrees indicate growing import of higher education in the country. Side by side, there have been increasing participation of educated manpower in foreign countries in the form of teachers, researchers and scientists and technicians which amount to export of educated manpower services on an increasing manner. While visa restrictions and immigration laws in advanced countries like USA, Canada and European countries act as hindrances to the growth of education exports through this mode, the tendency has been on the rise. For the entry of foreign educational institutions to India and offering degrees and courses to Indian students, competing with the Indian institutions, the relevant policy imperative has been the appropriate regulatory and accreditation mechanism to maintain the quality of educational services. This would involve approval and accreditation of courses offered by these foreign institutions, charging of fees, and acceptance of such degrees and diplomas in the Indian job market, in private as well public sectors. Trade policy reforms do not meet these requirements and the policies of state intervention and regulation in the field of higher education must address these issues, to preserve the quality of higher education in the country. Side by side, one must remember the fact that higher education sector, despite its phenomenal growth over the last five decades, has not yet been able to cover a vast majority of education-seekers in our country, and international trade in higher education through the different modes of GATS cannot provide any solution to this gap. Only resources would be diverted from domestic use to foreign use through this process. Foreign Direct Investment in this sector appears to be thin and cannot substitute for the requirements of massive investment by the government in the field of higher education in the country. With emphasis on inclusive growth in the XI Five Year Plan, there is some increase in the projected government expenditure on higher education, but the impact on actual expansion of higher education supply in the country would be judged only after the process is completed and actual investment takes place.

5

Cost of Higher Education in India

5.1. INTRODUCTION

The basis of international trade is comparative advantage. That is, one has to compare the relative cost of a product at home as well as abroad to find out whether the country has comparative cost advantage over the foreign country for the product. For a multi-commodity, multi-factor world, which in fact is the reality, such calculations are complicated as the basis of comparison would warrant unchanged forms of production across different activities, which are not always the case in real life for number of services like education. Moreover, there are inherent lumpiness in the costs of providing services like education, and since there are subsidies and grants that are embedded in the provision of educational services in a country like India, it is difficult to separate the production cost from the maintenance/sustenance cost. The costs are not covered by market forces. There exists elements of subsidy from the government, either as infra-structural support/investment under different plans as well as payment of salaries and allowances to teachers and supportive staffs in government/ semi-government institutions, colleges and universities, and in some private colleges also. It is difficult to apportion the total cost of providing a unit of higher education by the component of financing them—tuition fees, subsidies, grants, scholarships, etc. With the introduction of economic reforms embracing globalisation in our country, there have an increasing trend to cover the unit cost of the higher education through hike in tuition fees, so as to cover increasing portion of the costs through private contributions. And it is a general trend worldwide that there are sharp increases in the tuition fees, user charges for lodging and food, and in the diminution of grants for students. With the extension of private sector in the field of higher education, this trend has been gaining in India, although there are obstacles to increase in fees in government sponsored educational institutions, basically on considerations of social equity. With the idea of inclusive growth embedded in our XI Plan framework, there have been renewed emphasis on extension of scholarships for students belonging to SC, ST, OBC and Muslim minorities. While this trend has increased the expenditure by the central government on higher education, the overall cost of obtaining higher education in India is still much lower compared to many other countries offering similar types of educational services. But the decomposition of such costs as production cost, subsidy or social cost, and maintenance cost is difficult, as there are cross-subsidisation such that poor students are offered scholarships or free studentship, while students belonging to higher income brackets are to pay higher fees. There exists the trade-off between social objectives of higher education and the business objective of making the educational services profitable and viable.

The structure of the present chapter is as follows. Section 5.2 summarises the theoretical rationale for comparative cost analysis for multiple products as the basis of international trade. Section 5.3 discusses the per student cost of higher education in India and selected educational institutions in our country. Section 5.4 discusses the cost structure of higher education in some countries of the world, which are major competitors of India in the field of trade in higher education. Section 5.5

summarises the assessment of trade potentials of India's higher education sector on the basis of comparative cost principle.

5.2. THEORETICAL BASIS OF TRADE

The notion of comparative advantage as the basis of international trade between nations had been propounded by David Ricardo, who argued that for a one factor full-employed economy producing two commodities using only labour input with constant-coefficient technology, the comparative cost ratios represented by the marginal cost ratios between the two goods in a nation must be less than that in another country to reflect comparative advantage, and when international terms of trade lies between the comparative cost ratios of the two countries then both countries would gain from international trade and there shall be complete specialisation in each country in the commodity in which the country has comparative advantage. The basic presumption is the international identity of given demand conditions, so that the basis of comparative advantage is the differences in technology and efficiency of resource-use. The other factors that may cause difference in pre-trade price and hence marginal cost ratio, may be differences in factor supplies and differences in demand conditions and differences in market structures and economies of scale. While in principle such cost differences indicate differences in market potentials for gainful participation in international trade, there may also be quality differences between products produced in different countries, and given price-income situations, such quality differences may also be reflected in the differences in pre-trade price ratios and hence motivates gainful trade among nations. In practice, there are number of commodities produced in each trading countries and the world consists of more than two countries. Let us explain, using the Ricardian framework, the cases for international trade among nations for (i) two goods and n countries, and (ii) m goods and n countries.

5.2.1. Two Goods and n Countries

A necessary condition for international trade to take place when there are n countries is that at least two of these have different comparative costs, for it is self-evident that, if all had the same comparative cost, there would be no incentive to engage in international trade, exactly as in the two-country case. Once this condition is satisfied, it is not very relevant whether all countries have different comparative costs or whether there exists subsets of countries with the same comparative cost; to simplify the treatment, we shall adopt the former assumption.

No loss of generally is involved in assuming that the countries can be ordered in such a way that

$$\frac{a_1}{b_1} < \frac{a_2}{b_2} < \ldots\ldots < \frac{a_n}{b_n} \tag{5.1}$$

Now, once the necessary condition is met, the sufficient condition is that the terms of trade are strictly included between the two extreme comparative costs,

$$\frac{a_1}{b_1} < R_s < \ldots\ldots < \frac{a_n}{b_n} \tag{5.2}$$

A new complication should be noted : even if (5.2) is satisfied, R_s may happen to coincide with some intermediate comparative cost. In this case, the country concerned will not participate in international trade, which will involve the remaining n-1 countries. In any case we shall find a certain number of countries with a comparative cost lower that R_s while the remaining ones will have a comparative cost higher than R_s, namely

$$\frac{a_1}{b_1} < \ldots\ldots < \frac{a_i}{b_i} \leq R_s \leq \frac{a_{i+1}}{b_{i+1}} < \ldots\ldots < \frac{a_n}{b_n} \tag{5.3}$$

where i=2, 3,…, n-1 denotes any country other than the first and the last. If the equality sign holds in the weak inequality $a_i/b_i \leq R_s$, then country I will not engage in international trade.

Once condition (5.3) is satisfied, international trade will take place between the countries with a comparative cost lower than R_s, on the one hand, and the countries with a comparative cost higher than R_s, on the other. The former group of countries will specialize entirely in the production of y: therefore, x will be exported by the former to the latter group, and *vice versa* for y.

5.2.2. m Goods and n Countries

Let us begin by examining the case of m goods and 2 countries. For this purpose, it is expedient to adopt the alternative definition of comparative cost, namely, the ratio between the absolute unit costs of the same good in the two countries. Without loss of generality, we can order the comparative costs in an increasing manner (namely in order of diminishing country 1 comparative advantage), that is :

$$\frac{a_2}{a_1} > \frac{b_2}{b_1} > \frac{c_2}{c_1} > \ldots\ldots > \frac{m_2}{m_1} \qquad (5.4)$$

For motives that will become clear further on, it is expedient to introduce the ratio between the two countries' unit money wage rates, both expressed in a common monetary unit, say gold (as the exchange rate is assumed to be perfectly rigid, it can be set at one without loss of generality). Let this ratio be $w=w_1/w_2$.

It can then be shown that the condition for international trade to take place is that w is strictly included between the two extreme comparative costs, i.e.

$$\frac{a_2}{a_1} > w > \ldots\ldots \frac{m_2}{m_1} \qquad (5.5)$$

It can also be shown that all goods with a comparative cost lower than w will be exported by country 2, which will specialize entirely in their production, whilst all goods having a comparative cost higher than w will be exported by country 1, which will specialize entirely in their production. In the particular case in which there is a good having a comparative cost exactly equal to w, this good will, in general, be produced by both countries and will not be internationally traded.

To prove these statements, we begin by observing that, given the money wage rate w_1 and w_2, the (monetary) unit cost of production and so the (monetary) price of the various goods in the two countries, before international trade is opened, will be :

$$\begin{aligned} &PA_1=w_1a_1, \quad PA_2=w_2a_2, \\ &PB_1=w_1b_1, \quad PB_2=w_2b_2, \\ &\ldots\ldots\ldots\ldots\ldots\ldots\ldots\ldots\ldots \\ &PM_1=w_1m_1, \quad PM_2=w_2m_2, \end{aligned} \qquad (5.6)$$

Now, given the assumptions of free trade, perfect competition and no transport costs, each good will be bought where it costs least. Therefore if—for example—we have $pc_1<pc_2$, country 2 will buy good C from country 1 (which will become an exporter of this good) instead of producing it internally, and *vice versa*. Furthermore, since, in the pure of theory of international trade, imports must be paid for by exports, each country must be able to export some good. It is now obvious that, if it were

$$w \geq \frac{a_2}{a_1}, \tag{5.7}$$

country 2 would produce all goods at a lower price than country 1, which could not then engage in international trade, being unable to export anything. In fact, since $w=w_1/w_2$ by definition, from Eq. (5.7), we get

$$1 > \frac{a_2 w_2}{a_1 w_1} \tag{5.8}$$

whence, given Equation (5.7),

$$PA_1 \geq PA_2 \tag{5.9}$$

So that country 1 produces good A at a price higher than (or at most equal to) country 2. Now, account being taken of Eq. (5.1), if (5.8) holds, it will also be true that w is higher than all other comparative costs and so, by similar reasoning, that the price of B, C, ... is higher in country 1. There is, therefore, no scope for international trade.

In a similar way it can be proved that if $w \leq m_2/m_1$, country 2 produces good M at a price higher than (or at most equal to) country 1 etc., so that, also in this case, there can be no international trade.

If, on the contrary, inequality (5.8) holds, by considering the left-hand side of it, we get

$$PA_1<PA_2 \tag{5.10}$$

whilst by considering the right-hand side, we have

$$PM_2<PM_1 \tag{5.11}$$

so that there exists at least one good (A) which country 1 can export and at least one good (M) exportable by country 2.

If we now indicate by the subscript w a generic good and by q the corresponding technical coefficient, it can easily be seen that $q_1/q_2<w$ is equivalent to $pW_2>pW_1$ (good W will be exported by country 1). This demonstrates the second part of the proposition.

The above analysis is based on the Ricardian pattern of specialisation using only one factor of production, where technology differences between nations is considered as the source of comparative advantage. In the modern Heckscher-Ohlin theory of international trade, factor endowment differences between nations constitute the basis of comparative cost differences, and hence international trade, even with identical technological knowledge, and identical demand conditions. For multi-country case, the predictions of the Heckscher-Ohlin theory can be generalised in the following way. Suppose, there are n>2 countries, which can be classified in the order of factor abundance on the basis of either physical or price definition, i.e., assume that

$$L_1/K_1 < L_2/K_2 < \ldots\ldots. < \ldots\ldots\ldots\ldots\ldots < L_n/K_n \qquad (5.12)$$

Where K_i is the total capital endowment of country i, and L_i is the total labour endowment of country i. Using the Physical definition of abundance, we can say that first country is capital abundant relative to the second, the second country is capital abundant relative to the third and so on upto the nth country, and assuming identical and homothetic tastes and no factor intensity reversals, the following inequality would hold good as the basis of international trade:

$$p_1 < p_2 < \ldots\ldots\ldots\ldots\ldots\ldots\ldots\ldots\ldots\ldots < p_n, \qquad (5.13)$$

where p_i refers to pre-trade price ratios equalling marginal cost ratios between the two goods (X and Y) in the ith country under perfectly competitive conditions.

That is, considering any pair of countries, we can argue that the capital abundant country is producing the capital intensive commodity X more cheaply than the labour abundant country prior to trade. The first country, under this condition, shall be exporting the commodity X in exchange for commodity Y, and the nth country shall export Y in exchange for commodity X, but the direction of trade between countries (2, 3, ... n-1) cannot be ascertained unless one introduces the demand conditions to break the chain of comparative advantage between exporters of X and exporters of Y. If, for example, the third country exports commodity X and imports commodity Y, then the first two countries, must also export X and import Y. When the analysis is extended to two countries and many commodities (m>2), unique ranking of commodities according to comparative advantage, as above, cannot uniquely be done, and one needs to find the additional condition, given homotheticity and identity of preference in both countries, that the weighted average of labour-capital ratio of country A's imported commodities must be higher than the weighted average of labour-capital ratios of A's exportable commodities, the weights being given by the relative amounts of capital absorbed by each commodity within each group. Thus the capital abundant country shall be exporting capital in exchange for labour only by exporting the capital intensive commodity in exchange for labour-intensive commodity, both defined as a group.

It may be noted that comparative cost differences as the basis of international trade and specialisation as discussed above according to the Ricardian and Heckscher-Ohlin theories of international trade do not strictly follow in case of trade in services, particularly higher education, where quality differences and differences in demand pattern are also important. The subsidisation made by the government in the field of education, particularly higher education is quite significant for a country like India, where not only market solutions, but also equity considerations occupy centre stage in the decision on investment in education and its pricing. Merit goods nature of education, plus its role in skill formation over time makes the cost comparisons under perfectly competitive market condition as inappropriate basis for judging the true export potentials of higher education. Moreover, there exists externalities between investment in primary and secondary education and in higher education, and therefore resource allocation on the basis of competitive market principle are not optimal. What is more, many of the institutes of higher learning in India, i.e. universities, are supported directly by the grants from the government—central or states, or both, and the pricing of higher education like public utility pricing in the social sector, do not correspond to the marginal cost pricing under competitive market conditions. Cost comparisons alone would perhaps indicate India's comparative advantage in the different fields of higher education *vis-a-vis* its major competitors, but India is not exporting education on that basis. Hitherto non-traded input of services are now made tradable thanks to the WTO agreements and cost comparison is only one of the considerations for trading the educational services.

5.3. COST OF HIGHER EDUCATION IN INDIA

In most of the countries, public funding of higher education is limited, and there is emphasis more on cost sharing for fulfilling the growing demand of higher education. In a poor developing country like India, higher education receive state funding primarily from social point of view. There is huge subsidy given by the state, and although the students are to pay for their enrolment in higher education, they pay only partly to cover the cost of education. Cost sharing of higher education is shared between four parties (a) Government or tax payers, (b) Parents; (c) Students, and (d) Individual or institutional donors. The source of cost shared by government, is basically the people who pay taxes. Most citizens directly and visibly or indirectly and largely invisible ways pay taxes from which the government expenditure or subsidies are paid. Parents pay some of the costs of higher education through payment of tuition, or bear some of the costs of students, the third party often shares the burden through term loans. The last party is donor, whose contributions may go either towards improving the quality of the university or institution budget or to students in form of grants or scholarships. Cost sharing is mostly associated with tuition fees or user charges especially on government institutions. In private institutions, who are not recipients of government grants or subsidies, tuition fees and other charges are directly levied upon all students to cover some or all portion of the costs of institution providing educational services. India has experience a slow shift in the direction of greater cost recovery, though at a very modest pace. In India, funding for higher education comes mainly from the central and state governments, student fees and donations and endowments come from the community. The relative shares of various sources in the total expenditure on higher education in India have changed considerably over the years. The UGC (University Grant Commission) is the apex body for providing grants to the universities and higher education sector. It provides two types of grants : Development grants (plan), and Maintenance grant (non-plan). It provides both planned and non-planned grants to central universities and planned grants to the state universities. Table 5.1 provides a picture of budget allocation and grants released (plan and non-plan) by UGC to inter-university centers in India during 2002-03.

TABLE 5.1

Budget Allocation and Grants Released (Plan and Non-plan) by UGC to Inter-University Centers in India (2002-03)

(*Rs. in lakhs*)

Name of Center	*Plan*		*Non-Plan*	
	Budget allocation	*Released of Grants*	*Budget allocation*	*Release of Grants*
NSC, New Delhi	800	800	890	744.25
IUCAA, Pune	230	230	495	373
IUC, deaf., Indore	450	375	570	101
NAAC, Bangalore	120	110	150	112.5
Inflibnet, Ahmedabad	200	117.29	195	138.75
CEC/media Center	500	500	700	609.36

Source : UGC.

The total expenditure incurred on higher education by Government in India mainly on university and higher education from 1990-2004 shows that slow increasing trend, but the public expenditure per student in higher education has declined continuously, with the increase in number of enrolment of students. With government's policy on subsidizing higher education for the benefit of weaker section of the student in form of scholarship, expenditure on scholarship had increased over the years, but at a slow rate, and only in recent years with more emphasis on inclusiveness in higher education in the XI plan has the number and amount of scholarship had increased substantially. Tables 5.2, 5.3 and 5.4 provide a summary picture on total government expenditure on higher education, per student expenditure and expenditure on scholarship over the years.

It is clear from the tables that the expenditure per student is quite low, and show a declining trend, and this accounts for limited increase in the access to higher education in the country over the years. The decline in public expenditure shows the scarcity of resource to the government. As result, the cost of burden of higher education is shared between government and students or parents, i.e., the government recovers a part of the cost of higher education through students fees.

Among the different recommendation made by UGC, that attracted the attention of the government, the following are important : (a) Raising fee levels; (b) Raising of resources by the institutions through consultancy and sale of other services; (c) Introduction of self-financing courses; (d) Introduction of student exchange. As a result, many universities have made very significant upward revisions in fee levels, besides introducing different kinds of fees. A study by Tilak and Rani (2000) found that out of 39 universities studied, more than half a dozen universities have raised fee rates in such a way that they generate more than 50% of the total recurring income of the respective universities from student fees, and another 13 universities could generate more than 20% of their recurring incomes. But for a large number of universities, raising resources through upward revision of students' fees became difficult in view of stiff opposition from students, and consideration of equity-based treatment for students coming from poorer sections of society. Thus, financing of higher education in India have been balancing acts in the context of conflict and competition between certain social values, as such equality and liberalism. A fee structure that is dictated by the market principle of demand and supply in education often led to profiteering in education, so much so that the government

TABLE 5.2

Expenditure on University and Higher Education by Level of Education in India (Rs. In Crore) (1990-91 to 2003-04)

Year	*Total Expenditure on Education and Trg. (Rev.) by Education and other Departments*							
	University & Higher Education			*Total*			*Total Expenditure on all Sectors (Rev.)*	*GDP at Current prices (at factor cost) base year 1993-94*
	Expenditure	*% of GDP*	*% to total Expenditure on all Sectors*	*Expenditure*	*% of GDP*	*% to total Expenditure on all Sectors*		
(1)	(2)	(3)	(4)	(5)	(6)	(7)	(8)	(9)
1990-91	3956.09	0.77	2.7	19615.9	3.84	13.37	146712	510954
1991-92	4396.78	0.75	2.58	22393.7	3.8	13.14	170370	589086
1992-93	4922.9	0.73	2.59	25030.3	3.72	13.15	190327	673221
1993-94	5557.2	0.71	2.54	28279.7	3.62	12.94	218535	781345
1994-95	6299.53	0.69	2.5	32606.2	3.56	12.95	251692	917058
1995-96	6954.07	0.65	2.43	38178.1	3.56	13.34	286195	1073271
1996-97	7983.11	0.64	2.42	43896.5	3.53	13.33	329390	1243546
1997-98	8595.67	0.62	2.32	48552.1	3.49	13.09	370838	1390048
1998-99	11097.42	0.69	2.52	61578.9	3.85	14	439768	1598127
1999-2000	15112.89	0.86	2.95	74816.1	4.25	14.6	512519	1761838
2000-01	16928.21	0.89	2.96	82486.4	4.33	14.42	572160	1902998
2001-02	14323.32	0.69	2.31	79865.7	3.82	12.89	619713	2090957
2002-03*	15858.83	0.7	2.34	85507.3	3.8	12.6	678548	2249493
2003-04 (RE)**	17064.13	0.68	2.22	94652.5	3.76	12.31	768852	2519785

and the judiciary in India had to intervene in the matter of financing of education though student fees. For e.g. the recent decision of the ministry of human resource development (MHRD) was to lower student fees in the Indian Institutes Of Management. UGC in 1993 recommended that recovery of a reasonable or meaningful proportion of academic cost should be made from the student. This recommendation is same as the issue of cost sharing, and in India cost sharing could take place only with limit. Keeping in view the increasing demand for higher education and inability of the state-funded universities and colleges to cope with the pressure effectively, the participation of private sector in higher education had been encouraged, particularly after the introduction of liberal economic regime, which had led to growth of many private educational institutions in the field of higher education, but the regulatory role of the government in ensuring quality, spread as well as equity, assume importance in this changing scenario.

TABLE 5.3

Public Expenditure on Higher Education Per Student in India (Rupees) (1990-91 to 2002-03)

Year	*In Current Prices*	*In 1993-94 Prices*	*Index*
1990-91	5652	7676	100
1991-92	5636	6727	87.64
1992-93	6111	6710	87.42
1993-94	6738	6738	87.78
1994-95	7329	6687	87.12
1995-96	6944	5812	75.72
1996-97	7207	5619	73.2
1997-98	7793	5692	74.15
1998-99	9536	6448	84
1999-00	10683	6954	90.59
2000-01	10543	6367	82.95
2001-02	9669	5582	72.72
2002-03 RE	9446	5522	71.93

Source : National Institute of Educational Planning Administration.

TABLE 5.4
Public Expenditure on Scholarships in Higher Education in India (Rs. in Crore) (1990-91 to 2003-04)

Year	*In Current Prices*	*In 1993-94 Prices*	*% of Total Expenditure on Higher Education*
1990-91	11.3	15.35	0.49
1991-92	13	15.52	0.53
1992-93	12.6	13.83	0.47
1993-94	13.4	13.4	0.43
1994-95	14	12.77	0.4
1995-96	14.7	12.3	0.38
1996-97	17.1	13.33	0.4
1997-98	13.4	9.79	0.28
1998-99	20.3	13.73	0.33
1999-2000	18.99	15.85	0.15
2000-01	15.31	9.64	0.22
2001-02	11.55	7.03	0.18
2002-03 RE	20.81	12.17	0.29
2003-04 BE	23.77	13.49	0.32

Source : National Institute of Educational Planning Administration.

Now let us compare the average cost of different types of undergraduate and postgraduate courses in some countries. Here we mainly consider the countries like India, Australia, Singapore, United Kingdom, USA and Canada. However, considering the cost of science courses in under-graduate and post-graduate level, we see that the average cost of studying in India is only about ¼th of course fee when compared to a similar course in the western universities. The average institutional costs (tuition feed + accommodation charges) for under-graduate programmes range from 2000-12000 USD per year depending on the course of study. Analysis of the data of fee structure of different universities in different countries (Australia, Singapore, United Kingdom, USA, Canada and India) shows that the tuition fee is comparatively very low in India. In the USA, cost of higher education is highest with respect to any other countries. Since we do not have data on total intake of students in other countries, we cannot calculate the cost per students; instead we present the cost per course in different universities in these countries. Table 5.5 summarises the picture.

TABLE 5.5

Average Cost Per Course (US $)
Including Tuition Fees and Living Cost

Science

Country	*Under-graduate*	*Post-graduate*
India	10860 (3 years)	10000 (2 years)
Australia	41890 (3 years)	29342 (2 years)
UK	66660 (3 years)	22220 (1 year)
US Public	80872 (4 years)	37915 (2 years)
US Private	102758 (3 years)	67574 (2 years)

Source : UGC.

It is clear that the comparative cost ratio between under-graduate and post-graduate studies is least in India (1.086) compared to 1.428 in Australia, 3.0 in UK, 2.133 in US public, and 1.521 in US Private. This would mean that world resources should be redistributed in such a way that India specializes in under-graduate courses and USA in post-graduate courses. But the comparative cost is not the sole basis of specialization and patterns of trade—therefore under a liberal trading regime export of education from India shall not necessarily be confined to under-graduate courses. Quality is an important determinant of trade induced specialization, given world demand, and domestic demand pattern constitutes the basis of resource allocation and patterns of specialization of different types of educational services—under-graduate general, technical or post-graduate levels, etc. But that does not mean that cost comparisons are unimportant is discussions of trade in higher education—it is one of the major determinants of the country's export potentials.

We now move to the fee structure of higher education in different institutions in India in different courses. Again there are large variation across courses and across universities in India, but there is a tendency for such fees to move over time. First, we consider the fee structure of Jawaharlal Nehru University (JNU) in New Delhi, which is a Central Government University, between the time periods 1999-2005. The fee structure of JNU shows an increasing trend—although the annual tuition fee remained same all over the period (1999-2005), but the other fees had increased in 2005. The subsidy component is quite high, the tuition charges paid by the students do not reflect the true cost of education in this university. Table 5.6 summarises the picture. Similar, though a bit diverse, fee structure prevails in other central universities as well.

TABLE 5.6
Fee Structure of JNU, 1999-2005

Courses	*1999*	*2000*	*2001*	*2002*	*2005*
MA, MSc., MCA					
Tuition fee (annual) *	216	216	216	216	216
Sport fee	16..5	16..5	16..5	16..5	16..5
Literary and cultural fee					16.5
Student union fee	15	15	15	15	15
Library fee	6	6	6	6	6
Medical fee					9
Medical booklet					12
Student aid fund	5	5	5	5	4.5
Admission fee					5
Enrolment fee					5
Security deposit					40
Student hostel and general — Information guide					15
Identity card fold					10
Total	258.5	258.5	258.5	258.5	370.5

Source : Website of JNU.

One of the top quality educational institutions in the country, the Indian Institutes of Management at different locations of India, are providing high quality management education at high fees charged from the students. Table 5.7 below provides a snapshot of the fee structure in IIMs for the MBA Programmes in rupees, as well as percentage from year to year. Upto 2003, although there have been further increments in recent years. The cost per student varied between IIMs, and it ranges fro Rs. 450 plus per year to Rs. 16,000 plus per year depending upon intakes and specialization. Such high fee structure is necessarily exclusionary in nature, as poor students cannot afford to undertake such costs for MBA programmes, but this high fee do nor deter the export potentials of these IIMs degrees. There are also many other private and semi-government management institutes in India, and their fees vary diversely for the MBA programme. There is an increasing tendency for foreign sponsored students to come for management studies in many of these IIMs as well as in other institutions, but the number is not very large. Given the opening up of educational services trade, this tendency is likely to go up, as the cost of such MBA programmes are still cheaper compared to many other countries, including the USA.

In the field of higher technical education, the Indian Institutes of Technology (IIT) at different centers provide the best quality education with high costs Fee structure of India Institute of Technology (IIT), Kharagpur, for different courses in IIT in 2001 (Table 5.8) shows that the fee ranges between Rs. 21900 to Rs. 100000 per annum for general students, and for SC/ST students Rs. 8400 to Rs. 7700. There also state-aided universities where there are subsidies by the government and fees paid by students are very low, whereas in the private engineering colleges, where the quality of technical education is variable, the fees paid by the students also vary considerably across regions, courses and specializations.

TABLE 5.7

Fee Structure Post-graduate Programme in Management (in Rs.) in IIMs vis-a-vis Percentage Increase in Fees Year to Year

Year	*IIMA*	*IIMB*	*IIMC*	*IIML*	*IIMI*	*IIMK*
1990	6625	3823	5430	5675		
1991	6750	3823	5430	10650		
	2%			87.66		
1992	13250	13125	12575	12450		
	96.3	24.3	56.81	16.9		
1993	15100	17575	17675	12450		
	13.96	34	40.56			
1994	35200	35000	25425	19000		
	133.11	99	43.65	52.61		
1995	44500	45000	40750	35800		
	26.42	29	60.27	88.42		
1996	56450	54000	46250	50050		
	26.85	20	13.5	39.8		
1997	69250	70000	51250	59900		
	22.67	30	10	19.68		
1998	76200	80000		70000	95750	
	10.4	14		38.54	16.86	
1999	80500	90000	80500	85000	103750	77350
	5.64	12.5	13.38	21.43	3.45	
2000	92300	100000	100000	95000	116150	84100
	14.66	10	24.22	11.76	10.62	9.11
2001	109300	110000	110100	110000	120575	100000
	18.42	10	10.1	15.79	16021	18.48
2002	119760	12500	124100	125000	134050	105000
	9.56	14	12.72	13.66	11.18	5
2003	147100	150000	127000	125000	148000	105000
	22.83	20	2.34		10.48	

IIMA - Indian Institute of Management, Ahmedabad.
IIMB - Indian Institute of Management, Bangalore.
IIMC - Indian Institute of Management, Calcutta.
IIML - Indian Institute of Management, Lucknow.
IIMI - Indian Institute of Management, Indore.
IIMK - Indian Institute of Management, Kozhikode.
Source : IIM websites.

Table 5.8
Fee Structure of IIT, Kharagpur, 2001

Courses	Semester Fee		Caution Money Deposit	No. of Semesters	One time Fee	Total	
	General	SC/ST				General	SC/ST
1. B.Tech., dual degree (upto 4th year)	15600	2100	4000	8	2300	21900	8400
2. B.Arch, integrated M.Sc.	15600	2100	4000	10	2300	21900	8400
3. 2 year, M.Sc.	5100	2200	4000	4	2300	11400	8500
4. M.Tech., MCP	4700	2200	4000	4	1500	10200	7700
5. Mmstd	4700	2200	4000	6	1500	10200	7700
6. Ph.D.	4700	2200	4000		1500	10200	7700
7. MS	4700	2200	4000		1500	10200	7700
8. MBA	45000	—		4		45000	
9. PGDBA	45000	—		4		45000	
10. PGDIT	50000	—		2		50000	
11. PGMOM	100000	—				100000	

Source : Website of IIT, Kharagpur.

5.4. CASE STUDIES

Cost of Higher Education in Australia

We now move to the consideration of costs of higher education in Australia, one India's major competitor in the field of export of higher educational services. In the last twenty years, the higher education sector in Australia has undergone tremendous changes in terms of organization, supervision, participation, and financing. From the early 1970s through 1988, tertiary education in Australia was made up of three separate sectors: universities, colleges of advanced educations (CAEs) and technical and further education schools and was overseen by the Commonwealth Tertiary Education Commission. The financial system in higher education, and the government's role in it, had also changed in Australia dramatically since the early 1970s. Prior to 1974, students were expected to pay partial fees. These were removed in 1974 and for more than 10 years, Australian higher education was free of tuition fees except for some contributions demanded from students to fund student facilities. Fees began to appear again in 1985. First, the government established a "Higher Education Administration Charge" (A $ 250 per student) followed by the introduction of fees for certain Australian post-graduate students in 1986. Since 1989, most Australian students had been contributing to the cost of their higher education through the Higher Education Contribution Scheme (HECS), which was introduced in the Higher Education Funding Act of 1988. Students in Australia enrolling for higher education, now pay between 25 and 35 percent of their tuition costs.

Table 5.9A portrays the fee status of Western Australian University from 1996-2004. It shows that fees for post-graduate and under-graduate courses had increased continuously, and cost per student also had increased, albeit at a slower rate (showing a slowly increasing trend). The fee of University of New South Wales, Sydney shows a fee status around Rs. 13 lakhs to Rs. 17 lakhs in a year (2006)[Table 5.9B]. Fee of University Of Western Australia is about Rs. 52742007, which increased in the next year (2007) to Rs. 55124111 [Table 5.9C].

TABLE 5.9A

Enrolment and Tuition fee (in $) of Western Australian University, 1996-2004

Year	*Post-graduate*	*Under-graduate*	*Total*	*Fee*	*Cost per Student*
1996	1253	10926	13653	23729	1.738006
1997	1287	11204	14114	33451	2.370058
1998	1331	11155	14100	33304	2.361986
1999	1488	11361	14536	34092	2.345349
2000	1479	11524	14687	39404	2.682917
2001	1638	11867	15166	43487	2.867401
2002	1881	11971	15529	50124	3.227767
2003	2308	12363	16358	49430	3.021763
2004	2377	12530	16659	53520	3.212678

Source : Australian High Commission.

TABLE 5.9B

Tuition Fee of the University of New South Wales—Sydney, Australia, 2006

Courses	*Under-graduate*	*Post-graduate*		*Research*
	Local and International	*International*	*Local*	*International*
Arts and Social Sciences	14350	13650	11577	13650
College of fine Arts	2680	2340	1830	2340
Commerce and Economics	5800	7225	5500	5175
Engineering	11910	11570	8975	12480
Law	1850	1170	915	1035
Medicine	10655 +na	2010 +na	945 +na	4665 +na
Science	12695	12565	8175	12000
Total in $	49285	48520	36972	46680
Total in INR	2680	1732829	1320407	1667116

Source : Australian High Commission.

TABLE 5.9C
Tuition Fee of Under-graduate Students, University of Western Australia, 2006 and 2007

Courses	*2007*	*2006*
Architecture and Fine Arts	57000	55500
Arts	105000	102000
Computer Sc. and Software	63500	61200
Economics and Commerce	40000	38000
Education		
Engineering	22500	22000
Health Sciences	47000	44000
Law	38000	37000
Life and Physical Sc.	493000	467400
Medicine and Dentistry	73000	71000
Music	52500	51000
Natural and Agricultural Sc.	493500	471500
Psychology	58500	56200
Total in $	1543500	1476800
Total in INR	57000	*52742007*

Source : Australian High Commission.

Cost of Higher Education in Singapore

Singapore has an educational system similar to that of the UK. At tertiary level it has two universities (National University of Singapore and Nan Yang Technological University) and four polytechnics, which are all public. Tuition and fees of the two universities and four polytechnics are moderate and do not vary much. Tuition for international students is generally 10% more than that for Singapore students. At the National University of Singapore (NUS), the tuition fee for medicine and dentistry is Singapore dollar (S$) 15,450 for 1999-2000 academic year, and the tuition for all other programs is S$5,000 (US$1=S$1.68 as of May, 2000). At Nan Yang Technological University the tuition fee is S$5,500 for all students. The tuition for the four polytechnics is same that is S$1,800. The Singaporean government highly subsidizes its higher education through the tuition grant. The fee status of National University of Singapore, Nan Yang Technological University and Singapore Polytechnics is almost similar in the year 2003-04. But the enrolment of student had increased from 2002-04 onwards. Table 5.10 below summarises the picture for 2003 and 2004.

TABLE 5.10

Cost of Higher Education in Universities of Singapore

Year	*Total Enrolment*	*Fee in S$*	*Cost Per Student*
	National University of Singapore		
2003	22149	126000	5.689
2004	21781	126000	5.785
	Nan Yang Technological University		
2003	15764	40700	2.582
2004	16837	407000	2.417
	Singapore Polytechnics		
2003	14371	37440	2.605
2004	13709	42314	3.087

Source : University Websites.

Cost of Higher Education in United Kingdom

United Kingdom or Great Britain had traditionally been the source of higher education in the world. The nineteenth-century British higher education system was fundamentally under private endeavors. In the twentieth century, many of the British Universities were converted into state universities in terms of grants received from the government. During the decade of 1990s, there was rapid expansion of the higher education sector in UK. The number of full-time students had increased by almost 70 percent between 1989 and 1995, and one in three young people now enter higher education, compared with one in six in 1989. In 1998/99 academic year, tuition fee of £ 1,000 was introduced to full time. undergraduate students from UK and EU countries. The British Government increased the fee to £ 1,025 for 1999/2000, reflecting an inflation of 2.5 percent.

The fee status of the universities in United Kingdom is different between domestic students and overseas students. For example, at the University of Bath the that difference between fee of domestic and overseas students is very high (overseas – domestic = Rs. 6035255 – Rs. 2294366) [Table 5.11A]. Difference also exists between full time and part time students, and this difference is spread across the domestic and foreign students. Table 5.11 below presents the schedule of tuition fees of different postgraduate students at the University of Bath during 2005-06.

TABLE 5.11

Schedule of Tuition Fees (in £) for Postgraduate programme, University of Bath, UK, 2005-06

Postgraduate Program	*Full Time*		*Part Time*	
	Domestic	*International*	*Domestic*	*International*
Architecture and Civil Engineering	28971	41459	7260	19470
Chemical Engineering	35000	113600	1750	5500
Electronic and Electrical Engineering	24500	79352	1750	5500
Mechanical Engineering	35000	113600	12810	39700
Biology and Biochemistry	7000	22400	3500	11200
Chemistry	7000	22400	1750	5500
Computer Science	14000	45200	3500	11200
Mathematical Science	11500	33800	5750	16900
Pharmacy and Pharmacology	21600	65290	14750	33090
Economics and International Development	43622	97600	19869	42865
Education	25290	68984	4896	11720
European Studies and Modern Language	34460	81300	5250	13200
Psychology	24698	59464	11674	26980
Social and Policy Science	28204	67942	12938	31010
School of Management	42956	66404	40994	71470
Total Fees in £	383801	978795	148441	345305
Total Fees *in INR*	33790475	86174731	13068991	30401223

Source : University Websites.

TABLE 5.11A

Annual Tuition Fees in £ for Selected Postgraduate Programme, University of Bath, UK, 2006-07

Programme	*Domestic Fee*	*Overseas Fee*
M.Sc. Health Psychology	3660	9300
M.Sc. Health Psychology (Part time)	1830	4650
M.Sc. Human Communication and Computing	1830	5950
Master of Research in Psychology (Part time)	1830	4650
Master of Research in Psychology (Full time)	3660	9300
M.Phil. (Full-time)	3660	9000
(Part time)	1830	4500
Ph.D. (Full-time)	4100	9300
(Part time)	3660	11900
Total Tuition Fees in £	26060	68550
Total Tuition Fees in *INR*	2294366	6035255

Source : University Websites.

TABLE 5.12

Tuition Fees of Postgraduate and Undergraduate Students of University of Bristol

Programme	*Full Time*		*Part Time*	
	Domestic	*Overseas*	*Domestic*	*Overseas*
(1)	*(2)*	*(3)*	*(4)*	*(5)*
2005-06	Tuition Fees for Postgraduate Courses			
Arts	180930	174385	90015	202450
Science	36929	69900	8125	1750
Medicine	7000	23400	3500	5850
Engineering	63500	155940	23600	63500
Social Science and Law	188976	429076	88465	168250
Total in £	477335	852701	213705	441800
Total in *INR*	42025363	75073206	18814942	38896803

2006-07				
Arts	175885	432240	88640	196800
Science	38494	74400	10350	24800
Medicine	18500	94100	15430	62670
Engineering	37000	124000	18500	62000
social science and law	219960	487560	95200	174425
Total in £	489839	1212300	228120	520695
Total in *INR*	43126236	166732897	20084062	45842849
2006-07	Tuition Fees for Undergraduate Courses			
Arts	129000	113982	51600	248894
Science	195000	623039	78000	531042
Medicine	33000	113396	13200	138595
Social Sciencs	13899	288379	52800	52800
Total in £	370899	1138796	195600	971331
Total in *INR*	32654561	100261483	17220948	845517588
2005-06				
Arts	55225	444600	—	—
Science	77550	772200		
Medical and Veterinaryine	65900	478100		
Medicine and Dentistry	134384	169100		
Engineering	12925	169100		
Social Science and Law	138996	288379		
Total in £	484980	2321479		
Total in *INR*	42698441	204386851		

Source : University Websites.

When we look at the fee structure in the, University of Liverpool during 2007-07, we find a variety of tuition fees spread across courses. The tuition fee ranges from £8350 for UG and PG courses in Arts and Humanities and Mathematical Sciences to £ 16650 for UG Medicine courses. The postgraduate tuition fee of University of Bristol (Table 5.12) for full time students ranges from Rs. 42 lakhs to Rs. 16 lakhs, overseas students have to pay Rs. 75 lakhs to Rs. 16 lakhs in 2005-07 and for the part time domestic students the fee varies from Rs. 18 lakhs to Rs. 20 lakhs and for full time overseas students, the fee ranges from Rs. 38 lakhs to Rs. 45 lakhs. The full time undergraduate domestic students have to pay fees in the range from Rs. 32 lakhs to Rs. 42 lakhs, and fees for overseas full time students ranges from Rs. 10 lakhs to Rs. 20 lakhs, and for part time domestic students it is Rs. 17 lakhs and for overseas part-time students, it is Rs. 84 lakhs.

TABLE 5.12A

Tuition Fees for Postgraduate Research at Bristol University, 2005-06 and 2006-07

Programme	*Full Time*		*Part Time*	
	Domestic	*Overseas*	*Domestic*	*Overseas*
2005-06	Tuition Fees for Postgraduate Research at Bristol University			
Arts	3085	8600	1545	4300
Science	3085	11400	1545	5700
Medical and Veterinary[a]	3085	11400	1545	5700
Medical and Veterinary[b]	3085	21000	1545	10500
Medical and Dentistry[a]	3085	11400	1545	5700
Medical and Dentistry[b]	3085	21000	1545	10500
Total in £	18510	84800	9270	42400
Total in *INR*	1629651	7465932	816146	3732966
2006-07				
Arts	3168	8900	1584	4450
Science	3168	11700	1584	5850
Medical and Veterinary[a]	3168	11700	1584	5850
Medical and Veterinary[b]	3168	21600	1584	10800
Medical and Dentistry[a]	3168	11700	1584	5850
Medical and Dentistry[b]	3168	21600	1584	10800
Total in £	19008	87200	9504	43600
Total in *INR*	1673496	7677232	836748	3838616

a : Science-based; b : Clinically-based.

Source : University Websites.

One interesting feature of the fee structure is that fees for postgraduate courses are higher than for undergraduate courses, and among the courses, the fees in science, medicine and engineering subjects are higher compared to arts and social sciences, with the exception of law, where the fee is slightly higher compared to other social science subjects. Fees for part-time students are lower compared to full-time students, both for domestic as well as overseas or foreign students. In the fields of postgraduate studies related to research degrees, the fees for both domestic and foreign students are higher than the undergraduate and postgraduate courses on a year to year basis, and the extent of scholarship offered by British government are very meager both in number and amount. As a result, the cost of higher education in British universities are on the higher side compared to many other universities in other countries. While some of these extra costs reflect higher living costs and lower fiscal subsidy amount by the government, for overseas students from India, it also reflects the relative weakness of Indian rupee *vis-a-vis* pound sterling. The export potentials of education from British Universities, however, do not solely depend on cost comparisons, other factors like quality, specialization and brand name, etc. are also important determinants of such export of education by Britain. One does not envisage equalization of fee structure across the globe following globalisation of educational services a la the WTO modes; in fact one would expect further accentuation of differences in fee structure across courses following greater mobility of foreign students, using up scarce infrastructure and capacities, such that fee augmentation in advanced countries like the UK would make the process of knowledge spillover more non-inclusive in nature. Poorer domestic students would face exclusion from participating in higher education and learning simply because they would not be in a position to pay for hike in fees in the field of higher education in market-based economies like the UK.

Cost of Higher Education in USA

The higher education sector in the USA is a mixed pack of state-aided and purely private institutions. Therefore, costs (i.e. tuition expenditures) vary enormously by institution, by sector, by program and by access to revenue. The US educational institutions with essentially the same programme profile, in general spend a great deal on education if they are highly endowed and/or if they can charge a high tuition fee, but spend much more modest amount per-student if they lack a large endowment, or a generous state budget, or the ability to charge high tuitions in the very competitive US higher education market. In fact, these revenue determinants go hand in hand, i.e., the most heavily endowed institutions are also the institutions that can charge the highest tuitions because affluent parents are willing to pay this premium to be able to send their sons and daughters to the most prestigious institutions. Comparing institutional expenditures is difficult because of heavy expenditures in some institutions on sponsored research, or public service, or hospitals and clinics, or auxiliary enterprises. Not only are the underlying per-student costs high in most US colleges and universities, but also the share borne by parents and students are also higher than in other countries. This is due principally to four factors: (1) grand size of the largely tuition-dependent private sector, (2) the fact that virtually all public colleges and non-instructional costs are unsubsidized; and (4) the general affluence of the US, reflecting higher ability to pay, combined with a cultural tradition of parental financial responsibility for at least the undergraduate higher education of dependent children. Many US universities offer scholarships and teaching assistantships to overseas postgraduate and doctoral students, the extent of scholarship, however, varying between universities. International mobility of students to such postgraduate and doctoral programmes are quite high in the USA, and cost differences alone is not the source of such service trade. Establishment of foreign educational institutions in the USA are not permitted by state laws, despite the GATS, and in general export of education by US universities and institutions are not significant in nature. We take the sample cases of the fee structure of some average typical US universities to know the fee status of universities in US.

In Table 5.13, we present the fee structure of the Eastern Connecticut State University, which shows that fee for domestic students in the year 2005-07 ranges from about Rs. 31 lakhs to

Rs. 35 lakhs. And for the international students it is about Rs. 68 lakhs to Rs. 72 lakhs. The Eastern New Mexico University shows that the fee status for the year 2006-07 in both states (domestic and out of state (international) is about Rs. 20 lakhs and Rs. 33 lakhs respectively for undergraduate students [Table 5.14]. And in Boston University the tuition fee for undergraduate courses in 2006-07 is Rs. 2175052 [Table 5.15].

TABLE 5.13

Tuition Fee of Full-time Undergraduate Students (in $) in Eastern Connecticut State University

	2005-06		2006-07	
Accounts	*Domestic*	*International*	*Domestic*	*International*
Tuition	3034	9820	3187	10315
State university fee	792	1945	820	2014
University general fee	1775	1775	2072	2072
Activity fee	140	140	140	140
Technology fee	223	223	223	223
Student loan fee	130	130	130	130
Registration fee				
Undergraduate	277	277	291	291
Graduate	320	320	336	336
Total	6691	14630	7199	15521
Total *in INR*	311633	9820	335293	722891

Source : University Websites.

Cost of Higher Education in Canada

Provincial and territorial governments provide most of the direct funding for public education in Canada. The balance of public postsecondary education income is obtained from tuition fees, research grants, contracts with business and industry, government research contracts, donations, and investment income. Since the early 1990s, university tuition fees in Canada have accounted for an increasing proportion of university revenues. However, in recent years this trend has begun to stabilize. In 1999-2000 student fees accounted for 19 percent of

TABLE 5.14

Tuition Fee in Eastern New Mexico University for the Year 2006-07 (in $)

Item	*In state*	*Out of state*
Undergraduate		
Tuition	1068	3844
Fee	414	414
Tuition and fee	1482	4260
Id card fee	25	25
Registration fee	95	95
Residence	1089	1089
Meal	1195	1195
Insurance	172	172
Book and Supplies	400	400
Total	2976	2976
Total in $	4458	7236
Total in *INR*	207631	337017

Source : University Websites.

TABLE 5.15

Tuition Fee of Boston University in $ in 2006-07

Tuition	33,330.00
Room	6,760.00
Board	3,720.00
Fee	462.00
Books and Supplies	792.00
Personal Expenses	1,183.00
Local Transportation	453.00
Total in $	46,700.00
Total in *INR*	2,175,052.00

Source : University Websites.

total university revenues, compared with 20 percent in 1998-99. Average undergraduate university tuition rose by 76 percent through the 1990s, or by 6 percent a year, in inflation-adjusted dollars. In the late 1990s, increase in average general undergraduate tuition rates came to a halt while tuition increases in professional, graduate or second-entry programs surged. Tuition in dentistry and medical programs, in particular, had increased dramatically. From 1980 to 2001, average undergraduate tuition in Canada rose from $1,600 to $3,550, and average graduate tuition has risen from $1,650 to $4,400 (in Canadian dollars). In 2000-01, Canada's total spending on public postsecondary education was expected to reach $26.8 billion, with $13.6 billion going to community college and trade-level programs, and $13.2 billion to universities. Since 1995, total government (federal and provincial) expenditure on post-secondary education remained unchanged in real dollars. However, there was a significant shift: Canadian governments—federal as well as provincial—were choosing to fund individuals and families rather than educational institutions. Total transfers to individuals for the purpose of post-secondary education in 2001 amounted to $4.25 billion. The average student could cover his/her costs using summer earnings and debt financing. The fee structure of some universities will show us the cost condition of Canadian universities.

The fee structure of University of Ontario Institute of Technology shows that the fee for domestic students was Rs. 4161180 in INR, and for international students it was Rs. 3183288 in INR [Table 5.16]. Again the St. Thomas University in the academic year 2006-07 charged Rs. 79 lakhs for Canadian students, and Rs. 156 lakhs for international students. [Table 5.17]. The fee status of University of Alberta shows that the fee for full time Canadian students was Rs. 31 lakhs and for international students it was Rs. 16 lakhs. And for part time Canadian students it was Rs. 10 lakhs and Rs. 53 lakhs for part-time international students [Table 5.18]. The University of Northern British Columbia shows that fee for full time students was Rs. 342875 and for part time students it was Rs. 180008 in 2006-07 [Table 5.19].

TABLE 5.16

Tuition Fee in 2006-07 (in $) of University of Ontario, Institute of Technology

Courses	*Domestic students*	*International students*
B.A., B.Sc., B.Ed., B.H.Sc., B.Sc. Mgmt.	21776	11550
B.Com.	17572	11550
Bit	23100	13650
B.Eng., B.Eng. and Mgmt.	23806	12600
Mits	14204	22050
M.A., M.Sc., M.Eng.	5400	
(+n/a)	17000	
Total in $	100458	76850
Total in INR	4161180	3183288

Source : University Websites.

TABLE 5.17

Tuition Fee in 2006-07 (in $) of St. Thomas University

Courses	*Canadian Students*	*International Students*
Bachelor of Arts	4355	8170
Post degree Bachelor of Education	6700	13400
Post degree Bachelor of Social Work	7100	14200
Part time	517	1006
Extension	489	978
Total in $	19161	37754
Total in *INR*	793689	1563850

Source : University Websites.

Table 5.18
Tuition Fee for Graduate Students in 2006-07 (in $) of University of Alberta

	Fall	*Winter*	*Total in $*	*Total in INR*
Full Time				
Canadian	3941.08	3622.03	7563.11	313280
International	2145.4	1826.35	3971.75	164518
Part Time				
Canadian	1247.04	1247.04	2494.08	103310
International	648.48	648.48	1296.96	53722.8

Source : University Websites.

Table 5.19
Tuition Fee for Graduate Students in 2006-07 (in $) of University of Northern British Columbia

Programme	*Full Time*	*Part time*
Master of Arts in Disability Management	1648.95	865.69
Master of Education	1775.79	932.29
Master of Science in Community Health Science	1648.95	865.69
Master of Science in Nursing	1648.95	865.69
Master of Social Work	1522.11	799.11
Total in $	8244.75	4328.47
Total in INR	342875.00	180008.00

Source : University Websites.

6

Policy Challenges under Globalisation

6.1. INTRODUCTION

Education is an important activity that transforms mankind from the world of darkness due to ignorance to the beaming world of knowledge. Even from the ancient days, therefore emphasis on education continued in human society and we have varied examples of education and character-building in our history and epics depicting the importance of education in social transformation. Now that the process of globalisation has started engulfing various walks of life, the prospect of globalising our education system has loomed large, and this has raised many important issues some of which have important implications for the policy.

Globalisation of the services under the GATS has opened up not only opportunities for trade-related gains in different forms, but also put challenges for national governments, particularly in developing countries. In the field of higher education, such challenges are enormous, in view of the complex nature of the prevailing educational system in many developing countries like India, particularly in view of the duality of the presence excellence in quality and also poor quality and gross inefficiency at the same time. The incidence of poverty as are existing in India, makes the task of measuring the gains from educational trade in India extremely difficult, as there are asymmetries and inequalities that haunt the system and create distortionary impacts.

6.2. ISSUES

As a backdrop of the emerging debate on globalisation of education in India, it is worth emphasizing that this is not a new concept or event, but its order and magnitude are likely to expand in the coming years. This follows the decision of the WTO to globalise trade in services including education, which was traditionally viewed as a non-traded activity. It is imperative to argue that this tendency to transform a non-tradable sector to a tradable one, not only alters the rules of resource allocation in the sense of altered regulatory framework, but also imparts socio-cultural impulses of far-reaching nature. This is because education empowers people and forms their skill which are essential for economic development. In India, there are hierarchical structure of education—primary, secondary, higher education—general, technical and vocational. School education is a highly sensitive to state subsidies and such subsidies are important for social justice aspect of education spread.

When India began its globalisation experiment on a full scale about nineteen years back, the focus was on reform in trade and industry—later agricultural sector was brought under its ambit through WTO's articles of agreement on agriculture. Social sector like health and education always received lowest priority in our overall policy designs, and also in our selection of the reform agenda under a globalised regime. But the GATS, which has brought into focus the WTO's recent emphasis on liberalizing trade in services, has identified educational services, health services, and financial services as the key entrant in the first phase of globalisation of services and that free trade in these services would commence from April 2004. In this context, we have to judge the tradability of the educational services in our country, as such a trade would have far reaching consequences on our society, polity and of course on the economy. However, given the heterogeneity of educational variety and quality, it is important to note the cost-effectiveness as well as quality, which are primary determinants of exportability of educational services. Available evidence suggest that bulk of the higher education in the country are subsidized heavily by the central and state governments, so that the quantity as well as quality of higher education are not purely market-driven.

Due to the expansion of the knowledge economy across the globe, the demand for higher and adult education in professionally related courses and non-traditional delivery modes have been increasing, but the capacity of India's public sector to meet this need is limited due to fiscal constraint, and there have been increased emphasis on market economy and privatization. At the same time, innovation in the field of information and communication technologies are providing alternative virtual way to deliver higher education such as corporate universities, profit institution, media companies : they are providing education service across national borders to meet the need of other countries. The scenario is changing for both public and private providers of education services. This resulted in rather complex picture of higher education. The increasing demand for higher education resulted in increasing mobility of students, and teachers, who are not only moving but moving across borders under the GATS framework. The benefits of such globalisation of educational services can be reaped if measures are taken protect a robust and good quality higher education system. The government in such a situation has an important role in (a) Licensing and regulation procedure for foreign providers; (b) Quality assurance and accreditation for imported and exported education service; (c) Funding protocols including operating grants, loans, subsidies and scholarship, and (d) Qualification recognition and credit transfer system.

The increased demand for public service in the sphere of higher education and the limited financial capacity of the government have resulted in the emphasis placed more on financial burden of higher education through higher tuition fees of students, and asking the publicly funded educational institutions like the universities and institutes to seek alternate and additional sources of funds through entrepreneurial or commercial activities at home and abroad. In tune with the basic ethos of liberalization, the government is permitting private providers of education to deliver the specific education and training programmes. This has created the need to allow both domestic and foreign private educational service providers to tap the internal market left uncovered by gradual withdrawal of state agencies, and at the same time seek foreign markets in the field of education. A long-term macroeconomic policy frame is necessary for the government to provide for inclusive forms of spread of higher education and its regulation. In fact, critics of liberalization of trade in educational services point out that the access by students to the field of higher education may be more limited as trade will commercialise education, escalate costs, and perhaps lead to a two-tiered system, posing threats to education as a "public good". The impact of freer trade in higher education can be a double-edged sword with respect to funding, whether public/private, higher education teaching/ learning and research activities. A comprehensive regulatory framework is called for to serve national interest and protect the interest of different stakeholders (specially the students). Such a regulatory framework needs to be compatible with part of a large international framework, increase connectivity and interdependence among nations, and greater coherence between national frameworks. The regulatory framework is also to be consistent with national objectives that the private as well as public providers from home as well as foreign private providers are to compete with each other to meet the desired ends in spreading quality education across the seekers of higher education, and in the realm of accreditation for quality and recognition of degrees, such interventions by the regulatory bodies are needed to safeguard the interests of students, researchers, and potential employers of trained manpower. National treatment obligation under the GATS required all providers to meet certain conditions in the host country, and quality assurance and accreditation of cross border delivery's authority need to be examined and guided by stakeholders and bodies related to education, and not by market.

The impact of trade liberalization on higher education sector in a country like India are likely to be uneven and sometimes distortionary in nature. The commercial approach to education through increased pressure for trade may lead to contraction of education in traditional subjects like Philosophy, History, Anthropology, and basic sciences, and expansion of education in subjects like Management, Marketing and Information Technology etc., which is not strictly desirable from the standpoint of national education and manpower development. The real economic issue facing the policy-maker is whether the revenues raised from commercial education activities be used to subsidise domestic education in standard subjects and their spread across different socio-economic strata or to finance further internationalization activities or not. Many internationalization strategies might be jeopardized by academic mobility with no income generation and profit motive, and many others, and in such cases reliance on trade flows and market solutions would be harmful. Therefore, effort would be needed to protect the benefits and importance of non-profit internationalization, and to direct resources to the implementation and sustainability of international dimension of teaching and research. In fact, there is likely to be a greater mobility of our qualified academic manpower to move to places of better facilities within the country and abroad, and this would tend to jeopardize the prevailing system of education, unless the government takes measures to retain them in universities and institutes of higher learning which have been created with many years of state investment.

A commitment to fully cover educational service under existing GATS rules require that foreign education service provider be guaranteed access to the educational market including all modes of supply. Government would required to give degree-granting authority to foreign educational service provider and non-government bodies (that exercise delegated governmental authority) such as teachers' colleges or professional associations, and recognize degrees and diplomas granted by foreign educational service provider. Government would require providing foreign educational service provider the same grant, financial assistance and other advantages as like education service provider at home. And the problem is that commercialization of public institution would bring them in competition with private institution. Public grants or tax incentives for research and development by education institution would be problematic as this would require that people within the country be given preferential access to the benefit of that publicly supported researcher and development. Signing on to existing GATS in higher education would substantially affect the public nature of higher education. Once these issues are codified in GATS any changes will be a matter settled through dispute settlement mechanism at international level, not by negotiation within country. Usually public sector provides cheaper education than private provider under normal commercial condition because the public sector is subsidized by tax payers. When it is established that government-funded institutions have an unfair advantage, the trade agreement can support private sector to access money, must obvious is 'like' treatment. Thus while as per the GATS agreement, the public sector funding of educational institutions should be non-discriminatory and fair even to foreign private providers, the interest to protect the advantage in investment in research, patents and educational expansion need to be taken care of in the policy framework that Government of India would be required to formulate to meet the challenges of globalisation of education services.

6.3. VOCATIONAL EDUCATION AND SKILL FORMATION

India's transition to a knowledge-based economy requires a new generation of educated and skilled people. Its competitive edge will be determined by its people's ability to create, share and use knowledge effectively. To achieve this, India needs a flexible education system, which is attuned to new global environment by promoting creativity and improving the quality of education and training at all levels. Development of skills among workers are crucial to enhance the efficiency and flexibility of labour markets as skilled workers are more mobile and be absorbed with ease compared to the pool of unskilled workers. For this vocational training needs to be strengthened, but available evidence suggests that there is a gap between demand and supply of skilled workforce in India. Accumulation of human capital in rural areas remained low, and whatever growth took place concentrated mainly in urban areas. Only 40% of new jobs created between 1993-4 and 1999-2000 were in rural areas. Declines occurred in occupations that had been among the largest employers of workers with low educational attainments, including housekeepers, cooks and maids, and occupations based on agriculture and allied activities. Occupations in demand over the 1990s included administrative, executive and managerial workers, sales workers, low-skilled construction workers, toolmakers, and machine and transport equipment operators (see Table 6.1 below).

TABLE 6.1

Occupational Distribution of Employment by Rural-Urban Residence

Occupational Group	*1993-94 (%)*			*1999-2000 (%)*		
	Rural	*Urban*	*Total*	*Rural*	*Urban*	*Total*
Professional, technical-related workers	2.2	8.7	3.7	2.0	8.0	3.7
Administrative, executive, managerial	0.8	5.7	1.9	1.4	8.4	3.1
Clerical and related workers						
Sales workers						
Service Workers						
Farmers, fishermen, hunters, loggers						
Production and related workers, transport, equipment operators, labourers	11.8	38.4	17.6	13.7	38.5	19.7

Source : Narain (2005).

It is important to note that during the 1990s, the relative supplies of workers with vocational or technical skills had declined, while their relative wages had also registered decline during the same period. It is conceivable that the relative demand for skilled workers are high, but employers do not choose to find them among the people with technical/vocational qualifications, possibly because the employers perceive that quality of technical graduates churned out by the system are poor, and hence not employable. Although the number of workers with some education has grown over the years, the overall educational attainment remains low in absolute terms and in comparison with other countries. Between 1990 and 2002, the average years of education of the adult population rose from a little over three years to about five years. Although this is a positive development, it is still significantly lower than the more successful East Asian, Latin American and OECD countries (Table 6.2).

TABLE 6.2.

Levels and Distribution of Educational Attainment (Ages 25 years and Above)

Country	*Average years of Schooling*	*Proportion of Adult Population with*			
		No Education	*Some Primary*	*Some Secondary*	*Some Tertiary*
India	4.9	51.0	31.6	11.7	5.7
Argentina	8.5	5.8	49.6	24.9	19.7
Brazil	4.6	21.3	56.8	13.5	8.4
Chile	7.9	5.3	42.9	36.0	15.8
Mexico	6.7	12.4	47.3	29.0	11.3
Korea	10.5	8.0	26.6	47.4	25.8
Malaysia	7.9	13.9	35.6	43.0	7.5
Singapore	8.1	12.6	28.3	48.5	10.6
Australia	10.6	1.7	21.1	38.6	29.8
Norway	11.9	1.2	11.5	62.5	24.8

Source : World Bank Database.

Thus, although productivity growth has been increasing and education levels rising. India still needs to improve its educational attainments substantially. It has large deficit on important quantitative indicators of education, viz., average year of schooling and net secondary enrolment, and demands for workers with technical/vocational skills seems to show a declining trend. In the absence of required data, we cannot infer about qualitative indicators—since India does not participate in standardized international examinations, there are no good comparative measures of quality. In comparison, most East Asian and OECD countries have comparative surpluses in the quantitative measures, and India is performing quite poorly at par with some Latin American countries. The comparative shortfall in the number of educated workers in India reflects inadequate investment on education in the past, and to pre-empt future shortfall of the flow of quality technical manpower in the labour market, government needs to invest on higher education and formation of quality skills on a large scale to meet the growing demand for such quality manpower in the post-globalization period and with trade in educational services opened up thanks to GATS treaty, this assumes crucial importance to protect the rising trend in productivity growth and technological improvement. Of course, government expenditure on spreading vocational and technical education needs to be financed, either through additional taxation, or through partnership with private sector or through increasing participation of FDI. While the scope for in-service training needs to be strengthened, the accreditation of new private training and technological institutes on strict adherence to international quality is essential to stall the process of quality deterioration in skills of Indian workforce, and meet the growing demand for such manpower in the globalised framework.

6.4. FDI IN EDUCATION SECTOR

The implications of FDI inflows into the higher education sector are not simple, as it has its bearing not only in the higher education per se but also on the education sector and more broadly on the whole process of generation of knowledge. Development processes in an economy being dependent on knowledge, the implications of liberalization of foreign capital flow have far reaching consequences. The policy of FDI in sectors of education services is through automatic route. In the absence of any policy in this sector foreign capital may flow in or out by means of offshore foreign institutions' campus or through the tie-ups with the private partners in India. There is also no limit to foreign capital investment in education services. Since the foreign education providers are coming in unregulated manner, an unregulated inflow of foreign capital particularly in education sector is a cause of great concern. It is now felt that FDI in education must be guided by certain norms and control as it is a sensitive sector and its implications should be examined before any FDI policy for higher education is formulated.

There are three main issues in regard to FDI flows to higher education sector, viz., investment, export potentials and quality. In a fund-constrained government sector, the possibility of expansion of infrastructure on higher education crucially hinges on availability of funds from foreign countries, and FDI in the domain of higher education can be construed as an investment to expand the sector. The cynicism of cultural imperialism associated with FDI in education sector notwithstanding, the inflows are not generic, but are confined to certain specific sectors. Therefore, the impact of higher investment on growth of education sector's output are likely to sector-specific and lopsided and not general in nature. It is often argued that FDI in higher education coming through foreign institutions can bring quality programs with market orientation. Besides updated curricula, the teaching-learning processes and evaluation processes may be internationalized within educational institutions in India. FDI may also bring the benefits of improved managerial and organizational skills to run the institutions in India and it could promote competitiveness in the education system as a whole. But since FDIs would be confined to selected sectors only, the augmentation of quality could take place only in certain specific sectors where FDI flows takes place, whereas in mass education sectors, the spillover effect of quality may not be there. In fact it might lead to accentuation of dualism prevailing in India's higher education sector, and a Dutch disease type of contractionary expansion may take place, leaving it more exclusionary in nature.

Regarding export potential effects of liberal flows of FDIs into higher education sector, it is often argued that there exists a positive correlation between FDI and export. Thus, it is argued that allowing FDI in education might lead to export of Indian education abroad in which there are large potentials in South-East Asia, Africa, and Latin America, etc. Education services, may, therefore, turn out to be net exporter and earner of foreign exchange. One should is, however, note like in commodity sectors, that foreign institutions would be interested to exploit the large market in India, rater than exporting education from India, and there is also no empirical evidence to show the positive association between FDI and export of education. Therefore, the FDI policy should be linked to specific sectors and the specific objectives, and not in general.

One should also note that GATS is directly not an investment agreement—it is a trade agreement in services that is multilateral and guided by minimum rules principles. Hence, institutional and legal interlinkages under GATS also necessitate the FDI gearing to fulfilling trade-based needs arising from interlinkages. It should be noted that investment is one of several different ways of gaining access to market. There is no investment protection provision as found in bilateral agreement. Thus, if there is commitment to allow commercial presence in Mode III, no control in FDI is possible. The FDI follows automatically from what is there in the 'Schedule of Commitments'. If there are no MA and NT limitations or any other Horizontal limitations, FDI will also not be subject to any control. In case of limitation FDI will be restricted to those limitations only. There is no back tracking possible because of progressive liberalization of trade under GATS. GATS not only addressed the terms and conditions upon which a foreign investor may enter the market, but also deals with establishment 'trade' or in other words, the conditions of operating the post-Investment phase. As such FDI is not only one-shot affair, it happens to be continuous phenomena as well. The important point is that both existing and future bilateral and regional investment agreements will need to take its provisions fully into account including strong MFN commitment. It means that opening any sector today for any country would mean opening the sector probably for all countries under GATS. Any foreign universities—public or private—willing to open overseas campus in India may be allowed to do so under the regulatory control of Government/ Government agencies. Such FDI should be guided by minimum investment norms decided by the regulating authority. Further, any foreign private to public joint venture programme may also be allowed without any restrictions so far as FDI is concerned as public institution in India is already covered by the national system of regulation.

6.5. TASKS AHEAD

The opening up of trade in educational services through different modes poses challenges of policy reforms in the field of higher education in our country. To survive in the global competition in educational trade, India has to modernize its education system so as make export of higher education attractive to foreign buyers one may suggest enhancement of our capabilities in higher education through the introduction of educational testing services within GATS, using our advantage in information technology and communications. The expertise already developed through the Common Admission Tests (CAT) of the IIM, joint entrance examination (JEE) of the IITs national eligibility test (NET) of UGC and CSIR, graduate aptitude tests in engineering (GATE), and pre-medical tests (PMT) conducted by different central and state agencies, can be effectively utilised for screening of applications of foreign students for entry into Indian universities and institutes in the field of higher education. Such reform in the admission procedure by the Indian bodies with the concurrence from the UGC, needs be integrated with the upgradation of our higher education system based on semester system of evaluation and credit transfer and of course, upgradation of basic infrastructures in educational institutions, so that high quality education services could be provided to foreign students seeking entry to Indian educational institutions.

Secondly, the inflow of educational services by the foreign and private sources under the window of trade in services, needs to be regulated in an appropriate manner so that quality of such education can be ensured. Assessment by national accreditation agencies, and the recognition of degrees provided by such institutions in the global market including in India is necessary to ensure employability of such educated manpower. The MHRD must develop such regulatory mechanisms through assessment of the degrees and also determining the fee structure for such courses offered by foreign agencies, so that the poor Indian students are not discriminated against. The restrictions could relate to free movement of persons, immigration rules, nature of courses, modalities of repatriation of money, subsidies to local institutions, quality assurance mechanisms, etc. An exercise is to be undertaken by the MHRD to identify: (i) areas and aspects where national treatment cannot be accorded to foreign providers, (ii) areas where market access cannot be allowed to foreign providers; (iii) conditions for recognition of degrees in India as well as in the host countries, wherefrom the educational services are forthcoming; (iv) subsidies that are essential for promotion of Indian education, but have to be outside the purview of national treatment, and (v) adequate safeguards to Indian institutions providing educations, and so on. Since education is in the concurrent list, and state governments fund the salaries of the university and college teachers and staffs, the additional expenses that need to be undertaken by the state governments in improving the academic infrastructure including the salaries of the human resources, so as to cope with global competition in the field of higher education, also needs to be supplemented by national government committing itself to GATS treaty.

Increased cross-border education delivery and a set of legal rules and obligations in trade agreements require that urgent attention be given to quality assurance and accreditation of education providers. Not only is it important to have national mechanisms which have the capacity to address accreditation and quality assessment procedures for the academic programmes of new private and foreign providers, it is equally important to develop an international approach to such cross-border trade in education. With the increasing importance of cross-border trade in the field of higher education, the national quality assurance schemes are becoming challenged by the complexities of international education environment. While there may be increasing awareness of this problem, there is no consensus for international policy coordination for quality assurance. This becomes important in view of diversity in educational systems in different countries. Such heterogeneity stand in the way of fruitful trade of educational expertise across nations, and since quality is an important determinant of trade, there is a need for quality coordination between countries that participate in educational trade as per the WTO guidelines. The key point is that authority for quality assurance, regulation and accreditation of cross-border delivery needs to be examined by the stakeholders and legitimate bodies related to higher education sector, and not left to the designers and arbitrators of trade agreements.

Since internationalization of education takes place within the domestic market boundaries, the rise in the cost of education will put a brake to our competitiveness. Further such a rise in cost of higher education would induce exclusion of a vast majority of poor bright students from the ambit of good quality high education. Subsidies in the form of granting scholarships to the poor and meritorious students need to be enhanced so as to preempt the process of market-driven exclusion to these poor students. This requires additional government expenditure and its financing. Trade policy interventions to curb the import of foreign educational service cannot be undertaken as it will contravene with WTO's norm of non-discrimination.

There is no denying the fact that spread and consolidation of infrastructure in the field of higher education would warrant a larger investment by the state. Private expenditure on higher education in the form of new private colleges or universities would be supplementary to state investment, and cannot be a substitute in a country like India. Facing the global challenge in the form of trade in educational services would warrant improvement in infrastructure as well as training of manpower to meet the growing need, and the process of inclusion. The Eleventh Five Year Plan has drawn up such an emphasis towards education, and has increased the allocation to the higher education sector. The paucity of qualified manpower is posing a serious challenge to our growth of the economy and this is all the more binding in the field of higher education sector. It is not possible to improve the quality of manpower and of infrastructure without investment, and since education is a merit good its expansion and sustainability hinges on state's investment for expansion. Only then the intrinsic strength of our higher education sector could be realized so as to enable us to participate effectively in global trade in educational services.

The process of adjudging the qualitative hierarchy of educational institutions in our country is far from complete. There also exists lack of clarity at the levels of both comprehension as well as execution as to how such qualitative characterizations are to be ascertained in a methodologically compact way. Certain institutions owed or run by central government are kept outside the purview of accreditation by NAAC—there are other ways of review for such bodies. However, multiplicity of evaluation process make the end products non-comparable. Moreover, many colleges—general degree, technical as well as vocational—have not yet been evaluated; the process is unmistakably very slow, for a variety of reasons. Universities and institutes which provide degrees and diplomas, do not conform to common minimum standard with respect to either recruitment of teaching personnel or specification of course curriculum so that qualitative variability is very much in built in our educational architecture, not to speak of differences in physical infrastructure or access thereof. As a result, we are not in a position to face foreign competition on equal terms, because firstly, we are not equal either on quality and/or efficiency, and secondly, given the asymmetry, the effects of unfettered competition and differentiated products are likely to create a situation of monopolistic competition where collusion in part may turn out to be an optimal strategy for some variety of educational output. The prospects for such collaborations lie in the middle quality ladder—these institutions have some good infrastructure, good demand conditions, but inept and bad quality domestic supply, to be replaced by medium quality, more diversified to emerging market needs and well packaged foreign supply in the event of freer trade in educational services.

In the event of full-scale globalisation of the services of higher education in India, the following consequences are expected from medium to long-term periods. First of all, good quality and cost-effectively run educational institutions in India shall be in a position to export their services, particularly in countries in Asia, Africa, Latin America, and even in some parts of Europe in selected fields, where these institutions have over the years, developed dynamic comparative advantages. There is no reason to be panicky for such educational institutions as they do not run the risk of being winded-off because of lack of demand. Whatever be the nature of global competition in educational services, institutions like IITs, IIMs, Institute of Sciences and even general education in selected fields would always have buoyant domestic market and the gains in export orientation in these institutions would be tremendous for the Indian economy—either students from abroad would come on a large scale to India to get education from these institutions, or there shall be external campuses of such units to export knowledge in other countries. Secondly, the least quality tier of educational institutions shall over the years, gradually peter out as a result of competition abroad. This is mainly because most of these categories of educational units have not been able to improve the quality of education, either due to paucity of infra-structural investment and/or of good quality manpower, mismanagement and lack of planning over the years, and a results are loosing demand. The examples may be drawn from colleges, institutes as well as universities. Since most of these units either did not have enough resources, or whenever they had, those resources were inefficiently used up, the effect of such closure of these academic units, would release resources which would be utilized on the basis of market signals for alternative uses. May be the buildings of inefficiently run universities be converted into hotels or hospitals or market places, depending upon the demand in that region or place. Thirdly, as a short-term measure, there would be tendency to collaborate, and if possible institute joint venture educational enterprises between medium-ranked indigenous educational units and foreign enterprises. Such joint ventures would be attractive in the areas of distance on-line learning, management education, different courses that meet the emerging needs of the service sector, like marketing, hotels, travels and tourism, insurance and risk management and the likes, and the scope of traditional liberal Arts, or traditional science subjects would take back seats when these joint venture educational enterprises would choose their priority list of education in our country.

There is nothing surprising in this scenario as the foreign enterprises would be market-driven in their pursuit of profit motives and their Indian counterparts, having good infrastructure, but dwindling domestic markets (because they have failed to maintain themselves at the top quality ladder), would be interested in diversifying the menu they offer. This process would increase the participation of the private sector in higher education and would change the dominantly public good character of higher education in the country. But there is no guarantee that the degrees and certificates that these joint venture enterprises would churn out would always ensure free entry of skilled Indian manpower in foreign countries, particularly in Europe and America—Asia, Africa, Latin America, and of course the Indian markets would be the targets of the job-seekers trained in such institutions. Even if that directional change takes place, this would amount to export of trained manpower, immigration laws in different countries permitting, but such exports are likely to be short-lived because private foreign investment in education would also be attracted to these set of countries and there is no reason why the outcome of those investments would be ignored for long in favour of their Indian counterpart, unless we can undercut on cost-basis, but not through subsidies, which the WTO rules won't permit. So domestic market is the only hope for long-term viability of such joint-venture projects.

The regulatory mechanism of the Ministry of Human Resource Development (MHRD) in the present scenario of globalisation and opening up needs to be strengthened. It is not sufficient to have only recognition of courses by the UGC and AICTE and to allocate funding to newly established institutions. It is required to assess the accreditation of the institutions seeking to establish branches in India or to procure Indian studies for overseas studies in different disciplines. More importantly, are the degrees churned out by such institutions acceptable for employment in India as well as in the country of origin of the institutions or not ? This is important not only for the welfare of the students who paid for these degrees, but also for the quality of the trained human resources in the country, which is so essential for sustaining a high growth profile of the economy. The types of educational training imparted by such foreign institutions are often in the realm of emerging areas for which demand for trained personnel in India is limited, given the nature of economic expansion in the country, and in the foreign countries, these trained personnel have adequate supply from the countries of respective origin, such that expansion of training of such professional manpower from India, may lead to unemployment of trained manpower, which is not very good from the point of view of national interest—such trained unemployed people may not be absorbed in the traditional economic activities in the country like agriculture and manufacturing. This is the mismatch problem, to which the economy might land up if adequate safeguards and regulations are not in place for the providers of educational services by the foreign institutions. Blanket liberalization of mode of supply for educational services in a country like India may be germane to such problems being generated in the coming days. Educational trade in the form of joint ventures with Indian private institutions may in general have such consequences.

There is a huge gap between the provision of educational services and the demand for higher education. But trans-border supply of education through the WTO mode may not suffice in meeting these requirements. The types of educational services that transnational enterprises or country-specific foreign institutions provide are not always of the type for which the country seeks supply. The country has adequate expertise to develop and augment educational service provisions to the prospective education seekers in the field of IT, Computer-software and hardware, communication, but do not have enough capacities to enrol students in the field of general education in science, technology and professional courses like management, finance, and in these fields the inflow of foreign capital as well as enterprises are meager compared to our need. Although there are advanced centers, institutes and universities in India who are capable of even exporting high quality education to foreign countries, their exporting capabilities are limited by the national immigration rules in countries like the USA. Therefore, while export of very high quality education services from India is limited by the inadequate domestic capacity with high capability, and restriction of markets in developed northern countries, where entry restrictions exists despite WTO's direction for free trade in educational services. An appropriate mix of policies by the Union government is required to be designed to address to the mismatch between the types of educational services available for import and ready for export. In fact, the balance of payments statistics on current account of trade in education services in India indicate that our net earning from such service trade is still negative and negligible.

There is no denying the fact that our education system as it evolved over the years, has been successful on many fronts of education and training. The number of colleges and universities have gone up significantly, and many of them with state patronage and support. The technical education facilities have also expanded quite substantially and the scope for medical education and agricultural research have also been magnified over the years from a situation of almost scratch at the stroke of independence. But after sixty-one years of independence, the reach of higher education is still very restrictive and globalisation of higher education system in India as per the provisions of WTO instead of spreading the scope for higher education and learning to our population, are inducing cost-escalating and hence exclusionary educational processes further by establishment of foreign private institutions who compete with scarce domestic resources and whose degrees and hence end-term employment opportunities are not necessarily beneficial to the job-seeking youths in our country. The other impact of globalisation in educational services is the gradual withdrawal of state in the field of higher and technical education in the country The role of the private sector in the field of higher education in the domain of science, technology and high quality liberal arts, law, medicine is still very limited.

Bibliography

Acharyya and Jones (2001). Export Quality and Income Distribution in a Small Open Economy, *International Review of Economics and Finance,* 10, pp. 337-51.

Acharya Rajat (2005). Product Standards, Exports and Employment, Physica-Verlag, Hydelberg.

Anderson, J.E. (1979). A Theoretical Foundation for the Gravity Equation, *American Economic Review,* 69: 106-16.

Baine, M., F. Docquier and H. Rapoport (2001). "Brain Drain and Economic Growth: Theory and Evidence", *Journal of Development Economics,* 64 (1): 275-89.

Balassa, B., (1964). "The Purchasing Power Parity Doctrine: A Reappraisal", *Journal of Political Economy,* 72, 564-96

Baldwin, R.E. (1969). "The Case against Infant-Industry Tariff Protection", *Journal of Political Economy,* 77(3): 295-305.

Baumol, W.J., Blackman, S., and Wolff, E.N. (September 1985). "Unbalanced Growth Revisited: Asymptotic Stagnancy and New Evidence", *The American Economic Review,* 75, 806-17.

Bergoeing Raphael, and Kehoe Timothy, J. (2003). Trade Theory and Trade Facts, University of Minnesota and Federal Reserve Bank of Minneapolis Research Department Staff Report 284, October 2003.

Bhagwati, J.N. (1985). "Trade in Services and Developing Countries", London: Tenth Annual Geneva Convention at the London School of Economics.

Bhagwati, J.N. (June 1984a). "Why Are Services Cheaper in the Developing Countries?", *The Economic Journal,* 94, 279-86.

———, (June 1984b). "Splintering and Disembodiment of Services and Developing Nations", *The World Economy,* 133-44.

Bhushan, Shudanshu (2005). 'Foreign Education Providers in India—Research Study', National Institute of Educational Planning and Administration, New Delhi.

Bowen, H.P., Leamere, E., and Sveikauskals, (1987). Multicountry, Multifactor Tests of the Factor Abundance Theory. *American Economic Review,* **77,** 791-809.

Boylaud, O. and G. Nicolitti (2000). "Regulation Market Structure and Performance in Telecommunications", Working Paper No. 237ECO/WKP (2000), 10, Economics Department, OECD, Paris, April 12.

Brecher, R.A. and Diaz-Alejandro, F. (1977). 'Tariffs, Foreign Capital and Immiserizing Growth', *Journal of International Economics,* 7, 317-22.

Breining, C., R. Chadha and L.A. Winters (2003). "The Temporary Movement of Workers: GATS mode 4, Bridging the Differences: Analyses of Five Issues of the WTO Agenda", Jaipur, India: Consumer Unity Trust Society, pp. 111-46.

Brown, D. and R.M. Stern (2001). "Measurement and Modeling of the Economic Effects of Trade and Investment Barriers in Services," *Review of International Economics,* 9:262-86.

Burgess, D.F. (1978). 'On the Distributional Effects of Foreign Direct Investment', *Internatiorlal Economic Review,* 1, 9, 647-64.

Burgess, David F. (1995). Is Trade Liberalization in the Service Sector in the National Interest?, *Oxford Economic Papers,* New Series, Vol. 47, No. 1. (Jan., 1995), pp. 60-78.

Burgess, D.F. (1990). Services as Intermediate Goods: The Issue of Trade Liberalization. In R.W. Jones and A.D. Krueger (eds.), *The Political Economy of International Trade.* Oxford: Basil Blackwell, pp. 122-39.

Carzaniga, A. (2003). "The GATS, Mode 4, and Pattern of Commitments," in A. Mattoo and A. Carzaniga (eds.), *Moving People to Deliver Services,* Washington, D.C.: World Bank, 21-6.

Caves, R.E. (1971). 'International Corporations: The Industrial Economics of Foreign Investment'. *Economica*. 38, 1-27.

———, (1982), *Multinational Enterprises and Economic Analysis,* Cambridge University Press, London.

Clague, C.K. (1985). "A Model of Real National Price Levels", *Southern Economic Journal,* 51, 998-1017.

Clague, Christopher (1988), 'Comparative costs and economic development.' Unpublished manuscript, University of Maryland.

Clark, C. (1940). *The Conditions of Economic Progress.* London: Macmillan and Company.

Colecchia, A., 2000. "Measuring Barriers to Market Access for Services: A Pilot Study on Accountancy Services." in C. Findlay and T. Warren (eds.), Impediments to Trade in Services Measurement and Policy Implications. London and New York: Routledge.

Commander, S., M. Kangesniemi and L.A. Winters, 2004. "The Brai Drain: Curse or Boon? A Survey of the Literature," in R. Baldwin and L.A. Winters (eds.), *Challenges to Globalization: The Economic Analysis*. Chicago: Chicago University Press.

Copeland, B.R. 2001. "Benefits and Costs of Trade and Investment Liberalization in Services: Implications from Trade Theory," a paper prepared for the Department of Foreign Affairs and International Trade, Government of Canada.

Corden, W.M. (1967). 'Protection and Foreign Investment'. *Economic Record,* 43, 209-32.

Deardorfaf, V. (1985). 'Comparative Advantage and International Trade and Investment in Services', in R. Stern (ed.), *Trade and Investment in Services: Canada-US Perspectives,* Ontario Economic Council, Toronto.

Deardorff, A.V., 1998. "Determinants of Bilateral Trade: Does Gravity Work in a Neoclassical World?" in Jeffrey A. Frankel (ed.), *The Regionalization of the World Economy.* Chicago University of Chicago Press.

Deardorff, A.V. and R.M. Stern 1998. Measurement of Non-tariff Barriers. Ann Arbor: University of Michigan Press.

Dixit, A. and Norman, V., (1980). *Theory of International Trade: A Dual, General Equilibrium Approach.* London: Cambridge University Press.

Dixit, Avinash and Stiglitz, Joseph. "Monopolistic Competition and Optimum Product Diversity," *American Economic Review,* June 1977, *67,* 297-308.

Djajics and Kierzkowshki, H.I. (1989). 'Goods, Services and Trade', *Economica,* 56. 83-94.

Doove, S., O. Gabbitas, D. Nguyen-Hong and J. Owen, 2001. "Price Effects of Regulation: Telecommunication, Air Passsenger Transport and Electricity Supply," Productivity Commission Staff Research Paper, AusInfo, Canberra (October).

Edwards, Brian K. and Ross M. Stan (1987). 'A note on Indivisibilities, specialization, and Economies of Scale.' *American Economic Review,* 77, 192-4.

Estache, A.Q. Wondon and V. Foster (2001). "Accounting for Poverty in Infrastructure Reform: Learning from Latin America's Experience," Washington, D.C.: World Bank.

Ethier, W. (1982). "National and International Returns to Scale in the Modern Theory of International Trade," *American Economic Review,* June, 72: 492-506.

Ethier, Wilfred (1979). "Internationally Decreasing Costs and World Trade," *Journal of International Economics,* February 1979, *9,* 1-24.

———, (1982). "National and International Returns to Scale in the Modern Theory of International Trade," *American Economic Review,* June 1982, 72, 389-405.

Falvey, R. and Kierzkowski, H. (1987). Product Quality, Intra-Industry Trade and (Im) Perfect Competition, in H. Kierzkowski (ed.), *Protection and Competition in International Trade,* Basil Blackwell.

Fink, C., A. Mattoo, and I.C. Neagu (2002). "Trade in International Maritime Services: How Much Does Policy Mater?", *World Bank Economic Review,* 16: 81-108.

Fink *et. al.,* (2003). "An Assessment of Telecommunication Reform in Developing Countries," *Information Economics and Policy,* 15: 443-66.

Francisco, J. (1999). "Estimates of Barriers to Trade in Services," Erasmus University, Unpublished manuscript.

Francisco, J. (2003). "Barriers to the Temporary Migration of Filipino Service Providers," in A. Mattoo and A. Carzaniga (eds.), *Moving People to Deliver Services*. Washington, D.C.: World Bank, pp. 179-90.

Francois, Joseph F. (1988a). 'Trade in producer services and the realization of increasing returns due to specialization.' Doctoral dissertation, University of Maryland.

———, (1988b). 'Increasing Returns and the gains from trade in Services.' Unpublished manuscript, U.S. International Trade Commission.

———, (1988c). 'Trade in non-tradables: factor proximity requirements and the pattern of trade in services.' Unpublished manuscript, U.S. International Trade Commission.

———, (1990). 'Producer services, scale, and the division of labour.' *Oxford Economic Papers,* New Series, Vol. 42, No. 4, (Oct., 1990), pp. 715-29.

Francois, Joseph F. (1990). Trade in Producer Services and Returns due to Specialization under Monopolistic Competition. *The Canadian Journal of Economics/Revue canadienne d'Economique,* Vol. 23, No. 1. (Feb., 1990), pp. 109-24.

———, (1990) 'Producer Services, scale, and the division of labour.' *Oxford Economic Papers,* Findlay and Kierzkowski (1983), International Trade and Human Capital: A Simple General Equilibrium Model, *Journal of Political Economy,* 91, 957-70.

Gasiorek, M., Smith, A. and Venables, A.J. (1991). Completing the internal market in the EC: factor demands and Comparative advantage. In A.L. Winters and A.J. Venables (eds.), *European Integration: Trade and Industry.* Cambridge University Press, pp. 9-30.

Gold, B. (March 1981). "On Size, Scale, and Returns: A Survey", *Journal of Economic Literature,* 19, 5-33.

Gonenc, R. and G. Nicolleti (2001). "Regulation, Market Structure and Performance in Air Passenger Transportation," OECD Economics Studies, No. 32, OECD, Paris.

Greenfield, H.I. (1966). *Manpower and the Growth of Producer Services,* London: Columbia, University Press.

Gold, Bela (1981). 'On size, scale, and returns: a survey.' *Journal of Economic Literature,* 19, 5-33.

Grubel, H.G. and M.A. Walker (1988). 'Modem Service Sector Growth: Causes and Effects.' Manuscript, Simon Fraser University

Grubel, H.G. and Walker, M., (1989). *Service Industry Growth.* Vancouver: Fraser Institute

Gold, Bela (1981) 'On size, scale, and returns: a survey.' *Journal of Economic Literature,* 19, 5-33.

Hamilton, C. and J. Whalley, 1984. "Efficiency and Distributional Implications of Global Restrictions on Labour Mobility: Calculations and Policy Implications," *Journal of Development Economics,* 14 (1-2): 61-75.

Hardin, A. and L. Holmes. 1997. Services Trade and Foreign Direct Investment, Staff Research Paper, Industry Commission. Canberra: Australian Government Publishing Services.

Hartel, T.W. *et. al.* 1999. "Agricultural and Non-agricultural Liberalization in the Millennium Round." Available at:http://www.worldbank.org/research/trade/archive.html/

Hashim, S.R. (2005), 3rd Convocation Address at Indira Gandhi Institute of Development Research, Mumbai, 6 December, 2005.

Helpman, Elhanan, and Krugman, Paul, *Increasing Returns, Imperfect Markets, and International Trade,* Cambridge: MIT Press, 1985.

Helpman, Elhanan (1981). 'International trade in the presence of product differentiation, Economies of scale, and monopolistic competition.' *Journal of International Economics,* 11, 305-40.

Helpman, Elhanan (1981). 'International Trade in the Presence of Product differentiation, Economies of Scale, and Monopolistic Competition.' *Journal of International Economics* 11, 305-40.

Helpman, Elhanan and Paul R. Krugman (1985). *Market Structure and Foreign Trade: Increasing Returns, Imperfect Competition, and the International Economy,* (Cambridge, MA: MIT Press).

Helpman, E. and Grossman, G.M. (1991). *Innovation and Growth in the Global Economy.* Cambridge, Mass.: MIT Press.

Hill, T.P. (1977). 'On Goods and Services', *Review of Income and Wealth,* 23, 315-38.

Hoekman, B.M. (1993). New Issues in the Uruguay Round and beyond. *Economic Journal,* 103, 1528-39.

Hoekman, B. 1995, 1996, "Assessing the General Agreement on Trade in Services," in W. Martin and L.A. Winters (eds.), The Uruguay Round and the Developing Countries, World Bank Discussion Paper No. 307. Washington, D.C.: The World Bank. (Revised version published in W. Martin and L.A. Winters (eds.), Canbridge University Press, 1996).

Hoekman, B. and A. Mattoo (2002). "Financial Services and The GATS." Paper presented at a conference on "Further Liberalization on Global Financial Market?" Washington, D.C.: Institute for International Economics, June 5.

Hoekman, B. (1995). "Assessing the General Agreement on Trade in Services," in W. Martin and L.A. Winters (eds.), The Uruguey Round and the Developing Countries, World Bank Discussion Paper No. 307. Washington, D.C.: The World Bank. (Revised version published in W. Martine and L.A. Winters (eds.), Cambridge University Press, 1996).

Hoekman, B. (2000). "The Next Round of Services Negotiations: Identifying Priorities and Options," Federal Reserve Bank of St. Louis Review, 82: 31-47.

Holmes, L. and A. Hardin (2000). "Assessing Barriers to Services Sector Investment," in C. Findlay and T. Warren (eds.), Impediments to Trade in Services : Measurement and Policy Implications, London and New York: Routledge.

Johnson, M., T. Gregan, G. Gentle and P. Belin (2000). "Modeling the Benefits of Increasing Competition in International Air Services," in C. Findlay and T. Warren (eds.), Impediments to Trade in Services : Measurement and Policy Implications, London and New York: Routledge.

Johnson, H.G. (1967). 'The Possibility of Income Losses from Increased Efficiency or Factor Accumulation in the Presence of Tariffs', *Econornic Journal,* 77 : 151-4.

Jones, R.W. (1971). 'A Three Factor Model in Theory, Trade and History', in J. Bhagwati (ed.), *Trade, Balance of Payments, and Growth,* North-Holland. Amsterdam.

Jones, R.W. (1984). 'Protection and the Harmful Effects of Endogenous Capital Flows'. *Economics Letters.* 15, 325-30.

Jones, R.W. and Ruane, F.P. (1990). 'Appraising the Options for Intenational Trade in Services', *Oxford Economic Papers,* 42, 672-87.

Jones, Ronald W. and Henryk Kierzkowski (1988). 'The role of services in production and international trade: a theoretical framework.' Paper presented at the Spring 1988 Meetings of the Midwest International Economics Conference, University of Minnesota—Minneapolis.

Johnson. H.G. (1967). 'The Possibility of Income Losses from Increased Efficiency or Factor Accumulation in the Presence of Tariffs', *Econornic Journal,* 77, 151-4.

Jones, R.W. (1984). 'Protection and the Harmful Effects of Endogenous Capital Flows'. *Economics Letters.* 15, 325-30.

Jones, R.W. and Ruane, F. (1990). Appraising the options for international trade in services. *Oxford Economic Papers, 42,* 672-87.

Kaliranjan, K. 2000, "Restriction on Trade in Disribution Services," Productivity Commission Staff Research Paper, AusInfo, Canberra (August).

Kang, J.S. 2000. "Price Impact of Restrictions on Maritime Transport Servces," in C. Findlay and T. Warren (eds.), Impediments to Trade in Services : Measurement and Policy Implications, London and New York: Routledge.

Kangasniemi, M., L.A. Witers and S. Commander, 2004. "Is the Medical Brain Drain Beneficial? Evidence from Overseas Doctors in the UK." Mimeo, University of Sussex (April).

Karsenty, G. 2000. "Just How Big Are the Stakes? An Assessment of Trade in Services by Mode of Supply," in P. Sauve and R.M. Stern (eds.), Services 2000: New Directions in Services Trade Liberalization. Washington D.C.: Brookings Institution.

Katouzian, M.A., (1970). The Development of the Service Sector: A New Approach, *Oxford Economic Papers,* New Series, Vol. 22, No. 3. (Nov., 1970), pp. 362-82.

Kemp, S. (2000). "Trade in Education Services and the Impacts of Barriers on Trade," in C. Findlay and T. Warren (eds.), Impediments to Trade in Services : Measurement and Policy Implications, London and New York: Routledge.

Krugman, Paul R. (1979). 'Increasing Returns, Monopolistic Competition, and International Trade.' *Journal of International Economics* 9, 469-80.

———, (1980). 'Scale Economies, Product Differentiation, and the Pattern of Trade.' *American Economic Review,* 70, 950-9.

Lancaster, Kelvin J. (1966), A New Approach to Consumer Theory, *Journal of Political Economy,* Vol. 74, April, pp. 132-57.

Lancaster, Kelvin (1979). *Variety, Equity, and Efficiency: Product Variety in an Industrialized Society* (Cambridge: MIT Press).

Macdougal, G.L. (1960). 'The Benefits and Costs of Private Investment from Abroad: A Theoretical Approach', *Economic Record,* 36, 13-35.

Marko, M. 1998, "An Evaluation of the Basic Telecommunications Services Agreement," CIES Policy Discussion Paper 98/09, Centre for International Economic Studies, University of Adelaide.

Markusen, James R. and Melvin, James, R., "Trade, Factor Prices, and the Gains from Trade with Increasing Returns to Scale," *Canadian Journal of Economics,* August 1981, 14, 450-69.

Markusen, James R. and Melvin, J.R., (1984a). "The Gains from Trade Theorem with Increasing Returns to Scale," in Henry Kierzkowski, ed., *Monopolistic Competition and International Trade,* London: Oxford University Press, 1984, 10-33.

Markusen, James R., (1984b). *The Theory of International Trade and Its Canadian Applications,* Toronto: Butterworths, 1984.

Markusen, J.R. (1989). Trade in producer services and in other specialized intermediate inputs. *American Economic Review,* 79, 85-95.

———, (1986), Explaining the Volume of Trade : An Eclectic Approach, *American Economic Review,* Vol. 76, pp. 1002-1011.

———, "Production, Trade and Migration with Differentiated, Slulled Workers," *Canadian Journal of Economics,* August 1988, 21, 492-506.

———, "Production, Trade and Migration with Differentiated, Skilled Workers," *Canadian Journal of Economics,* August 1988, 21, 492-506.

Markusen, James R. (1988a) 'Trade in producer services and in other specialized intermediate inputs'. *American Economic Review.*

Markusen, James, R. and James, R. Melvin (1984) 'The gains from trade theorem with increasing returns to scale.' In Henryk Kierzkowski, ed., *Monopolistic Competition in International Trade* (Cambridge: University Press).

Markusen, J.R., and A.J. Venables 2000, "The Theory of Endowment, Intra-industry and Multinational Trade", *Journal of International Economics*, 52: 209-34.

Marrewijk Charles van, Stibora Joachim and Vaal Albert de (1996), Services Tradability, Trade Liberalization and Foreign Direct Investment, *Economica*, New Series, Vol. 63, No. 252. (Nov., 1996), pp. 611-31.

Mattoo, A. 1998, "Financial Services and the WTO: Liberalization in the Developing and Transition Economies", for presentation at the workshop, "Measuring Impediments to Trade in Services", Productivity Commission, Canberra, April 30-May 1, 1998.

Matto Aaditya, Robert M. Stern and Gianni Zanini (eds.) (2008): A Handbook of International Trade in Services, Oxford University Press, London, 2008.

McCulloch, N., L.A. Winters and X. CIrera, 2001, "Trade Liberalization and Poverty: A Handbook. London: CEPR.

McGuire, G. 1998, "Australia's Restrictions on Trade in Financial Services. *Staff Research Paper*, Productivity Commission, Canberra.

McGuire, G., M. Schuele and T. Smith (2000). "Restrictiveness of International Trade in Maritime Services," C. Findlay and T. Warren (eds.), *Impediments to Trade in Services : Measurement and Policy Implications*, London and New York: Routledge.

Melvin, J.R. (1987). 'Services: Dimensionality and the Intermediation in Economic Analysis'. *Working Paper, Institute for Research on Public Policy*, Victoria, BC.

———, (1989). 'Trade in Producer Services: A Heckscher-Ohlin Approach'. *Journal of Political Economy*, 97. 1180-96.

Mussa, M. (1974). 'Tariffs and the Distribution of Income'. *Journal of Political Economy*, 82, 1191-204.

MHRD (2003-4), *Selected Educational Statistics*, 2003-4, Ministry of Human Resource Development, Government of India.

Murphy K.M. and Shleifer Andrei (1997): Quality and Trade, *Journal of Development Economics*, Vol. 53, No. 1, pages 301-17.

Mussa, M. (1974). 'Tariffs and the Distribution of Income'. *Journal of Political Economy*, 82, 1191-204.

Narain, A. (2005): Labour Force Participation and its determinants in India, Draft working paper prepared for the study of labour Markets in India.

Ncear, Mimap (2003), *India Survey Report, The Well-Being of Indian Households*, NCEAR, Tata-McGraw Hill, New Delhi.

Neary, J. P. and Ruye, F.P. (1988). 'International Capital Mobility, Shadow Prices and the Cost of Protection', *International Economic Review*, 29, 571-86.

Nguyen-Hong, D. 2000. "Restrictions on Trade in Professional Services," Productivity Commission, Staff Research Paper, AusInfo, Canberra (August).

NIEPA (2004), 'Internationalization of Higher Education, Issues and Concerns', National Conference, 26-7 August 2004, National Institute of Educational Planning and Administration, New Delhi.

Nicoletti, G., S. Scarpetta and O. Boylaud, 2000. "Summary Indicators of Product Market Regulation with an Extension to Employment Protection Legislation," Working Paper No. 226, Economics Department, ECO/WKP(99) 18, OECD, Paris, April 13 (revised).

Nielson, J. and O. Cattaneo (2003). "Current Regimes for the Temporary Movement of Service Provides: Case Studies of Australia and United States," in A. Mattoo and A. Carzaniga (eds.), *Moving People to Direct Services*. Washington, D.C., World Bank , pp. 113-56.

Oye, K. (1992). Economic Discrimination and Political Exchange: World Political Economy in the 1930s and 1980s. Princeton, N.J.: University Press.

Panagariya, Arvind (1981) 'Variable returns to scale and patterns of specialization.' *American Economic Review*, 71, 221-30.

PECC (Pacific economic Cooperation Council). 1995, Survey of Impediments to Trade and Investment in the APEC Region. Singapore: PECC

Planning Commission (2006). An Approach to the 11th Five Year Plan, Government of India, 14 June, 2006.

Rivera-Batiz, Francisco, L. and Luis Rivera-Batiz (1988) 'The effects of direct foreign investment in the presence of increasing returns due to specialization.' Paper presented at the Spring 1988 Meetings of the Midwest International Economics Conference, University of Minnesota—Minneapolis

Rodrik, D. 1995, "Political Economy of Trade Policy," in G.M. Grossman and K. Rogoff (eds.), *Handbook of International Economics*. Amsterdam: Elsevier.

Romer, Paul M., "Growth Based on Increasing Returns Due to Specialization," *American Economic Review,* May 1987, 77, 56-62.

Romer, P.M., 1994. "New Goods, Old Theory, and the Welfare Costs of Trade Restrictions," *Journal of Development Economics,* 43(1): 5-38.

Sampson, Gary P. and Richard H. Snape (1985). 'Identifying the Issues in Trade in Services'. *The World Economy,* 8, 171-81.

Sanyal, Kalyan, K. and Jones, Ronald W., "The Theory of Trade in Middle Products," *American Economic Review,* March 1982, 72, 16-31.

Sapir, A. (2001). "Who's Afraid of Globaliztion?" in P. Sauve and A. Subramanian (eds.), *Efficiency, Equity and Ligitimacy: The Multilateral Trading System and the Millennium*. Chicago: Chocago University Press.

Shariff, Abusaleh (1999), Indian Human Development Report: A Profile of Indian States in 1990s, NCEAR and Oxford University Press, New Delhi.

Singh, R.P. (ed.) (1998), Indian Universities—Towards Nation Building, University Grants Commission, New Delhi.

Steiner, F. (2000). "Regulation, Industry Structure and Performance in the Electricity Supply Industry," *Working Paper No. 238,* ECO/WKP (2000), Economics Department, OECD, Paris April 12.

Stern, R.M. (2002). "Quantifying Barriers to Trade in Services," in B. Hoekman, A. Mattoo, and P. English (eds.) *Development, Trade, and the WTO: A Handbook*. Washington, D.C.: The World Bank.

Tang, P.J.G. and A. Wood (1999). "Globalization, Co-operation Costs and Wage inequalities (January) Mimeo. Brighton, *Institute of Development Studies*, University of Sussex.

Tilak, J.B.G. (2006). "Education—A saga of Spectacular Achievements and Conspicuous Failure', in *Indian Social Development Report*, Council for Social Development, Oxford University Press, New Delhi.

Trewin, R. (2000). "A Price-Impact Measure of Impediments to Trade in Telecommunications Services," in C. Findlay and T. Warren (eds.), *Impediments to Trade in Services : Measurement and Policy Implications*, London and New York: Routledge.

Walmsley, T.L. and L.A. Winters (2002). An Analysis of the Removal of Restrictions on the Temporary Movement of Natural Persons. *Discussion Paper No. 3719*. London: CEPR.

Warren, T. (2000a). "The Identification of Impediments to Trade and Investment in Telecommunications Services," in C. Findlay and T. Warren (eds.), *Impediments to Trade in Services : Measurement and Policy Implications*, London and New York: Routledge.

Warren, T. (2000b). "The Impact on Output of Impediments to Trade and Investment in Telecommunications Services," in C. Findlay and T. Warren (eds.), *Impediments to Trade in Services : Measurement and Policy Implications*, London and New York: Routledge.

Winter, L.A. (1991). International Economics. London: Routledge.

Winters, L.A. (2002). "Trade, Trade Policy and Poverty: What Are the Links?" *The World Economy*, 25(9): 1339-67.

Winters, L.A., T.L. Walmsley, Z.K. Wang, and R. Gryberg (2003a). Negotiating the Liberalization of the Temporary Movement of Natural Persons. London: Commonwealth Secretariate, *Economic Paper No. 53*.

Winters, L.A., N. McCulloch, and A. McKay (2004). "Trade Liberalization and Poverty: The Evidence So Far," *Journal of Economic Literature*, 42(1): 72-115.

World Bank (2006). Skill Development in India—The Vocational Education and Training System, Human Develoment Unit, South Asia Region, The World Bank, January 2006.

Index